SOCIALISMS AND DEVELOPMENT

SOCIALISMS AND DEVELOPMENT

* * *

René Dumont with Marcel Mazoyer

Translated by Rupert Cunningham

PRAEGER PUBLISHERS
New York · Washington

BOOKS THAT MATTER

Published in the United States of America in 1973
by Praeger Publishers, Inc., 111 Fourth Avenue,
New York, N.Y. 10003
Published in France under the title
"DEVELOPPEMENT ET SOCIALISMES"

© 1969 by Editions du Seuil
English translation © 1973 by André Deutsch
All rights reserved

Library of Congress Catalog Card Number:
73-125388

Printed in Great Britain

To Jan Palach, who freely sacrificed himself for the sake of a humane socialist endeavour.

To Andrei Sakharov, who is defending intellectual freedom in the USSR.

To young workers, schoolchildren and students who would like to live under socialism in freedom.

Contents

Part Two THREE CONTINENTS IN SEARCH OF
SUITABLE FORMS OF SOCIALISM
René Dumont

5. KENNETH KAUNDA'S HUMANIST SOCIALISM IN ZAMBIA

Preface

Following my work on the unexpectedly rapid recovery of French agriculture during the postwar period, I devoted an increasing amount of time (almost all of it from 1957 on) to the rural, technical, and economic problems of backward countries, especially the socialist countries. After two attempts to describe agrarian economics throughout the world, in order to emphasize their extreme diversity,[1] I decided to write a series of hasty notes on a number of African regions.

In 1962, I felt it urgent to point out in a rather harshly titled pamphlet that there had been a *False Start in Africa*.[2] Since students in what we call the Third World[3] had often opted for revolutionary or reformist socialism, I tried to the best of my ability to enlighten them on the meaning of their choice. It was also with the youth of backward countries in mind that I later studied the agrarian problems of the USSR, Cuba and China.[4] Partisans of revolution too often underestimate post-revolutionary difficulties, and receive some very rude awakenings.

For a long time now, socialism has been the great hope of large numbers of workers, starting with the European working class who, in the last century, paid dearly for the beginnings of development in the industrial revolution. How glorious was the Republic under the Empire, and how splendid socialism, when capitalism alone reigned, confident of its divine right. Jean Jaurès, whose writings beguiled my youth, dreamed of a fraternal social republic that would bring peace and social justice to the world, and in the end he gave his life for it. But after the Paris commune, 1871, revolution met with failure in Russia in 1905 and flared up again in Mexico from 1911 to 1921.

Since then, differing types of socialism have come to power in numerous states both large and small and at various stages of development: 1917 in the USSR, 1945 in eastern Europe and North Korea, 1949 for the whole of China, 1954 for North Vietnam, 1959 for Cuba, Guinea and Mali, 1967 in Tanzania. As a result, we are no longer dealing with theoretical conceptions of future societies. Marxism-Leninism,[5] one variant of socialism, has proved to be capable of taking and keeping power. A socialist concept has thus been exposed to everyday difficulties, submitted to the critique of events, to the objectivity of concrete economic results and – even more important – to the appraisal of the inhabitants of the countries where it prevails.

The cold-war world of 1950 seemed to be divided into two great blocs, which the East referred to as 'socialism and capitalism' and the West 'communism and free enterprise'. The under-developed regions were largely colonial. Twenty years later, in 1970, the world seems infinitely more complicated. It was around 1950 that a specific notion of underdevelopment, until then in-correctly equated with the backwardness of the Middle Ages (it was Rostow who wrote that all countries must pass through the same stages of development) began to emerge. At the time, several of us thought that co-ordinated and very vigorous action on the part of the rich and the poor, spurred on by the newly independent nations, would be able to control it relatively quickly.[6] As the next decade, the sixties, approached, modern decoloniza-tion, which had begun with India and Pakistan in 1947 and had already affected a large part of Asia, spread like wildfire across the whole of Africa, often peacefully.

At John F. Kennedy's request, the United Nations then pro-claimed the 'Decade of Development', aimed at accelerating the economic progress of countries in the early stages of industrializa-tion. But we are forced to admit that progress made in the eco-nomic field in the sixties, has been checked: the 5 per cent annual growth rate has not often been reached. Even in the united field of food production it has been a resounding failure. Whatever certain erroneous or falsified production statistics may claim, the overall food supply has increased a little less rapidly since 1959 than the Third World's population. The more fully documented increase in food imports in countries as different as Tunisia and the UAR, for example, provides proof that can hardly be refuted. Around 1965, the dangers of famine became so explicit that we decided to write another very serious warning entitled *Nous allons à famine*.[7]

We were not the only ones to be worried. At the end of 1966, shortly after it appeared, our study was echoed rather disturbingly from the other side of the Atlantic by the Paddock brothers. The subtitle of their work *Famine 1975* was quite clear: *America's decision: who will survive?*[8] Our work had called attention to the serious dangers of food shortage and widespread famine, should the mistakes we pointed out continue; but at the same time we had emphasized that these catastrophes might be avoided through the more rapid extension of birth control, accelerated agricultural development, greater co-operation of the wealthy nations, decrease in the exploitation of the Three Continents through a more rational organization of the world economy and exchange, and so on.

For the Paddocks, on the other hand, widespread famine after 1975 is absolutely inevitable. With no apparent emotion, they announce the death of tens of millions of men by starvation because 'the time of famines will succeed the atomic age'. A disturbing conjunction. Accordingly, they propose a *policy of selection*, with the United States deciding whom it is in their interest to aid during the 'time of famines': Tunisia and Pakistan are mentioned as deserving countries. The undeserving, of which examples given range from Haiti to India by way of Egypt, should abandon all hope of being saved, *lasciate ogni speranza*.[9] With the bad countries thus practically wiped off the map, it will be possible, state the Paddocks, 'to build a better world'. A last judgement on almost medieval lines!

Since he has been head of the FAO, M. Boerma has stressed the obvious fact that hunger can be overcome, but will it be? That is quite another matter. I read in the summary of his address to the UNESCO Conference on 4 September 1968 that, according to M. Boerma, there is no reason why most of the developing countries' yields should not increase at the same rate as those of the more highly developed, temperate lands. M. Boerma seems not to have grasped all of the handicaps which make up the very essence of underdevelopment, and he would be wise to read Gunnar Myrdal's *Asian Drama*, to which we refer in Chapter Ten. The 1968 report of the FAO recognizes that the good harvest of 1967 succeeded in closing only part of the gap in food production per head incurred in the course of the previous two years by the Three Continents, so no celebrations are called for.

The Paddocks' warning may therefore be taken very seriously. It shows that the underdeveloped world must rely on its own resources immediately, accelerating its development in order to cope with its population explosion. The population explosion must in turn be controlled unless it can be fully matched by the growth in food production. But what economic structure can best promote this development? In many states a socialist one is favoured. Yet from Senghor in Senegal to Mao Tse-Tung, through Boumedienne in Algeria, Kaunda in Zambia, Nasser in the UAR, Keita in Mali,[10] Nyerere in Tanzania, Touré in Guinea, Tito, Dubçek and Kadar in Yugoslavia, Czechoslovakia and Hungary, not to mention Brezhnev, Castro and many, many others, these socialist regimes vary very widely in conception ... which is a very fortunate thing.

In all the struggles between these ideologies, which are put into effect in such very different ways, there are many people – especially in Moscow and Peking, but in plenty of other places as well – who still have the effrontery to claim that they possess the truth in politics. We shall see that such dogmatism is undoubtedly dangerous for the very future of socialist regimes; there is a serious risk that they may ossify, for it is in the interest of the groups in power to maintain the status quo by every means – including military occupation by the 'allies', as when Prague attempted a possibly contagious programme of liberalization.

In the first section of this book, we show that the successes of capitalism in developed countries are offset by many of its results: world wars and alienation, but most of all underdevelopment. We then study some aspects of various socialist experiments. These have some positive results to their credit, but also some very indifferent and even wholly negative ones. In their various guises, from the economic reforms of eastern Europe to the revolutions of the proletarian civilizations of China and Cuba, all are critically reviewed here.

It would be dishonest to equate – as the hardened dogmatists do – all attempts to move with the times or adapt to local conditions with the denial or betrayal of socialism. We should have to agree upon what each of us understands by socialism and we shall soon find that there are irreconcilable differences on numerous points. We shall therefore try to clarify our own ideas of socialism, in which the importance of freedom and individual fulfilment in dedication to the community are stressed, but we make not the slightest claim of holding a monopoly of socialism which allows us to condemn all pretensions to such a monopoly on the part of others. We have seen in Prague recently the extent to which this claim may lead to the abandonment of the basic principles of socialism.

In the second part, I attempt a critical study of various systems which have been put into practice in the Third World and which call themselves socialist. From Zambia's humanist socialism we move on to Tanzania's, which is more pronounced; then to the United Arab Republic, where it is becoming bureaucratized. India provides an example of hypocritical socialism, as does Mexico, though in a very different setting. I also compare various economies calling themselves liberal, such as that of the Ivory Coast, or even anticommunist, as in South Korea.

Marcel Mazoyer, in the third part, examines some of the Algerian phenomenon in depth. He explains why he considers that liberal capitalism has very little chance of quickly removing underdevelopment from the Three Continents. I am seeking a way of reconciling socialism with greater economic efficiency and fuller liberty, which are so necessary to win general support for the effort of development. Humanity is trying to strike a balance, constantly in danger of being upset, between necessary authority, indispensable liberty and desirable justice. Socialists want to reduce[11] social inequalities; this quest will continue into the mists of time without ever being satisfactorily resolved, but honest men are trying, and will try, to pursue it.

Concrete socialism, or socialism in power, entered upon its second half-century in 1967. At such an age, the time is ripe for it to embark on a series of *aggiornamenti*, or elucidations, which should from now on continue without interruption. In this book we try to make a modest contribution to that difficult undertaking,[12] and in order to provide a concrete example within these pages of the multiplicity of socialist options and of our rejection of any one transcendent and unique, true socialism (or even, as far as I am concerned, of any socialism that is rigorously scientific), I have asked Marcel Mazoyer to contribute to this work with his outlook on socialism, which differs from my own. We have never looked for compromises, such as the Negro-white proposal of the radical congresses of the thirties. We do not wish this dialogue to be limited to the two authors; as with my previous books, those readers, young and not so young, whose ideas have not been fixed *a priori* are cordially invited to take part.[13]

RENE DUMONT

NOTES

1 *Types of rural economy, studies in world agriculture*, Methuen, London, 1957. *Lands Alive*, Merlin Press, London, 1965.
2 *False Start in Africa*, André Deutsch, London, Rev. ed., 1969.
3 Since the Tricontinental of Havana, revolutionaries have preferred to call it the Three Continents. We use both terms.
4 Studies published by Editions du Seuil, Paris, in 1964 and 1965.
5 Which claims to have monopoly of it.
6 Because, from 1949–53 to 1953–7, agricultural progress in the non-communist bloc of underdeveloped countries accelerated at a rate of 3·5 per cent per annum, as Paul Bairoch tells us, *op. cit.*, Chapter One. Since then it has been decelerating almost without interruption even though I had hoped for improvement.
7 With Bernard Rosier, Editions du Seuil, Paris, 1966 (translated as *The Hungry Future*, André Deutsch, London, 1969). Since then we have intensified our discussions, many of them organized by Ascofam, 82 rue Saint-Lazare, Paris 9e.
8 Little, Brown, Boston, USA.
9 'Abandon all hope', the warning at the gate of Dante's Inferno.
10 Has fallen from power since these lines were written.
11 It would be utopian to aim at suppressing them.

12 Towards the end of May 1968, a student explained to me that this work would be useless: we must henceforth 'rely on the revolutionary spontaneity of the masses . . .'.

13 Being unable to thank all who have helped us with this work, we will mention only Mlles H. de Chaponnay and Erica Eugène, MM Samir Amin, Gérard Belkin Chambard, Gilbert Etienne and Georges Séverac, who constructively criticized some of the chapters.

PART ONE

The Need for 'Aggiornamento'[1] in Socialisms

RENE DUMONT

CHAPTER ONE

The Light and Shade of Capitalist Development: The American Empire

1. The Agricultural Foundation of Development

Three thousand prelates and dignitaries of the Catholic Church, assembled for the second Vatican Council, have made a modest attempt to clarify the Church's position. If Populorum Progressio[2] represents real progress for the backward countries, the appeal of this encyclical remains essentially an appeal to the generosity of rich countries, and its effect has been considerably weakened by Paul's subsequent commentaries. There is no question of carrying out any similar design with regard to socialism, for we are dealing here not with a church setting forth new interpretations of its dogmas but with increasingly multiform schools of thought. If socialist thought continues to become dogmatic as it develops – and this is hardly an assumption for there are too many instances of it in recent history – it will become fixed and ossified, losing its chance of progressive evolution. Moscow's pressure on Prague, culminating in the harsh and stupid occupation, is fresh evidence of this. We must first of all take a rapid survey of some of the features of capitalist development, for capitalism is still a formidable and often underrated rival to socialism.

Commercial capital was being accumulated in western Europe as early as the thirteenth century, but it was chiefly invested in the purchase of land as all else was destroyed by the endless wars. The Renaissance and the great voyages of discovery created fresh fortunes, but at first it was the Medici and other rich patrons who fostered the arts. The youthful states warred among themselves to establish unity or to extend their conquests. Accelerating and self-perpetuating technical progress – the real 'moment of take-off' – only came with the English industrial revolution at the end of the eighteenth century. We should bear in mind, as P. Bairoch does, the predominant role which previous agricultural progress played in this development; if, as it is said, the productivity of the agricultural labourer in the British Isles went up about 40 per cent between 1730 and 1780.

Georges Séverac[3] traces it even further back, stressing the fact that in temperate countries, the climate did not favour productivity adapted to the gathering of natural resources. Thus, in order to survive in those conditions, an agricultural method which allied the peasant's labour with economic forethought had to be established. This has led to the development of an increasingly efficient agricultural technology. Capitalist industry had its origins in temperate climates, where an ethic of peasant labour and saving was necessary for the population to survive. This individual saving was quite distinct from the feudal accumulation of wealth that was frequently squandered by parasites.

Protestantism, which saw wealth as a sign of divine favour but was also eager to reinvest it, played an important role at the start of industrialization. It is true that certain resources were furnished by colonial exploitation, but after close analysis P. Bairoch considers that this can hardly be called a determining factor in the expansion of European capitalism. Surpluses levied from colonial peoples did not give rise to any real capitalist development in Spain or Portugal, where they were highest, or even in Bordeaux or Nantes, where they were often wasted in extravagant expenditure.[4] Germany, the Scandinavian countries and even the United States have developed, as Séverac reminds us, without directly expropriating colonial surpluses.

Local agricultural progress is therefore essential to begin with, and the poor countries should not forget this. The 'take-off' extended through Europe, then spread to the United States, under economic and human conditions which though natural were quite exceptional and not to be reproduced in backward countries which cannot follow Rostow's[5] scheme, for all its claim to universality.

2. *The Human Toll of the Industrial Revolution*

Development has completely upset the relations of production and the economic structure, and has transformed our living conditions. Those who support capitalism nowadays generally tend to forget that this technical revolution at first brought terrible misery to the working class. At times it more than halved the actual living standard in England, producing slavery and the systematic killing of children; the cost in human terms was quite scandalous.

When economic chaos, crises and depressions checked the increased potentialities of production, the working class, subject to increasing suffering, protested, became organized and revolted, even breaking the machines which were sometimes the cause of unemployment.[6] Socialist thought developed; its aim was a revolt that was to usher in a world of brotherhood which would be the antithesis of this inhuman society with its terrifying injustices. In the long run this confrontation helped to raise the living conditions and wages of the workers, something that could not have been accomplished by charity alone. The scope of the hateful law of wages was rapidly curtailed. Capitalism was forced to share out a greater fund of purchasing power and from this, in spite of itself, it gained fresh impetus which in turn enabled it to damp down the cycle of depressions in which recession and unemployment had alternated with prosperity and expansion.

From then on expanded development enabled the productivity of labour to reach even higher levels and permitted some very remarkable growth rates to be attained. When feudal discipline persists within a framework of capitalism, when the entire population has long been accustomed to hard work[7] and a modest wage, when the artisans' skill and intelligence are combined with a mystique of patriotism and a national will to surpass the 'western barbarian' – under these conditions a miracle such as that of Japan can take place within the space of a century. Since 1947 they have outstripped all other growth records, whether capitalist or socialist, chiefly through their outstanding organization and by keeping the rate of investment in the neighbourhood of one-third of gross production. Once again, this is a miracle beyond the reach of the backward countries, who are starting out a century too late.

The atom will increase our energy resources tenfold; automation will still further multiply productivity, while computers make it easier to plan, programme and administer giant complexes. The size of the North American economy, its spirit of free enterprise combined with its increasing exploitation of the poor countries, and a hegemony that does not hesitate to take action to maintain its power – these factors have brought into being the American Empire, whose machinery of violence, masked by puritan hypocrisy, have been exposed by Claude Julien.[8] All this leaves Europe, at the end of the nineteenth century still mistress of the world, concerned about her relative backwardness. Even in agriculture, where progress has been most difficult, automatic machinery has brought about specialization in industrial workshops or what are in effect agricultural factories.[9] The United States, with an agricultural force making up 7 per cent of the working population, can overfeed its 200 million inhabitants and squander food, while exporting more than 15 per cent of its production. The 3 per cent who work on the large farms produce enough to feed the whole population; the peasants are a social group on the verge of disappearing.

3. A Darker Side of the Picture

Progress is made in capitalist society according to the law of personal profit, which leads to competition, which in turn contributes to productivity; it is also the law of the jungle. Nevertheless, large sections of the capitalist world, such as the police, the army, teaching, the railways, the roads and so on, are not regulated by competition, which makes an internal contradiction in this regime. Nationalist feeling, so highly developed in the nineteenth century, combined with the exacerbated rivalry of capitalism's phase of imperialism,[10] helped to produce a general climate of chauvinism. The arms race makes large and easy profits for the arms dealers. At Fez, in 1923, an old Moroccan settler told me how these firms had given him instructions to distribute arms to tribes hostile to the ruling Maghzen; they hoped that the disturbances this triggered off would provoke European intervention, thus increasing the chance of profitable conflicts on a world scale. But for Joseph Caillaus, they could have started making money in 1911 instead of having to wait until 1914!

In affirming its economic and moral superiority and consecrating itself the 'free world', the world of free enterprise has forgotten its share of responsibility in the colonial wars and in the two world wars. The latter have set a term to the European hegemony in politics, made possible the appearance of socialism in the world and hastened decolonization. We must not let these positive aspects blind us to what it cost in blood and ruin, both material and, more especially, human. It also aggravated the relative backwardness of Europe's economy and contributed to the emergence of two new supreme powers: the United States and the Soviet Union and their respective imperialisms.

Would that war had at last been recognized as the supreme evil it is, now that it can lead to atomic suicide! The eminent economist Galbraith, however, has no hesitation in introducing, if not writing, such a book as *La paix indésirable*, which sets out to show the many uses which military preparation serves. It creates an artificial demand[11] and its wasteful expenditure helps the economy. It provides the basis for the acceptance by everyone of political authority; it has enabled societies to maintain the necessary distinctions between the classes and has assured the citizens' subordination to the state. The author concludes that it would be necessary to make very careful preparations for the eventuality of peace, not that we should consider it necessarily desirable that war should end.

Jaurès had already reached the conclusion that capitalism gave rise to war, as surely as a thundercloud brings on a storm. Unfortunately, we have to add here that the socialist states also avail themselves of force and damnation and are not exempt from the possibility of war. The stronger ones even have the effrontery to claim, as Moscow did when it withdrew its experts from China and when it invaded Czechoslovakia, that they were acting in defence of socialism – when what they were primarily defending was the continuance of their own prerogatives. In 1914 the soldiers were supposed to be defending freedom, not dying for the arms trader.

4. *And Another: The Condition of the Working Class in the Waste-making Society*

In the developed countries where the industrial revolution flourished social injustices continue to exist. Even in the richest of them, such as the United States, there remains a considerable margin of poverty[12] and unemployment which it has not been possible to eradicate. This predominantly affects the black population, thus aggravating a racial problem already highly charged with memories of slavery. Black Power,[13] exacerbated by the war in Vietnam, is becoming a serious threat to the power of North America; the students there are beginning to stir, boycotting, for example, the recruitment activities of Dow Chemical, which manufactures the genocidal napalm.[14]

Even in France, on the very doorstep of Nanterre University, as in many other suburban areas, the sub-proletariat of the slums provides living proof of the continued existence of excessive inequalities – which are even more indefensible when you consider our rapidly increased capacity for production and the way we squander fruit and butter. Though the old, the out-of-work and the immigrants from Portugal or Africa cannot be decently housed, the number of week-end retreats and second houses continues to multiply: the luxuries of the rich continue to have an intolerable priority over proper housing for every working family. The worst jobs are handed over more and more to these foreigners, who are the real proletariat of the wealthy nations, highlighting the extent to which we have become a privileged group, freed from the necessity of doing menial work.

The skilled worker sees his material conditions improving; absolute impoverishment is no longer acceptable in developed countries. Yet in many underdeveloped areas within the rich countries, relative poverty still continues, providing grounds for increasingly virulent protests from the peasants and unemployed of Brittany, for example. The sons of workers[15] may get into universities, but they make up only 6 to 8 per cent of students, while agricultural workers make up 5 per cent. It generally takes two or three intermediate generations before the offspring of poor peasants complete their rise in the social scale. Though a minimum standard of material comfort is vitally necessary for a full life, a higher standard is no longer the essential foundation of human dignity.[16] As a step towards self-management, some workers are also demanding joint management of their own enterprises and communities, rather than a deceptive share in profits that may be all too easily disguised.

In May–June 1968, students finally revolted against the bourgeois culture still meted out by universities that have scarcely shaken off the authoritarianism of the Napoleonic era or the alleged infallibility of *magister dixit*. The best of the students refuse to become instruments of capitalist exploitation and challenge the whole of our consumer society, which is incapable of providing them with any uplifting ideal or any sense of human solidarity; although the latter is taught by so-called humanism, no attempt is actually made to practise it.

They are not sufficiently aware of the extent to which this society exploits the Three Continents, a problem which was not fully aired during the historic days at the Sorbonne. Nevertheless, even if their challenge of imperialism seems to us too sketchy and one-sided – for, especially since August 1968 in Prague, there is also Soviet imperialism to be considered – it is still a healthy reaction. This brings us to the most serious charge that must be levelled against development: its antithesis, underdevelopment, which is the biggest disgrace of modern times.

5. Underdevelopment and the Population Explosion

After the Age of Reason, the nineteenth century was one of progress and science, when people thought that an era of universal happiness was close at hand. The industrial revolution was propagated easily enough to begin with, when it only affected European countries whose level of knowledge differed little from that of Britain, its starting-point. But as it developed and spread farther afield the technological gap increased, making it ever more difficult to transmit industrialization. Colonization had by then affected all of Africa and the greater part of Asia; each European industry set aside colonies as sources of raw materials and protected markets for their industrial products. At the end of the last century Jules Méline, defending the interests of the textile factory-owners of the Vosges, savagely opposed the establishment of any industry in 'our' colonies.

In Latin America the landed oligarchy, which had seized power for its own ends from the Iberian monarchies, maintained an economy that continued to depend on Europe, providing sugar, tobacco, cotton, coffee, precious metals and oats, the cereals and meat of Argentina, in exchange for industrial products – consumer goods rather than equipment. The existence of slavery and colonization, which favoured archaic political and economic structures, is prolonged by the fact that the economy is still subject to external domination and that industrialization is going ahead too slowly. The recent deterioration of the terms of trade, which was most pronounced during the years 1954–62, has made the situation worse. It has now reached the point, as Pierre Jalée[17] reminds us, where the Third World is virtually being pillaged.

Medical techniques have spread very quickly in milieus still sociologically unsuited to rapid economic development.[18] This fact has at length given rise, especially in the last twenty years, to a population explosion absolutely without precedent in the history of mankind. Gunnar Myrdal even considers that 'the only great economic and social revolution in the underdeveloped world, up to the present, has been the explosion of its population'. To those who, like the Pope, still doubt the inevitability and urgency of birth control Maurice Guernier's[19] reply is that at the present mean rate of population growth – very slightly in excess of 2 per cent a year – we should have an average of 1,500 inhabitants per square metre by the year 3000. In historical terms this date is not very remote, and a new situation must be met by new solutions.

6. *Exploitation and Imperialism: Towards an Uninhabitable World*

The expropriation of the colonialists which, as I have said, played no essential part in initiating the development of the wealthy nations does seem, on the other hand, to have been a decisive factor in arresting the backward countries' growth. For one thing, a given amount of money is more significant to the much weaker economy; next, neo-colonial exploitation, even more than colonialism, has shown itself able to exploit by under paying for primary products and overcharging for exports. This is especially true of the last period, when the colonies no longer controlled the metropolitan budgets[20] since expenditure on social services (education and health) and infrastructure had increased. Séverac reminds us that colonialism was even more harmful as a force corrupting society than as the direct instrument for expropriating surpluses. Like the proletariat, the colonized peoples were not allowed to manage their own economic and political affairs, were denied the power to decide their own code of conduct and their own fate. And then, when it came, independence favoured the rise to power of privileged minorities who exploited the country to their own advantage.

Claude Julien estimates[21] that during the period 1959–65 the profits sent back to the United States from Latin America and Asia were more than nine thousand million dollars in excess of the value of that country's new investments in these parts of the world. This net inflow of investment income, combined with the ability to incur unpaid debts, held abroad as dollar reserves, is making it possible for the United States progressively to take control of all the leading industries of Europe. Our own economic subjection is thus being added to that of the Three Continents and, as in the case of the backward countries, we are largely financing it ourselves.

When the United States advises the poor countries to follow their example in the matter of development, they forget that their 6 per cent of the world population consumes between 14 and 40 per cent of the chief raw materials used in the world, and that this has necessitated the development of a very cunning and wide-spread network of captive sources of supply, thanks to the preferential treatment given to export development. Under such conditions, the slogans so frequently heard even in socialist countries which propose 'catching up with America' would appear to be unrealizable. Without running the risk of speedily exhausting numerous mineral reserves, of destroying soils and flora and of polluting the air and ocean to an intolerable degree, it would be impossible to produce enough to give the rapidly expanding population of the world a standard of living like that of North America. Besides, this cannot provide the material basis of any uplifting ideal for the young. American imperialism and the population explosion will leave future generations, the ever deteriorating heritage of a world unfit to live in. How will three private cars per family manage to circulate in the overpopulated deltas of Asia? Will there be enough oxygen left at the end of the next millennium? We must be suffering from some collective insanity!

7. Famines and Growth of Injustice on a World Scale

Tropical agricultural products for export have risen fairly quickly during the last fifteen or twenty years, to the point at which supplies of coffee, cotton, sugar, sisal, jute, rubber, oils, pepper, etc., are more or less in excess of the effective demand. Only the demand for cocoa has recently exceeded supply, but a few years ago it was the other way round. With sugar and sisal the fall in prices is catastrophic, for nobody can produce it at 'world' prices any more, even taking only current expenditure into account and neglecting investment and amortization costs.

Potential rivalry from synthetic fibres makes it impossible to hope for any notable rise in the price of sisal; competition from synthetic products is becoming increasingly serious for rubber and cotton, and jute will soon be affected in the same way. The rich countries have a decreasing need for many raw materials. Coffee is protected by an international agreement of the Malthusian type, which certainly protects the producer but also acts to prevent the spread of its consumption. This would not be acceptable in the case of basic foodstuffs. When the agreement was renewed in 1968, the United States was opposed to Brazil developing the manufacture of soluble coffee, since they wanted to keep all the profits of the process to themselves. In the end they made the Brazilian soluble coffee factories go bankrupt and bought them up cheaply . . . in order to close them down. This is what they call 'alliance for progress' (whose progress?).

On the other hand, the situation with regard to foodstuffs in the backward countries, which we described at length in an earlier study, is much more serious. Since 1959, that is for a full decade now, the increase in the production of foodstuffs for the Third World as a whole has barely kept pace with its population.[22] Shortly after the last war the food imports of these countries cost them slightly less than half the value of their agricultural exports. In 1965 there were 9·5 thousand million dollars of exports and 8 thousand million dollars of imports (one-third higher than in 1962). By 1968 the two figures had converged. The cereal deficit in the underdeveloped countries is continually deteriorating: in 1967 and 1968 it was 27 million tons a year. The corn and maize silos of the United States and Canada, which in 1969 were much fuller than at the beginning of 1967, are still not as full as in 1957.

Social inequalities have never been as great, on a world scale, as they are today, and never has the gulf widened so rapidly. Our generation is very quick to pat itself on the back for its generosity and morality even while, passively at any rate, contributing to the ruin and massacre of more determined or deprived peoples, from North Vietnamese peasants to the Indians of central Brazil, who are going the way of those of California.[23] Yet no age in history has been responsible for evils so inexcusable, in that at last we have the technical and economic means to end almost all of them fairly rapidly. Our predecessors did not have this chance – which makes our own responsibilities all the heavier. But the political means for using it have not yet been discovered.

How splendid was the American Dream of 1900 to 1945, as officially presented. The United States chose to appear as the ark

of the world's liberties, setting itself up as the defender of democracy in 1917 and 1941 and as the liberator of the oppressed by its
anti-colonialist stance on Indonesia and Indo-China in 1945, and
on Algeria in 1954–60. Yet it has superseded the old-style colonialism of Europe with an even more grasping neo-colonialism, and
it has ended up having a war of its own in Indo-China and instigat-
ing massacres in Indonesia. Of course the United States supplies
India and many other countries with a lot of corn, but that is to
check communism in these areas. There are more dictatorships
now than there were before 1960 in Latin America, where the
United States supports the most corrupt governments, as I saw
for myself in Nicaragua. Caste or family interests are protected
together with those of the North American companies.

The backward countries will never emerge from their underdevelopment except by banding together to contest, by force if
necessary, the established disorder of the strong imperialist nations
who exploit them both at home and abroad. An amusing road-
safety poster (showing a little girl and her dog crossing the road in
front of a powerful car) reminds us that 'the right of might is
never best'. Did its authors realize how revolutionary that is?

As the gulf widens between nations, as between individuals,
men are born less and less 'free and equal'[24] in fact, if not in law.
A man born into a rich family in a developed country may very
well have health, education, ease and even fortune, while the son
of a *fellah* in the Moroccan Rif, of a *conuco* of southern Venezuela,
of a Brazilian *caboclo*, of a Chilean *inquilino* or a South Vietnamese
nha-que[25] has none of the same chances. At least the latter is fighting
to get a better deal for himself, or for his children.

8. The Benefits of Developed Societies should not be Lost

We have the right to reject such injustices and to revolt against
this kind of 'institutionalized anarchy'. We should not, however,
cling to the belief that capitalism has reached the ultimate stage of
its development, that American imperialism will collapse more or
less of its own accord. The fear of communist competition has

considerably reinforced it, by compelling it to correct its chief shortcomings. After the war people were seriously proclaiming the inevitability of another great slump comparable to the one of 1929–38, which nearly proved disastrous for the system, but the present outlook cannot justify any similar predictions.[26] Capitalism is now better able to avail itself of the state's growing economic power to give fresh impetus to an expansion that is slackening off. Neither controlled finance nor a certain degree of planning hold any terrors for capitalism, which can turn them to its own advantage while continuing grudgingly to deny their efficacy. Anyway, planning has become indispensable to the running of very big business. This added flexibility makes capitalism even more formidable as a rival to socialism; the real danger is that it may give it the upper hand for a long time to come, if socialism meanwhile becomes more rigid in outlook.

Nevertheless, in the absence of any world currency the monetary situation gives rise to very serious problems which the experts do not know how to resolve. The great depression of 1929–33 coincided with serious internal difficulties within the USSR. Today a certain irresolution is to be seen in the socialist camp; when capitalism begins to have less fear of competition, it quickly tends to fall back into its old habits.

The United States' political sagacity hardly seems to have increased in proportion to its wealth; rather the opposite. The colour problem and the student revolt could undermine its empire from within. The best way of responding to the 'American challenge', however, is not simply to deny its technological ability, the quality of its teaching (which is an old subject of debate in the universities)[27] or its organizational methods. Competition is not always evident within the framework of monopolies, but it is far from having disappeared and continues on the whole to operate in favour of economic efficiency. But the more absolute socialist monopolies have a greater tendency to become inefficient and bureaucratic than the capitalist ones.

Though the cost in human terms has been very high,[28] capitalist economy has a very long experience upon which to draw, since it started out several centuries before socialism and reached a high level of development earlier. Socialism cannot afford to overlook the qualities of professional thoroughness, hard work and technical and economic discipline which seem to be a heritage of protestant puritanism and a consequence of development.

We showed, in our recent studies of agricultural problems in the USSR, Cuba and China, how socialism, in the early days, imprudently rejected a number of economic laws, many of which remain valid under socialism. It has taken the USSR nearly half a century to rediscover them one by one, and during this period ground has been lost that will be very difficult to recover. However, we do not accept that socialism has been permanently surpassed, or that the socialist idea is incapable of contributing to the future of mankind.[29]

Nor do these findings make us at all happy at the way in which the world economy is falling into the hands of the giant North American companies. It has been estimated that if the present trend towards concentration continues, by 1985 two hundred companies could control three-quarters of the 'free world's' industry. The 'Student Commune' (to use Edgar Morin's happy phrase) of May 1968 was intended as a rejection of a consumer society based on profit, self-advancement and the denial of human solidarity. It tried, amid the confusion inseparable from any attempt at total reappraisal, to found a society based on communal participation. Various political currents became involved, tending to temper the excessive rigidity of Marxism with some libertarian ideas, insisting that the whole man should be treated with greater respect instead of being regarded simply as a producer or consumer. The students should also bear witness to their concern for the more unfortunate by refraining from exploiting the backward countries in any way; not only urging them to violent revolt but also seeking to give them more and truer aid, at once,[30] even under their present regimes, so as to improve their position and make them better able to carry on the struggle.

If socialism responds to the American challenge[31] solely in material terms, it may very well be defeated. The response should seek to bring about a renewed socialism which would be capable of greater economic efficiency and also of more respect for man and of greater solidarity with the Third World. A pan-European socialism[32] might have offered a common front with the backward countries against the greatest threat of our times, the economic and political hegemony of the North American or Soviet imperialism,[33] but we still need a society really better in many respects to contrast with the so-called free world; and this does not seem so easy now as it did at the beginning of the century, for the first age of experienced and embodied socialism has all too often proved even worse than capitalism.

NOTES TO CHAPTER I

1 In May–June 1968, people talked at the Sorbonne of 'cleaning up' the university; the insufficiently destalinized French communists were compelled to coexist peacefully with the Maoists, Trotskyites, anarchists, Christian revolutionaries and other 'heretics'.
2 My analysis of this encyclical was published in *Esprit*, May 1967.
3 Lecturer in rural economy at the *Institut national agronomique*.
4 These benefited the rich less than they harmed the poor, which does not excuse the rich.
5 *Les Etapes de la croissance économique*, Editions du Seuil, Paris, 1960.
6 In the summer of 1952, in the province of Ferrara, we saw a platoon of carabinieri protecting a harvester–thresher, recently acquired by the Italian landlord, from being destroyed by agricultural labourers.
7 In the suburban trains of Tokyo, when these extremely overworked women were unable to find seats, the strapping young men never dreamed of giving up their own. (Seen in July 1968.)
8 *L'Empire Américain*, Grasset, Paris, 1968. (Translated as *America's Empire*, Pantheon Books, New York, 1971.)
9 I first used this term in 1924 to refer to a large mechanized cereal farm in northern Tunisia; it greatly alarmed my teacher, Henri Hitier.
10 It has not turned out to be the ultimate stage of capitalism as Lenin thought.
11 See *l'Evénement*, May 1968.
12 Read Oscar Lewis, *La Vida*, Secker & Warburg, London, 1967.
13 J. Loyer, *Black Power* EDI, 1968.
14 In 1967 there were more killings in Houston, Texas, than in the whole of England. Violence, aggravated by the extermination of the Indians and the lynching of Negroes, is characteristic of this society in which the communal sense of the frontier was finally limited to the colonizing, usually protestant, whites. See *L'Amérique Brûle* by James Hepburn, Nouvelles Frontières, Paris, 1968.
15 With an increased wage gap, the appalling state of housing and transport

and the difficulty of moving up the social ladder, working-class conditions still exist!

16 Alfred Sauvy in *Les Quatre Roues de la fortune*, Flammarion, Paris, 1968, indicates the danger of urban congestion resulting from the unjustifiable priority given to private cars over public transport.

17 Maspéro, Paris, 1965.

18 *Cf.* Albert Meister, *L'Afrique peut-elle partir?* Editions du Seuil, Paris, 1966.

19 *La Dernière Chance du Tiers-Monde*, Laffont, Paris, 1967.

20 But they still contributed to the giant companies (transport, public works).

21 *L'Empire Américain*, quoted above.

22 In his remarkable book *Diagnostic de l'évolution économique du Tiers-Monde 1900–1968* (Gauthier Villars, 1969), P. Bairoch gives 106 as an index of food production per head in the non-communist bloc of underdeveloped countries during 1958–62, 108 in 1964, and 105 in 1968. World-wide agricultural production per head works out at 106 in 1958–62 and 106 in 1968; so the former is regressing and the latter is stagnating.

23 Read the tragedy of California's last 'wild' Indian, Plon, Paris, 1968.

24 Unesco's motto that all men are born equal in right and dignity ignores the fact they are born unequal in wealth, and are therefore in practice unequal.

25 Names for the poor peasants of these various countries.

26 According to Flamant and Singer-Kerel, *Crises et récessions économiques, 1968*, periods of falling prices made up 42 per cent of the total period between 1918 and 1939, as against 18 per cent between 1945 and 1965. The later depressions were much milder than the pre-war ones.

27 The very dangerous tutelage of the business world is also of long standing.

28 In the early stages of development to begin with, and for the Third World now.

29 Otherwise this book would not have been written.

30 To defer aid until after a hypothetical revolution is an easy way out. But the aid must also be improved so that it does not help to increase exploitation and oppression; that is not easy.

31 In *La Vida*, mentioned above, Oscar Lewis quotes Stryker and Wallace to the effect that 'For some time now the diminution of the slum population (in Puerto Rico) has been less than 0·5 per cent a year; unless this rate changes the slum belt will persist for more than two centuries.' The American challenge is a two-edged sword.

32 It has been indefinitely postponed by the occupation of Prague. The French Communist party cannot make us forget that if we chose their path, we should give Moscow the right to come along one day and correct our probable heresies, *manu militari*.

33 Or an alliance between America and Russia against China, which is a possibility that can no longer be ruled out.

CHAPTER TWO

The Human Costs of European Socialisms

1. The Alienation of the Peasantry and the Intelligentsia

Our Soviet friends[1] will not be pleased with our using the word 'socialisms' in the plural. Yet there is a world of difference between the revolutionary atmosphere of an embattled communism surrounded by hostile forces and the hateful era of Stalinism, and the faltering steps of the post-Stalinist period! Socialism came to power in Russia through a soldiers' and workers' revolution which overthrew a newly-instated bourgeois government, too irresolute to end the unpopular war. It is doubtful whether the workers' revolt alone could have succeeded,[2] without the military defeat[3] and the growing disaffection of the soldiers, who were often of peasant origin.

A great deal is said about October 1917 in St Petersburg, but the numerous peasant revolts during the summer and autumn of 1917, so well described by Trotsky, are ignored. These helped the revolution, whereas the destruction of buildings and the ransacking of the big progressive farms, of which there were a few, only made it more difficult to spread their technical knowledge. Instead of dispersing pedigree livestock and modern equipment it would have been wiser to have established state farms right away, preferably under the old management.

A similar frenzy of destruction caused a lasting setback to Mexican agriculture after 1911–1921. The fine houses could have been used as schools and hospitals, as the more level-headed peasants realized; this lesson was not forgotten by the Chinese and Cubans.

There was, from the beginning, a dictatorship 'by the vanguard

of the working class', who did not worry overmuch about democratic scruples in the face of the even more unscrupulous class
enemy. Though the Bolsheviks were in a minority in the Soviet
Assembly, they kept the power in their own hands. It is by such
vanguards that the world is run, but all the same, they must
justify the powers they confer upon themselves by the humanity
and effectiveness of their measures. Fortunately the young Soviets
declared peace on the world. They nationalized all land in Russia,
leaving the majority of peasants in a very undecided frame of
mind.

Most of them would have preferred an agrarian reform by
which a portion of land was allotted to each family, with full
ownership, so that they did not have to submit to periodic redistributions of the lands of their commune. A veiled struggle soon
began between the Soviet power and the peasantry over the pressing need for requisitions of food for the workers. Lenin was
forced to climb down with the establishment of the NEP.[4] From
the outset the peasants were treated like children by the Soviet
regime. Trotsky claimed that 'They would never have brought
about an agrarian revolution through their own efforts ... they
had to be guided ... they must take the workers as their
guide.'

The Russian peasants, who made up the larger part of the population at that time, responded with passive resistance to this con-
temptuous attitude and, later, to Stalin's forced collectivizations.
This led to the semi-stagnation of agriculture which has continued
down to the present day.[5] As we have already stressed there was
one important exception: the strong – but short-lived – period of
expansion during the early days of Khrushchevism (50 per cent
between 1953 and 1958), when the most glaring errors of Stalin's
agrarian policy were being corrected.

A socialist state cannot force unwilling peasants to adopt an
economic structure of collective ownership based on principles
which were developed in the context of industry. They would be
unlikely to agree unless this form of production provided them
with considerable material advantages by the wholesale adoption
of modern techniques[6] – and not only mechanization. Otherwise

one would have to be able to rouse the countryside into a 'Chinese-type' state of political enthusiasm. Even so, the peasant should be able to have his say within the chosen structure and feel that he is participating, rather than being dragooned and eventually turned into a secondary proletariat by the state. One has only to see the servile attitude adopted by collective farm workers before some of their superiors, to realize that their dignity has not been respected (October 1962).[7]

Russian industry was from the outset impaired by the civil war, but also by the flight of the majority of intellectuals, ranging from engineers and technicians to members of the liberal professions. By 1921 production had fallen to 18 per cent of its 1913 level. This blow could have been softened if a different attitude had been adopted. The worst aspects of the old regime were those which it had inherited: its secret police and its bureaucracy, which preserved very firm traditions of tyranny.

2. The Stalinist Counter-revolution of a Mock 'Scientific' Socialism; and the New Freeze

The old bureaucracy, reinforced by an infusion of the working class, soon returned to dictatorship, totally perverting Lenin's democratic centralism which, though open to criticism was at least meant to be founded on the people. This bureaucracy soon became the firmest support of a government that increasingly rejected the popular control so highly prized by Lenin.[8] After the suppression of Makhno and the Kronstadt rising of 1921, political groups were forbidden, even within the party, which already had the monopoly of power; this was another setback for democracy. Militants were degraded to the status of propagandists, transmitting orders from the top,[9] which was the only place where ideas could originate. Stalin played off the differences between right and left in order to concentrate all the power into his own hands, and instituted frightful despotism on Asiatic lines. It is true that dangerous enemies of the revolution still existed in Russia, but such an exaggerated and ultimately ridiculous personality cult was

certainly not the best way of neutralizing them or, as has happened
in China, of winning over the best men.

From the time of Lenin's revolution, with its aim of establishing
a social republic to free the proletariat, up to the cult of Stalin, a
neo-despotic state and a real counter-revolution progressively
developed, flouting almost every socialist principle.[10] While setting out to dispel working-class alienation, another, and much
harsher alienation was introduced. This was a fundamental
outrage to human dignity, for which the handing over of the
principal means of production to the state (not the workers) cannot
compensate. The human cost of this early socialism appears, in
some respects, to have been as high or even higher than that of
capitalism.[11]

It is true that under this regime the basis of the economy was
removed from capitalist dominion, but only to be transferred to a
bureaucracy, ruled by a tyrant, under absolutely intolerable conditions. Planned terror, as Che Guevara said, ended in the virtual
raping of men's consciences. Stalin's appetite for power led him
far beyond what was strictly necessary for the political safety of
his regime. The millions killed or exiled make the human toll of
capitalism and of this earliest 'socialism' roughly equal.

Stalin should not be made to take all the blame; his bureaucracy must bear a large part of the responsibility. He is the prime
offender, but to accuse only him, as Mr K did in 1956, is to try to
whitewash the system. Many aspects of the system are still dangerously intact as we can see from the evidence: Budapest in 1956,
Prague in 1968, the condemnation of writers, the stiffening of
censorship and so on. Those French intellectuals who once spread
Stalinist propaganda and have since dissociated themselves from
it, are still rather dismayed to think they could have accepted such
servitude.

When Marcel Prenant was pressed to answer for the pseudo-
genetic imbecilities of Lysenko, he resigned from the French
communist party. Even while pretending – in the absence of any
possible jury – to the title of the only truly scientific socialism,
Stalinism was engaged in shamelessly flouting the traditions of
science. These claims to possession of the truth are always very

dangerous and tend to promote intolerance: burnings at the stake in the days of the Inquisition, forced labour camps and military occupation today.

Séverac reminds us that the existence of a single truth is anyway incompatible with the philosophy of knowledge which stems from dialectical materialism. The orthodox justification of Prague is to say that, at any given time, there can be only one 'line' of conduct which conforms to the interests of the proletariat. While Marxist ideology emphasizes that the character of truth is relative to history and class, it attempts, at the same time, to extract from it a truth transcending history and class.

This contradiction could be resolved by a return to objectivity, to a recognition of the fact that all truth is relative – relative to the particular historical circumstances, but also to the level of intelligence and interests of those who hold this truth. This would mean admitting that other truths might exist, in which the role of the working class is less central. If this were recognized, minority dictatorships could find no basis for their legitimacy other than sheer force. We see every day how they give rise to power struggles between rival cliques and between socialist nations, whose interests are certainly not non-antagonistic, whatever Mao claimed in 1957.

The Party held that it alone was in the mainstream of history, and the Trotskyist heresy was punished by absolute excommunication; any means of rooting it out was permitted.[12] One would be tempted to soften these criticisms occasionally, if only the Russians would recognize the danger of their many falsifications of history and admit the millions of dead and exiled for which Stalinism must be held responsible. Destalinization is less and less able to bear scrutiny, and it is getting increasingly difficult to publish accounts of Stalinist atrocities. Censorship[13] is returning in a stricter form than before. A hard frost has followed the half-hearted thaw. Russian intellectuals have to choose between the gilded chains of propaganda and the harshest condemnation. It was the dread of contagion[14] which caused the ardent attack on the democratization of Prague.

3. Some Positive Results and Blocked Destalinization

We will not, however, subscribe to the arguments of Russia's enemies, who hanker for the indefensible despotism of the old regime, or partisans of the 'American way of life' and free enterprise. It is hard to be really objective about communism, as I have tried to be for several decades. I have attempted to steer a course between the slavish adherence of a fellow-traveller (the role of a *'potiche d'honneur'* as Vercors called it) and anti-communist propaganda, which soon falls back on self-interest and calumny.

A revolution was certainly necessary in Czarist Russia, to end its frightful miseries, unjustified massacres and crimes against human dignity. No revolution can be carried out in conditions of heavenly beatitude.[15] The situation of an educated collective farm worker of 1970 bears no comparison with that of his grandfather, the alcoholic and illiterate *moujik* of 1914. The price seems excessive, but the Stalinist bureaucrats cannot take all the blame. For we in western Europe gave help to the white armies in an effort to smother the revolution, which seemed distinctly positive at that time. Sufferings due to the Second World War must also be distinguished from those of Stalinism.

The parasitic social classes, opposed equally to economic progress and to recognizing the elementary human dignity of the workers, had to be removed. The imperial court where Rasputin held sway; the fun-loving Grand Dukes, the mainly parasitic rural nobility and the capitalist exploiters; all these people – with a few exceptions – deserved to be swept away. If the revolution is not, and cannot be, totally just, the system which preceded it certainly could not have been more unjust.

The Soviet regime was the first to develop and apply a centrally planned economy. Though some of its defects are now familiar, we should not overlook the fact that in some ways it represented an advance over the anarchic capitalism and its recurrent cyclical crises, which were often transmitted from abroad. We should also not forget that capitalism proved less effective in a backward context. This early experiment eased the way for later planning methods, including those of Monnet, Hirsch, Ripert and Massé, authors of the French plan.

The Soviets speeded up the development of heavy industry, without which they might have collapsed under the massive pressure of Hitler's aggression, which Munich attempted to divert on to Russia. Yet it was not necessary to pay for this at the expense of the peasant's liberties, by a bullying that culminated in the anti-kulak (or even anti-peasant) civil war of 1929–33. For at least two generations the Soviet people suffered its consequences by privations of every kind, particularly with regard to their liberties which have been affected even more than such things as food and clothing.

The Soviet regime justly prides itself on having hastened the spread of universal education at every level, even in the remotest regions of central Asia. It has had the sense to ensure that scientific and technical subjects predominate; a lesson which the backward countries, who follow our own inappropriately humanist model, would do well to bear in mind. The Russians have made great efforts to honour the worker and rehabilitate manual labour. Stakhanovites and other heroes of work are allotted the position on Soviet radio which we give to sportsmen and pop singers.

This utilitarian instruction, however, is still bounded by the limits and orientation of party dogma. For a long time it rejected cybernetics, without which Russia would never have been able to launch its sputniks and take the lead in the early days of the conquest of space. The French Gaullist ORTF, however, was in no position to give lessons in liberalism; the absence of free speech always debases the critical sense, produces docile followers and puts an end to any real development.

The freeze, which followed the period of destalinization, also had far-reaching economic consequences. It took many years for the Soviet planning authorities in Gosplan to recognize that their myth of coal and steel was out of date and for them to give higher priority to natural gas, petroleum, aluminium, plastics and all kinds of chemical industry. Meanwhile Soviet agriculture had been terribly short of fertilizer. Even Khrushchev had great difficulty in making himself heard. This atmosphere of hostility to criticism has considerably delayed the appearance, adoption and development of the famous economic reforms sometimes called Libermanism, after one of their best-known promoters. As late as 1962 it was considered doctrinally outrageous to admit[16] the part rates of interest played in economics, or the usefulness of having irrigation water actually paid for by the *kolkhoz* and *sovkhoz*.

The development of the spirit of initiative necessary for these reforms to be effective demands the appearance of a new type, the socialist entrepreneur, capable of taking risks, of being rewarded for his successes and punished for his failures. If he is to take on all the responsibility, for better or worse, he will have to be allowed more initiative. Recent developments have moved a little in this direction, and some of Gosplan's powers have shifted to the technical ministries and departments of economics. Though still held on a leash, enterprises are being given more autonomy. The technician is gaining ground at the expense of the administrator, but party membership still counts for the highest posts.

All grades are becoming more concerned about economic problems. If productivity can be increased by improving administration, working harder and cutting down waste, then a tenth of the profits realized over and above production costs could be set aside in bonuses for the staff.

They say that the Soviet workers are in power, but in fact, they are politically controlled by the party bureaucracy and their working lives are closely supervised by the technocrats. To be sure, they can suggest practical improvements in matters of detail or for the better organization of their works, but they are not free to discuss or propose basic reforms of fundamental economic or political principles, despite the fact that these constantly need adjusting. It is only the managers who have been given slightly more initiative; the workers still have no share in the running of the factories – which have been nationalized, rather than socialized.

In the international sphere, the Soviet state made decisive contributions to the defeat of Hitler and to decolonization. Yet the Kominform advised the Chinese very badly in the early days of their revolution and for a long time Stalin could not bring himself to recognize the Chinese communists' victory. On the other hand, Afro-Asian decolonization would undoubtedly have been less rapid but for the Soviet Union's support, even if this was only moral and indirect. The colonial powers hastened to give subject governments their independence rather than have them overthrown by socialist movements, as happened in the Cameroons. Though the Chinese may consider Russia's contribution to the Vietnamese resistance insufficient, without the Soviet force America would be in a far more dominating position.

The development of the Soviet economy is being held up by over-centralized planning. There is a privileged caste of party climbers who confer exorbitant powers upon themselves, which they are not in a position to take up and use effectively. Khrushchev showed great political courage in daring to initiate the process of destalinization. At that stage of the development of the Soviet economy, he could have given fresh impetus by reintroducing a certain amount of market competition, handing back power to the consumer and making enterprises autonomous.

Economic reform cannot be fully realized unless producers have more initiative and responsibility and the public greater critical awareness. But for this to happen, greater cultural, and therefore greater political freedom are required. This is where the Soviet yoke presses hardest, for when all is said and done it is only intended to safeguard the excessive privileges of the managerial caste. The structure's rigidity impedes economic progress and individual happiness. Happiness cannot be conferred, for it lies in its own achievement, through the possibility of creation and self-assertion, and this requires a structure which allows opposition and debate. If economic power were transferred to the managers and to the producers' and consumers' representatives, the party's power would dwindle, which, in turn, would lead to a reduction of the 'class increments' of Party members, and of their misappropriations from the national revenue. Such a state of affairs would not be tolerated by the new managing class who seek to protect their caste interests under the cloak of defending socialism, both at home and among their East European neighbours (Belgrade 1948, Budapest 1956, Prague 1968 . . .).

c

4. The Exportation of Socialism to the Peoples' Democracies

Proletarian internationalism declared that there would be no wars between socialist states when class and the power of monopolies had disappeared. The Soviet Union has nevertheless profited from its conquests and extended its frontiers from Finland to Moldavia, by way of the Baltic countries, East Prussia, Poland, subcarpathian Ruthenia and the Kuril Islands.

Worse still, since eastern Europe has been recognized as being within its sphere of influence, the Soviet Union has set up satellite regimes there. It began by exacting heavy war damages, especially from Germany and Hungary. The terms of trade were very much to the Soviet Union's advantage and though less so, still are today. It succeeded in establishing the communist party's dictatorship over eastern Europe, through the National Front, even in the countries where it was very much a minority, as in Hungary and Poland, or practically non-existent, as in Rumania. This type of socialism, copied from a foreign model even in the particulars of how it was applied, was a kind of neo-colonialism that flouted both national sentiment and the rights of the individual.

Though the Czechs (before 1968) and Bulgarians were often pro-Russian, the Poles, Germans, Rumanians and Hungarians were much less so and felt the yoke much more keenly. The Czechs had experienced the freedom of a bourgeois democracy; the Russians, having never known it, were amazed at the nostalgia of the people of Prague. The Yugoslavs, who had liberated themselves, were the first to rebel and, on that account, were soon excommunicated. Stalin believed he had only to lift his little finger to make them get back into line; but, as Mr K said, even lifting his whole arm did not avail.[17] Unduly prolonged economic Stalinism, which gave absolute priority to heavy industry, proved unfortunate in the very small countries, where metallurgy was seldom to be preferred economically. Especially in Germany and Czechoslovakia, centralized planning came up against extremely valuable traditions of local initiative and skill in industry.

It was in agriculture that the results were most often disastrous.

Agrarian reform often seemed necessary to overthrow the privileged minority in their rural feudalities, with which Hungary was
particularly afflicted. Yet partitioning the land into small holdings
'leased for a thousand years', as they said in Hungary in 1947,
often disorganized rational production units that were much
more up-to-date than the peasant farms. Production on the
Esterhazy estates in Hungary sank to about a third of its former
level.

At Easter, 1948, in the Puszta, I saw a great cattleshed able to
accommodate a hundred cows being pulled down so that the
stones could be used to build twenty-five small ones, holding four
cows each. Some of the peasants thought this cowshed might
possibly provide the basis of a *kolkhoz*, which they already dreaded.
In their zeal to destroy this hated symbol they were quite astonished
when I explained that the stones they obtained from it were
worth very much less than the building itself, and that many more
would be required for the construction of twenty-five small
sheds.

Such behaviour was all the more questionable in that, after the
Kominform's condemnation of the Titoist 'heresy' in June 1948,
collectivization on Soviet lines was undertaken, contrary to the
wishes of the great majority of the peasants, who were quickly
deprived of their much desired property. As the level of cultivation increased, so did taxes and compulsory expropriations; pressures by the administration and the police were stepped up. Many
resigned themselves to joining the scheme, but did not greatly
exert themselves, while others adopted a passive resistance by
falling back on a near-subsistence economy while most of their
land lay fallow. A village on the Hungarian plains in 1952 had a
hostile air, with its shut doors and set faces. Output sank to such
an extent that in 1953, Rakoci had to be replaced by the ill-fated
Imre Nagy in order to prevent the prolonged dearth being followed by widespread famine.

Stalin and his associates demanded endless trials and purges and
sent Mikoyan to Prague to have Slansky executed. They hanged
Rajk, the only communist leader whose honesty and austerity[18] I
heard praised in Budapest in 1948. The harsh suppression of the

German revolt of 1953 and particularly that of Hungary in 1956 by the Soviet army, emphasizes the unpopular character of these so-called democracies.

The victims of 1956 did not die quite in vain: in Poland destalinization became more marked for a while and Gomulka authorized the dissolution of the *kolkhozes*, which have since practically disappeared. Except in Yugoslavia, however, these producer co-operatives dominated agriculture in all the other people's democracies, including Albania and East Germany. The second wave of collectivization, initiated by Kadar in 1959, was relatively successful – not entirely because of the prevailing attitude of resignation – the new co-operatives are autonomous, make their own statutes, are free to choose even ex-kulaks as chairmen, and advance only by very easy stages towards collective ownership.

5. The Compromise of Self-management in Yugoslavia

The economic achievements of recent years have not been bad; but when communists want to prove that agricultural growth is more rapid in eastern Europe than in the western, they take 1952 as the starting-point for the curves, the year when as a result of peasant ill-will, production was catastrophic – much lower than before the war. The clearest examples of recovery are those of Poland since 1956 and Yugoslavia since 1953, which, in both cases followed a much desired decollectivization.

In Poland this progress was brought about chiefly by the activity of the rich peasants, but in Yugoslavia it came initially from big investments and from the high technical level of the agro-industrial combines; these cultivate the best land in the country, are continually buying more and receive the lion's share of agricultural investment. Peasants there seem even more reluctant to invest, despite efforts to enrol them in the general co-operatives.

Up to 1968, many notable Soviet economists were regarding this Yugoslav model with growing interest. Self-management is the attempt to hand over the basic power in a factory to the workers, though Albert Meister has shown us its limitations.[19]

National banks continue to decide investment and within certain limits, this control seems useful, if intelligently applied, for producers' interests do not necessarily coincide with those of the nation. A number of communes, likewise endowed with economic powers, have sought to cut down unemployment by creating factories, even unprofitable ones, which soon became known as 'political'.

When a new economic reform in 1965 decided not to subsidize these factories any longer, it became necessary to absorb 250,000 redundant men, some of whom had to go and look for jobs abroad. Western capital can now easily be invested[20] in Yugoslavia. The freedom of the market allows competition and enables the consumer ultimately to influence the direction of production. Confronted with solutions of this kind the 'pure' Chinese veil their faces and pronounce anathemas against the 'return of capitalism'. In June 1968, students in Belgrade protested against the unemployment and emigration, but they also protested against social inequalities and profiteers within the Party and the administration (the 'red bourgeoisie') and against wages of more than £120 a month. This maximum is not so far above the minimum of £75 claimed, during the same month, by the Renault workers in France.

They are experimenting, undogmatically, with a mixed economy based on planning and on competition. At Warsaw, in 1959, Bobrowski[21] reminded us that neither method can now claim the quasi-divine infallibility once genuinely ascribed to it, by its partisans. This is a model of great interest to the backward countries, who cannot institute too much collectivization until they attain a certain level of development; they should not slavishly initiate the Yugoslav system, but try to adapt some of its features to their local conditions. In Algeria, where self-management is developing in a different environment, it does not have the same possibilities as in Yugoslavia, mainly owing to the lack of trained personnel. Mazoyer will return to this point later.

6. *Different Approaches to Economic Reform*

In 1968 and 1969, Moscow's guardianship of socialist thought became more exacting. Rumania, though not totally destalinized internally, showed a more positive concern for national independence than the others, and has not been afraid to defend occupied Czechoslovakia. This sort of nationalism is more acceptable to the USSR than democratization.[22] Meanwhile economic thought is continuing to free itself from the yoke of Soviet dogma, and young economists from eastern Europe are able to come to study the West's results, such as the French plan or their industrialized agriculture.

From 1964 to 1968 then, there has been a whole series of economic reforms, in sympathy with each other to the extent that they attempt to correct the same fundamental errors. The reintroduction of interest rates is proposed, even for loans from state banks to the same state's enterprises. These enterprises' deficits are no longer made up almost automatically, following some politico-administrative observations, but are now submitted to the banks, who take economic rather than 'political' factors into consideration. Profits from the units of production do not serve to redistribute the return on capital, but are taken as a measure of their efficiency. For a long time the administration limited itself to finding out whether the quota of bulk production had been fulfilled, according to a plan more or less badly adjusted to the actual possibilities of production (often according to the report of the director of the enterprise).

This check referred mainly to gross quantity, while quality, being too difficult to measure, was long neglected. The plan is now tending to become more flexible, giving a few basic pointers rather than a whole series of rigid constraints – which leaves a little more autonomy and initiative at the base, such as I, and many others, have been demanding for years.[23] Since decisions can now be taken closer to the site of execution, they will be more relevant to local conditions and actual difficulties. Contracts between groups of agricultural producers and processing plants means that a vertical integration is set up comparable to that of the capitalist world.

By accepting that a certain degree of human imperfection is inevitable, these countries are allowing personal interest to play a larger role. Sometimes the salary range has a tendency to broaden, as in Hungary where bonuses derived from profits can constitute as much as 80 per cent of a director's salary, or 40 per cent for trained personnel, though it shrinks to 20 per cent for the workers. Miners and tractor-drivers formerly used to earn more than young doctors, teachers and agronomists.

Of the many problems remaining to be solved, that of prices seems to be one of the most intractable. Until now they have often been arbitrary, or even quite unrelated to the costs of production. Since they cannot be adjusted *wholly* in accordance with the law of supply and demand, it is difficult to see how the socialist 'fair price' can be determined.[24] Nor is it practicable to correct the most glaring errors by means of successive approximations. If the rates of interest are generally too low, it hardly seems possible to fix them rationally in the absence of a capital market.[25] One is often tempted to look to capitalist economies for the correct fundamental principles, but this too is unsatisfactory.

Within this general trend, however, certain differences became apparent, to some extent linked with the liberalization in politics. The revival of economic thinking in eastern Europe was producing work of value comparable to that in the USSR. Economic structures were thus undergoing, through successive pragmatic experiments, changes which resulted in clear differences between them. There are basic differences in the field of agriculture between pro-Chinese Albania and the mixed economy of Yugoslavia, even within the group of countries which still deserve to be called peoples' democracies.

Poland has retained its state farms; these constitute 13 per cent of its agricultural land, while less than 1 per cent is taken up by *kolkhozes*. Every effort is being made there to raise the level of the peasants by enrolling them in agricultural co-operatives with compulsory rates of investment – but in view of the fact that the countryside is still overpopulated, the bias towards mechanization which these have is disproportionate. The state co-operatives and factories buy the produce and so take a part in deciding the balance of production.

Most of the land in Hungary, Rumania and Bulgaria is culti-vated by producer co-operatives. In Hungary, however, they are given more latitude and initiative; the renting of land has been reintroduced, and the metayage system adopted for remunerating certain kinds of manual labour, while quasi-private cultivation is permitted within the framework of special co-operatives. Though Bulgaria has decided against moving in the direction of the Chinese people's communes, *kolkhoz* organization there, as in Rumania, was recently still very rigid and centralized.

Many other differences could be noted in other sectors of pro-duction or distribution and we cannot say which is the best system; this can only emerge from prolonged experience. Experi-mentation, with errors being constantly corrected, is the only basis upon which socialism can be constructed. It would be very danger-ous to rely on a foundation of time-honoured theories and dogmas whose interpretation becomes ever more delicate. Fortunately these reforms evolved in a freer atmosphere, after long talks in which western economists also participated. Several of us were summoned to Hungary for this purpose.

7. *The Difficulties of Czechoslovakian Agriculture*

Czechoslovakia was fairly prosperous before the war – though there was a marked difference between the development of the Czech lands, which were quite progressive, and Slovakia, which was more backward – more 'east European'. I was very struck in July 1938, by the land-hunger of the small Moravian peasants, who were even forced to grow beet on the sloping banks of road-side ditches. By the agrarian reform of 1947 the large estates were disbanded, while the peasant cultivations were still further frag-mented. From the end of 1948, when the government became entirely communist, more or less compulsory collectivization was introduced. As early as 1946, some dedicated pioneers, such as

Weber at Kydnié, south of Pilzen, had already formed a few small voluntary producer co-operatives, in the midst of great difficulties. Economic constraints, excessive taxation and heavy administrative and police pressures were necessary to convince the mass of peasants. A peasant requesting admission for his son to the secondary school, for instance, could often only obtain it by joining the co-operative.

Many peasants preferred to change their work – especially since agriculture was heavily taxed by the state and the factories paid better wages. This massive rural exodus, without compensating modernization, together with the recalcitrance of the co-operative workers, caused a big drop in agricultural production, which until 1954 remained around 15 per cent below the pre-war level. In the face of this disastrous situation, in 1953 levies on the co-operative funds and forced deliveries were reduced; the pressures towards collectivization were relaxed and production revived a little. These modest results quickly prompted another drive of collectivization; by 1959 it had for the most part been achieved. By 1969 only about 9 per cent of the land was still privately owned – but that included numerous small private gardens and allotments, as well as the more or less isolated small holdings in the mountains.

Since output had only just reached its pre-war level by about 1960, other solutions were sought. The more unsatisfactory co-operatives, especially those in the Sudeten areas, were transformed into state farms; there are 343 of these altogether, with an average area of 4,300 hectares. Together with the research stations and other school and state enterprises, they account for nearly 30 per cent of the agricultural terrain. The individual co-operatives have been regrouped, and in 1967 they numbered 6,450, cultivating on average 616 hectares each. Production did not rise above the pre-war level again until 1965, after a long series of attempts to correct the chief faults in a system that had clearly miscarried.

8. The Failure of Centralized Management and the Anti-peasant Policy

In their note on the 'transformation of agricultural economy in Czechoslovakia',[26] Téran and Lamzer showed that the latter was more or less 'a miniaturization of the Soviet model', in which heavy industry was given absolute priority. On the other hand, the industries which provide the means of modernizing agriculture or of processing its products, had no direct link with the units of production and, being relatively neglected, were unable to play their key role in the industrialization of agriculture. The latter, which received scarcely any funds, had to develop on its own – constituting a 'socialist variant of an agrarianist policy'.

All economic decisions were in the hands of the state planning commission, which regulated the economic life of the state farms and co-operatives down to the smallest details (such as the area of each cultivated plot) through the intermediary of the regional administrations of agricultural production. Téran and Lamzer specify that 'the more hazardous an activity is, the more it requires a decentralized form of management'. But two neighbouring units were unable to communicate except by referring back through the entire hierarchy. All buying of agricultural produce and all selling of industrial products to agriculture were carried out by a state monopoly. The plan only took account of quantity and industries who had no direct contact with their clients neglected quality. This meant that in 1967 the country had a million crowns' worth[27] of unsaleable agricultural machinery on its hands, yet there was never enough food of adequate quality for the cattle ... and so on.

Only bulk production was controlled, and costs were not taken into account; this encouraged free spending and the waste of equipment and manpower on the state farms, so that almost all of them were in the red. Without competition there was no incentive to speed up technical progress. In the co-operatives, forced collectivization without adequate equipment ended by breaking the peasant's sentimental attachment to his land and livestock (the milk yield per cow dropped); in short, it proletarianized him and took away his interest in a structure of traditional large-scale agriculture which lacked the compensations of technical progress.

Though Czechoslovakia had been making extensive studies[28] since 1930, to find the best sites for each crop, the planning commission was afraid of causing further discontent and shared out all the plots more or less proportionally, since some of them did not pay well. As a result, corn and sugar-beet had to be grown in the mountains of Bohemia, where potatoes and natural or artificial meadows would have been more suitable. It was the height of stupidity to try to make the best stock-breeders in these mountains adopt Lysenko's methods of animal selection – yet those who refused, like Weber, who incurred the personal hatred of Novotny were considered traitors!

Since prices were fixed too low, subsidies which made up 13 per cent of the co-operatives' receipts were necessary; this proportion had to be raised to 35 per cent for the state farms, despite the fact that they were highly privileged from every point of view (supplies, buildings, equipment, qualified technicians and so on). The quality most appreciated in the management of these enterprises was not competence, but docility, which was very necessary when so little independence was permitted. Industry paid better and spread across the whole country, which is covered by a dense network of bus services. As the less common articles of diet remained dear – in urban households, 58 per cent of the budget goes on food – many rural families solved the difficulty by sending their sons or husbands to work in factories, while the old people and women stayed on at the co-operative, where they could feed themselves cheaply from their individual allotment and had no problem of accommodation. This progressive ageing and feminizing of the work-force makes modernization even more difficult.

Since before the war, the Czechoslovak communist party had been represented in the Moscow Komintern by Gottwald, who was of working-class origin. He took little account of the peasants and considered agriculture only as one branch of the total economy, without recognizing its specific character. During the war the Germans favoured the big landowners, while the patriotic peasants formed an anti-German coalition with the communists, who dominated the resistance. This bond was strengthened by the desire for agrarian reform, for at that time some members of the party wanted a national agricultural policy with firm historical roots, based on the progressive development of voluntary co-operation.

These hopes were dashed by the Kominform's decision of June 1948, condemning national policies. The party and the ministry took a tougher line and with compulsory collectivization 'the alliance of workers and peasants' came to an end. The centralization of control set up an almost feudal relationship, in which sons of peasants were sometimes forbidden to attend non-agricultural schools – this is in some respects reminiscent of serfdom. It was not until 1968 that the peasants were represented in the National Front! At agricultural conferences, party and government representatives would expound the official aims to delegates of the agricultural and co-operative workers, who had to pass them – unanimously.

9. Economic Reform

After rallying slightly, agricultural production in Czechoslovakia made no further progress between 1960 and 1964, when the national revenue stagnated or even diminished. This socialist system was thus a total failure, in spite of its claim to be the only one capable of promoting a continued high level of growth – as against capitalism with its cyclical depressions. An economic reform was then initiated, under the direction of Professor Ota Sik, which, while retaining collective ownership of the means of production, sought to decentralize decisions and introduce some positive elements of a market[29] economy to regulate the production units – which would then also have to be concerned with their sales. Gross profits, not gross production, were to be supervised, and expenditure was at last to be taken into account. The planning commission was to limit itself to future plans and the general direction of the economy – the latter no longer being achieved by authoritarian directives, but by economic means such as prices, credits, subsidies and taxes. Enterprises, placed on a similar footing by the free play of the price mechanism according to natural regions, would thus enter into competition, and the consumer would also have his say. Within these enterprises, to offset the administration, there would be management councils representing the workers. Economic success would then largely depend on the managers' competence, and only this quality would henceforth bring promotion.

The Czechoslovak leaders hesitated to adopt reforms in agriculture, fearing that the confusion they might cause would add to their already difficult task of getting the country's food-supply on its feet again. In 1967, however, the regional administrations of agricultural production in each district were replaced by 'agrocomplexes'. There were co-operative unions between production enterprises, such as state farms and co-operatives, and industries connected with agriculture. Nevertheless, many agricultural workers, confronted with this departmental initiative, see these agrocomplexes as a new version of state control, particularly as they have to protect the frequently conflicting interests of the state and the producers.

It seems that not many agrocomplexes proved viable, and since the marked political liberalization in 1968, many have stopped functioning. This is not to say that the state should not keep a watch over the economy – but that is as far as it should go. Within broad limits set by the state, agricultural enterprises should be left free to make their own economic decisions and allowed to participate in the management of the factories they supply and by which they are supplied (vertical integration); and there should be greater mobility of the factors of production – both men and land. The state, in short, should no longer interfere with day-to-day running, but try to set up a stable market by using prices, investments and incomes.

It should supply grants for modernization, but only if the improvements are really up-to-date. In the Bohemian mountains they are still building cowsheds in which the animals are hobbled, although the present preference is for free stalling. If Czechoslovak agronomists were to travel more widely, they might not fall so far behind.

10. *The Spring of Prague, and the Winter*

The military occupation by the Russian army and its 'allies' has not put an end to Prague's economic reform, but has made it much more difficult. There is a shortage of coal, because the trucks have been requisitioned by the occupying forces. The instability of the Czechoslovak balance of payments chiefly reflects the inadequate quality of its industrial production. This could have been remedied by the acquisition, with the aid of loans, of a great deal of modern equipment from the West, such as Germany could have provided. This would have loosened Soviet control over the Czechoslovak economy.

The launching of such a reform also requires marked liberalization in politics, for when initiative is handed back to the base, the latter must be in a position to criticize, which rules out censorship.

Bohemia, Moravia and Slovakia are the only socialist countries to have known the so-called fundamental liberties, and they greatly appreciated them. It was amidst almost universal[30] joy that they were rediscovered, at the time of the Spring of Prague,[31] when the communist leaders were made into national heroes to an even greater extent than Gomulka was in 1956.

This kind of initiative posed a threat to those neighbours who had remained hard, such as Ulbricht, or those who had hardened again, such as Gomulka and the Polish partisans. Above all it threatened the excessive advantages of the privileged Soviet minority, the party climbers, the 'new class' whom Djilas denounced. The abrupt return of winter after 21 August, with the occupation of Prague, is after all nothing but an attempt to prolong these privileges, just when they have ceased to be in any way justifiable. The United States' failure to react was only to be expected, since liberal socialism would be a much more effective rival than totalitarian communism.[32]

The military occupation has also shown how soldiers are treated in a 'socialist' army. The old Czech militants were outraged by the accounts of Soviet soldiers being summarily executed when infected with typhus, or for refusing to crush young Czechs who lay down in front of their tanks. Though the USSR claims to be a socialist country, it has repudiated the fundamental tenets of socialism: respect for the ideas of other people, whether Soviet intellectuals or Czechoslovak citizens[33] – and respect for life.

11. The Differing Transitions to Socialisms

Charles Bettelheim has recently published a book called *La Transition vers l'économie socialiste*.[34] In this he employs the singular throughout, as though there were henceforth only one conceivable type of evolution open to a socialist economy, based on the sacred texts of Marx and Engels, Lenin or Mao Tse-Tung, and dependent only on the historical background, the natural conditions and the level of development attained. Bettelheim grapples with a most interesting 'assortment of theoretical and practical questions'. Yet he gives no precise analysis of the practical difficulties which he[35] himself encountered in applying his theories on the ground, especially in Guinea between 1959 and 1961, and Cuba since 1961. This would seem much more urgent to me than a lot of historical and theoretical analyses, such as 'The price system in the Soviet Union in the early fifties'.

Though he emphasizes in the title that there is only one socialist economy, Bettelheim from time to time corrects himself. Thus, on the very first page (page 9), he says: 'This transition, or rather, these transitions . . . by the scientific methods which Marx elaborated, the problems of *the* transition may be correctly stated and resolved.' Here the suggestion, in my opinion, untenable, again appears that for problems of such complexity there can be only one correct way (*mine*, be it understood) of stating or of solving them.

Let me assert once more that in this study I expound my own opinions, based on inadequate knowledge and not always immaculate reasoning; I do not pretend they are more correct than other people's. By the same token, I refuse to recognize any other analysis as being the only correct one, not even if it is originated by the dogmatic pro-Chinese disciples of Althusser from the *Normale supérieur*; their vehemence adds nothing to the quality of their reasoning. True scientific method requires experiments, which are impossible to carry out in the field of history.

The idea that there can be only one form of transition to one precise stage, socialism, which will prepare the ground for the definitive move to communism seems to me to be a reversion to Utopianism, from which Marx himself was not always completely free. The world has entered upon an age of accelerated evolution, constantly producing new and fundamental changes. The human solutions that will be brought to bear can never prove entirely satisfactory, nor always be adapted to fit production conditions which are in a constant state of flux: 1917, 1949 and 1959 are obviously dates of great historical significance, as were 1789, 1848 and 1871 – the last two especially. But this series has certainly not come to an end, and 1968 will not be forgotten; Prague and her students were fighting for us all.

Several passages in Bettelheim's book project the idea of an attainable state of perfection. Thus, on page 75 we find: '*The socialization* of the means of production will be *complete* . . . when society is truly able to use all the forces of production . . . in order to satisfy the needs *it recognizes*.' (The italics are my own.) But who is it who is going to recognize the needs to be satisfied? – this is an essential problem, which will always remain 'to be solved correctly'. Who is to lead society? Who is to represent the citizen, the producer and the consumer 'correctly'? The point at which socialization becomes 'complete' should also be more precisely specified. 'To each according to his needs' may serve as a yardstick for a minimum standard but who is going to say what their needs are, or even whether they are needs, or just desires which are limitless.

12. Tolerance and the Impossibility of a Perfect Socialism

It was inevitable that there should be several paths open to socialism, paths which, though starting at the same point, became increasingly divergent, and there is no strict scientific criterion for deciding which of them is best. Popular wisdom reminds us that perfection is not of this world – nor will it ever be, but that does not mean we should resign ourselves to the most disgraceful imperfections and inequalities. Society may be improved, and this is the general aim of all true socialists' activity, even if they cannot agree upon what *the* socialist society should be like, nor, above all, on the best means of attaining it.

Yet, if there is no one aim that is indisputably the best, the very spirit of the struggle must change. Since nobody possesses the truth, everyone should respect the thoughts and opinions of others and, whenever possible, prefer discussion. Violence may be justifiable in a genuinely liberating revolution, which aims to establish an obviously better society – if no other course remains open, as seems true in a number of Latin American countries. But in this context there can be no justification for Budapest in 1956 or, above all, Prague in 1968, which seem to me as open to criticism as Santo Domingo or Vietnam. Only a genuinely liberating revolution can be justified. The rule of the proletariat must no longer be transformed into rule *over* the proletariat (as J.-P. Sartre expressed it on 20 May 1968 at the Sorbonne). Socialism and freedom must be reconciled. Bettelheim thought that one day society would be able to fully determine its own needs; but I tend rather to believe that this objective will become more and more difficult to realize.

In the already developed countries, such as western and central Europe, it is becoming harder to define what the limits of planning are, since everyone's minimum requirements have been satisfied. These needs, being modest, are all that can be easily defined. It is of course indispensable that there should be criticism of our society of consumption and leisure, increasingly modelled on the United States. We must, however, improve on the Sorbonne's definition of the basic principles of what we wish to substitute for it. At the present stage we could make it our first aim to give workers and students real participation[36] in the running of their enterprise or university.

This is a reformist objective, linked with the fact that the CGT and the communist party, in May–June 1968, categorically repudiated the insurrectional strike.[37] It would seem possible – again, this is only my own opinion – to aim, at every stage, at improvements within the present regime, and at the same time at a total revolutionary transformation when this becomes necessary. But such a revolution, rejected by the communist party as long ago as 1944, and again in 1968, would attract the French in greater numbers, if its pattern for the future were more clearly defined, particularly on the political plane, and if it affirmed its respect for the fundamental liberties[38] – instead of confining itself to economic proposals difficult to carry out effectively within the present framework.

Few of us are still convinced, with the example of the Japanese rate of growth before us, of socialism's clear *economic* superiority, in developed countries. So the attraction of socialism is that it offers a more worthwhile ideal of life – a society of greater political justice and freedom – than the capitalist jungle. This modified socialism should show itself capable of diminishing the old barriers without introducing as many new ones, which might prove even more restrictive. It will not be easy, but the essential purpose of this work is to help those backward countries which have decided of their own accord to adopt a socialist course. It would be paternalistic to try to make the choice for them. To see what really *can* happen, we should look at what is going on in China, North Vietnam and Cuba, countries which are doing their utmost to create a *new man*.

NOTES TO CHAPTER 2

1 This term does not apply to the Soviet leaders responsible for August 1968, who have by their action denied the very essence of socialism: respect for others.

2 'If the agrarian question had been solved ... the Russian proletariat would never have managed to take power in 1917', wrote Leon Trotsky, *History of the Russian Revolution*, Gollancz, London, 1965.

3 1789 followed a financial failure.

4 New Economic Policy, which authorized the renting of land, or even labourers, from less enterprising neighbours, allowed free markets, and so on.

5 Between 1959 and 1965, according to a recent statement by Brezhnev, the growth was 10 per cent, instead of the 70 per cent ambitiously forecast. The growth achieved is not appreciably greater than the population growth.

6   Including education through dialogue.

7   *Cf.* René Dumont, *Sovkhoz, kolkhoz ou le problématique communisme*, Editions du Seuil, Paris 1964.

8   'Lenin, Wake Up! Brezhnev's Mad!', said the posters on the walls of Prague, on 24 August 1968.

9   Which were not always very comprehensible anyway, with the insidious changes of line.

10 This was written in May 1968, and unfortunately born out by the events in Prague at the end of August. On this subject, see the magazine *Politique aujourd'hui*, No. 1, 1968, which is mainly devoted to Czechoslovakia. This magazine was condemned by the French communist party, which has not had the courage to dissociate itself from Moscow's action to the same extent as the Italian party.

11 We must not forget, however, countless instances of capitalism's human toll: the revolt of the silk-weavers of Lyons in 1831, Birmingham in 1820, children working in the mines, Elbeuf and Mulhouse in 1840, the killing of militant syndicalists in Sicily and the United States, Shanghai in 1927, Batista in Cuba – and Samoza to this day in Nicaragua, where many agricultural workers are not even allowed to *buy* milk on the estate for their children.

12 Including the eventual assassination of Trotsky himself.

13 A cultural attaché from the USSR embassy justified censorship during the 'friendship month' of the Montargis lycée, in July 1968. The re-establishment of censorship was one of the basic objects of Prague's occupation one month later.

14 Firstly of Ulbricht and Gomulka, then of Brezhnev.

15 On the barricades in the rue Gay-Lussac, in May 1968, one little old man was weeping over his burnt-out car: 'There go all my savings!' Yet these barricades achieved positive results at a very moderate cost compared to Mexico in October 1968, and the imprisonment of students in Tunisia (the trials of September 1968) and Madrid, etc.

16 As I did at the Agricultural University of Alma-Ata, at the end of October.

17 Brezhnev, in 1968, had not profited by the lesson.

18 At Prague, in October 1948, a communist friend of mine who was at that time devoted to the cause, advised me to read in the bulletin of the Komin-form (which had just removed from Belgrade to Bucharest) an article in which a Polish leader, Gomulka, was accused of chauvinistic, right-wing deviationism. He had just informed me that in Bohemia people often refused to speak German, and was upset when I asked him whether this attitude did not also smack of chauvinism. He unhesitatingly admitted that it was very difficult, even for a staunch supporter who wished to conform, to comply with all the Party's excessively vague directives.

19 *Socialisme et autogestion, l'expérience yougoslave*, Editions du Seuil, Paris, 1964.

20 Lenin himself envisaged this solution in the early days of the Soviet Union; he did not get many takers! However, the Japanese have invested in Siberia and the overseas Chinese in China – why then such narrow-minded severity?

21 An expert on Algeria; he recently mentioned his fear that he might die without having known *the* socialism.

22 Cl. Fuzier (*le Monde*, 28 and 29 July 1968) has written, apropos **Prague:**

'Nothing except the level of the communist movement's evolution determines the degree of common action possible between socialists and communists.' I quite agree about the need for communist evolution; but the socialists should also evolve, in particular by getting themselves out of the Americans' clutches. Le Populaire has long been subsidized by the Americans.

23 For an historical account of agricultural evolution in these countries, see especially: Types of rural economy, studies in world agriculture (Methuen, London, 1957, ch. XIV to XVI) and Lands Alive (Merlin Press, London, 1965, ch. XIV and XV), both by R. Dumont. For the general situation in these countries to the end of 1967, see the February 1968 issue of Esprit.

24 'Kantorovitch has shown that any optimal programme of production corresponds to only one optimal system of relative prices', writes Jean Marceczewski, in La découverte de la science économique en URSS, Le Monde, 7 January 1969.

25 Nor is it obviously rational for a Western country to change its bank rate in order to attract floating capital.

26 L'économie agricole tchécoslovaque en transformation, Institut national de la recherche agronomique, October 1968.

27 Three crowns are worth one franc, non-convertible currency.

28 Cf. René Dumont, Types of rural economy, studies in world agriculture, ch. XVI. Methuen, London, 1957.

29 'We are seeking to offset centralized planning through the creation of a market system to correct its subjective errors . . . errors or faults that could have been avoided had not a model developed elsewhere been transplanted wholesale, as being the universal, standard model . . . Intellectual inadequacy and the inability to surmount contradictions lead people to resort to force', wrote Ota Sik in April 1968, during the Spring of Prague; reproduced in Politique aujourd'hui, January 1969.

30 Including a large proportion of the 65,000 party members.

31 Read Pavel Tigrid's study Printemps de Prague, Editions du Seuil, 1968.

32 This was written before Jacques Madaule defended this idea in Le Monde, 23 February 1969, 'socialisme et liberté'.

33 Jan Palach's sacrifice, in January 1969, prompted the Czechoslovak leaders, who were tempted by 'realistic' compromises, to realize that they had plenty of room for manœuvre – which would have been increased if the French communists had continued to support them.

34 Maspéro, 1967.

35 Who speaks of 'progress and difficulties of planning'.

36 Not in the restrictive Gaullist sense of the term.

37 This position may be warranted by the danger of post-Gaullist military fascism.

38 Readers who have not entirely shaken off their Stalinist allegiance can read One day in the life of Ivan Denisovich, Penguin Books, London, 1963; La maison de Matriona, Juillard, 1967; Cancer Ward, Bodley Head, London (Part 1), 1969, (Part 2), 1970; The First Circle, Collins, London, 1968, Harper & Row, New York, 1968; all by Alexander Solzhenitsen.

CHAPTER THREE

The Ambitions and Problems of the Messianic Socialisms: China, North Vietnam and Cuba

1. *The Two-fold Development of China's National Socialism*

In the beginning few Europeans understood that, in China, social-ism had necessarily to develop in quite a different way; not only because Chinese industry was producing much less, in absolute terms, than Russian industry in 1913 – and infinitely less in propor-tion to its population – but also because in China the communist movement was national as much as social, since the country had been semi-colonized by Europe and Japan. After the failure of the working-class revolt, the torch was taken up by the peasants. The communist party eventually succeeded in rallying the mass of peasants to its standard chiefly because it took a very strong stand against the occupying Japanese, and not just against the native proprietors and money-lenders.

The movement that brought the Chinese party to power was predominantly rural, so that systematically anti-peasant policies like those of Stalin were never adopted.[1] Also, the party was able to make peace with the majority of the middle class, who responded readily to the call of national pride. This enabled production to return to a reasonable level not long after the revolution – much more rapidly than in the Soviet Union. There were, however, many other more subtle factors involved.

Old China held the Confucian belief that 'the idea of the moral code, the ancient *li*, was necessary and sufficient to cause universal social preace to prevail.[2] China had a pre-capitalist economy, and cultural traditions vastly different from those of Europe where, long after the Renaissance, socialism had been evolved during the nineteenth century as a post-capitalist solution.'

Chiang Kai Shek himself attempted something on the lines of 'moral rearmament', which was a complete failure.[3] The red army won over the mass of peasants by its good behaviour, which was very different from the pillaging of traditional sodiers.[4] From the beginning, Chinese socialism adopted a puritan ethic unlike the Russian revolution in its early days. Corruption, prostitution, drugs, gambling, begging and thieving were almost entirely suppressed. One feels much safer in a working-class district in China than in a comparable neighbourhood in Europe, or especially North America.

Yet China initially took Stalinist socialism as its model. In her book, which I have quoted above, Marthe Engelborghs estimates that 'between 1950 and 1957, out of 25 thousand million dollars of investments in China, 21·3 were devoted to heavy industry'. The 'people's republic blossoming from the Middle Kingdom' still believed this version to be the only true one, just as in the old days they would hark back to Confucius as the custodian of all wisdom. This new truth had been revealed by the Party, which was very upset when, in 1956, at its twentieth congress, their 'brother' party in Russia tore down the almost sacred image of Stalin which they had taught the Chinese people to revere. The Chinese will seldom admit to having been so grossly deceived, for fear of 'losing face'.

China broke with the Soviet Union gradually but totally and with gathering vigour began to denounce its modern revisionism, imperialist concessions and neo-colonialism. The priority for heavy industry has been abandoned; and since 1959 agriculture has come first. This was a result of the relative failure of the first plan to set up people's communes, suggested by Mao himself in 1958, which aimed at a rapid transition to communist[5] – and also the total failure of the small country blast-furnaces, which were the final, exaggerated manifestation of the absolute priority given to cast iron and steel production.

On the other hand, about this time a change appeared in the development of socialism. This new trend is of great significance to backward countries who wish to progress by their own efforts, relying on their own resources. Two-fold development means using modern techniques to the full – but as these are, at first, limited, they are made to go hand in hand with improvement of the peasants' and artisans' traditional methods. This idea seems to me very important, because whenever modern industry has been developed in a vacuum, as in Mexico or the United Arab Republic, it has proved very difficult both to reabsorb the men it makes redundant, and to provide the rural population with adequate purchasing power. The main reason why the development of South American industry is at a standstill, is the lack of rural customers with money to spend.

2. The Religious Character of the Cultural Revolution

Since the early days of the revolution in the southern hills, between 1927 and 1933, and even more in the caves of Yenan, 1935–43, the Chinese leaders lived hard, austere lives, that were patterns of devotion to the community and sublimation of instinct, utterly dedicated to national liberation and social revolution. After the break with the Soviet Union, this tendency became more pronounced, especially following the relative failure of the 'great leap forward' in agriculture.

In 1958 it was still thought possible to progress rapidly towards the communism of plenty. In those days they used to say: 'Six years' hard work, for ten thousand years of happiness,' and: 'Communism is paradise and the people's commune is the ladder to it.' At the end of 1958, Chairman Mao promised that everyone should soon have 200 lb of meat a year! When the lean years of 1959–62 came along, he had to change his tune. Belief in the need to restrain the population explosion was accepted and understood fairly quickly.[6] As Marthe Engelborghs wrote: 'Mao's communism will be established without an abundance of material goods, in an atmosphere of puritanism, one might even say of sanctity.' The young French group, the Marchisio, abruptly transferred from swinging Paris to Peking in 1961, were particularly struck by this.

'Each member of the group,' adds Marthe Engelborghs, 'is perpetually striving to improve his virtue and let it shine forth, so as to bring about his own ideological transformation, the transformation of his colleagues and of the whole society.' This seems to contradict Albert Meister's view[7] that militancy and voluntarism cannot develop until a fairly high economic level had been reached, which China has not yet attained. He therefore considers it impossible for these sentiments to operate from now on, in tropical Africa,[8] as I had suggested they might.

Meister could certainly retort that there is no party in Africa with the same influence and authority over the entire population, as the communists possess in China. The correction of dogmatic errors of the 'great leap's' involved admitting that the Chinese peasant was still far from perfect; he was afforded a slight breathing-space in which the rates of investment were reduced, excessive efforts allowed to slacken off and the small (and inefficient) blast-furnaces demolished – while small collectives were made autonomous within the large communes. Above all, the sharing out of food 'according to need' in the public refectories was provisionally discontinued, and once again people were rewarded only according to their work.

Once the food-shortage had been averted in 1962–4, the external danger became clearer, calling for a boost in morale. The Party knew that it was threatened as much by the bureaucratic sclerosis of neo-mandarinism, as by the bourgeois tendencies of the young, who were the mortal enemies of socialism in power. There was in fact a drop in the recruitment of young volunteers to join the Party and the army at this time.

Mao Tse-Tung's economic powers were reduced after the partial failure of the 'great leap forward' of 1958. A number of 'small liberties' had had to be conceded to the peasants: private allotments, free markets, small family cottage industries[9] and so on. In 1966, to regain the power for his appointed successor, Lin Piao, and the army, Chairman Mao unleashed the 'revolution of the proletarian civilization', or cultural revolution, as we call it. His aims were to revive the habit of opposition, rekindle the flame of revolution and free himself from the growing influence of bureaucracy – which is a particularly dangerous reef when one cannot set up Lenin's type of popular control.

This revolution was a reaction against 'modern Soviet revisionism'. Han Suyin has very intelligently defended the rather simplistic, reverent and daunting[10] theses of the Chinese communist party. She stresses[11] 'the rottenness of opportunism, the infiltration of ideas of personal interest, which have given rise to cliques greedy for power ... administrocrats, rather than Marxist thinkers.'

It was also necessary in China 'to dispel the aura of superiority surrounding party members ... each successive generation must ask for, and obtain, its own fresh infusion of revolutionary spirit. ... Religious systems have already attempted such a conversion 'within man's soul', but without bringing scientific efficiency to bear, as Mao Tse-Tung has done', adds Han Suyin. This immense effort and effervescence on the part of the Chinese is of great interest to the backward countries, provided they are capable of adapting it intelligently to their own conditions, but whether this ideological orientation should be called scientific is debatable. Taken overall, the Chinese effort, carried out under very difficult conditions of underdevelopment and overpopulation, unquestionably deserves to be applauded; this done one is in a better position to make substantial reservations.

3. Can Man be Brought to Perfection in a Short Time?

The widespread Chinese system of education has many advantages. It consists half of study and half of non-academic work, a programme which I have also recommended for Africa. Since the pupils' education is largely paid for by their work, it is economical from the outset and can be rapidly extended – whereas the expense of schools in Africa has already become so great that it is impeding the continent's economic development. What is even more important for the future is that schools of this kind should foster respect for manual work, develop practical abilities and skills and allow for the possibility of innovation and fruitful discovery. African schools imitate our own aristocratic humanism too slavishly and this is inappropriate to their level of development; they fill the slums of African capitals with out-of-work 'intellectuals', while depriving the countryside of the young, dynamic element who should have been providing the stimulus for it to evolve.

Chinese socialism holds the optimistic view that men can be rapidly perfected, if the great majority are extremely dedicated to the revolution. Though the cultural revolution may favour a shake-up of ideas, nevertheless, according to Lin Piao, it remains strictly within the framework of 'correct and unified revolutionary thought'. Certainly, the general morality of the Chinese, like their devotion to the revolution, appears to foreign visitors to be much higher than that of the Russians.

I feel that the role of morality in development has been under-estimated by some sociologists and liberal economists, who often deny its existence. Protestant puritanism, however, has been a useful myth in the development of capitalism. Narrow material-ism is too sketchy a creed; a man's actions are not solely deter-mined by short-term interest. Here in China a type of civilization very different from our consumer society is beginning to take shape. Several generations must pass before it can aspire to the promised material abundance (but only for a post-industrial socialism) by Marx.

In the meantime, China may attain a vital minimum of material prosperity fairly quickly, together with a high level of culture, creating a society in which men's lives are dedicated, above all, to the community.[12] This concern, reminiscent of the ancient teach-ings, is not sufficiently present in the West: yet its very excess in China threatens to extinguish all possibility of individual develop-ment. Some compromise might be sought . . . but to our Chinese friends there is a smell of heresy about the very word 'com-promise' – a word we make great use of in this book. To dogmatists of any shade, free thinking has always seemed heretical. Dogmat-ism, with the police states to which it soon gives rise, is our greatest enemy in every country today.

What is most disquieting to an old western university teacher with liberal tendencies, is this imposition of a single frame of thought. Men have a right and duty to interpret these ideas, but their basic premises may only be questioned, under the threat of an excommunication even harsher than that of the Middle Ages, for 'having chosen the path of capitalism'. Intolerance is now the most serious threat to the future of socialism. Han Suyin admits that people wished to submit the intellectuals to all sorts of stupid pressures. Only those who have been through sessions of this kind of criticism know how paralysing such a psychological inquisition can be, and the loss of sleep and appetite it causes; too much of this petty persecution is certainly not conducive to research.

I sometimes tell my pupils that if I were a teacher at the Agricultural University of Peking, I should certainly have committed suicide by now, for in the spring of 1964[13] I was able to see at close quarters how little freedom of expression my Chinese colleagues in the chairs of rural economy enjoy. But how would I have reacted if I had been born in China and lived through Chiang Kai Shek's regime and the revolution? It is impossible to say. Yet I cannot help shuddering at the prospect, envisaged by Han Suyin, of 'revolts, leaps forward, and purges within the Party, until the communist society is brought into being – which may take a *thousand years*'. I believe that men will always remain largely imperfect, and that in some ways this is a good thing, and so I cannot see that an ideal communist society will ever come about; one may well hesitate before sacrificing the self-development of forty generations to it.

We should applaud the immense effort of the Chinese revolutionaries, for the backward nations have a great deal to learn from them. One of the sincerest tributes they ever received was from Kenneth Kaunda, president of the Zambian republic: on returning from China in June 1967, he confided to his colleague and Zambia's friend, Julius Nyerere, 'All these Chinese are hard workers and very dedicated to their community and their country. Evidently they are Christians.' Kaunda's lips could have framed no greater compliment; because although the heads of state in France and the United States and many other places proclaim themselves Christians, the Africans Nyerere and Kaunda really try to live like Christians, which is more difficult.

The leaders of the poor countries might take the harsh, austere lives of the Chinese leaders as an example, as Kaunda and Nyerere have done already to some extent. They would be courting certain failure, however, if they tried to regroup their peasants into popular communes by force, or impose any other extreme form of collectivization on them against their will – especially when one considers the mentality of the peasants and their present stage of development. The Chinese model, in short, like those of North America, Japan and Israel, cannot be reproduced under such very different human, historical and economic circumstances, except possibly to some extent in North Korea and Vietnam. China's civilization, evolved over thousands of years, is quite distinct from that of Europe, and almost equally removed from that of Africa.

Almost alone among the backward countries, China has been able to develop by relying on its own resources, primarily because of its agricultural independence.[14] Nevertheless, the productivity of Chinese agriculture, being higher than in south-east Asia generally (except for Thailand, Malaysia, Formosa and Korea), favours its industrial 'take-off'. The other countries would find it much harder to get off the ground without a great deal of outside aid – which at the moment is largely being channelled into the two Vietnams.

4. North Vietnam puts the World's Most Powerful Nation into Retreat

This French colony was first liberated by means of a hard-fought war, the start of which I saw at Yên Bay in 1930, and then by the peasant soviets of Nghê-An in 1931. On achieving independence in 1954, it initiated an agrarian reform which, in view of the rather different circumstances, was rather too closely modelled on that of China. Every village was required to give up and put on trial several landlords, who were often condemned. In the areas where, as I knew, small peasant farmers predominated, even those with no more than 1·5 hectares, which they often cultivated themselves, had to be baptized 'landlords'. As their service in the resistance was not always taken into account and some heroes were executed, it is easy to understand why the peasants of Thanh-Hoa revolted in 1956, when the army had to intervene.

Those responsible were dismissed and peace was restored. The spread of agrarian collectivization, between 1959 and 1961, made a high level of human investments possible, mainly directed towards the harnessing of hydraulic power. Yet the rise in the yield per hectare – so marked up to 1959[15] – slackened off during the period 1959–65, even before the bombardments started. It was as though many peasants were indicating their preference for working as individuals. Before that time moreover, 12 per cent of North Vietnamese soil had still been privately cultivated without any political, administrative or police pressure being put on the peasants to make them join the socialist or semi-socialist co-operatives.

In the report I gave to President Pham van Dong in March 1964,[16] I stressed the fact that the rate of increase in food-production did not appear to have reached 3 per cent a year since 1959 and that consequently the growth in population had overtaken it. Shortly afterwards widespread birth-control was initiated. In an interview published in Le Monde on 28 December 1967, Pham Ngoc Tam, the minister of health,[17] emphasized that the rate of population growth in Hanoi had dropped from 34 to 20 per thousand within three years.

Some demographers maintain that it takes a long time to produce any substantial reduction of the birthrate, but the exemplary discipline of the North Vietnamese provides an interesting contradiction to this, for the decrease is not due solely to the war. Unless the population explosion is quickly checked in the backward countries, where it is so hard to propagate agricultural progress at the best of times, the difficulties of constructing socialism there may well become insurmountable. Here again it will be necessary to abolish the taboos which still prevail among many revolutionaries, especially in Latin America.[18]

In North Vietnam too, industry started off rather too much on Soviet lines, so the large complexes at Vietri, the steel-works at

Thai Nguyen and the factories of Haiphong were easily destroyed by American bombers. Jean Chesneaux[19] mentions 'the weight of central planning machinery, the absolute priority given to basic industry, the preference for large-scale units . . .' The reaction of decentralization, with small plants following two-fold development, took place fairly rapidly even before the bombardments, which forced it to be generally adopted.

I mentioned, as an example, to women in Tanzania, who are still all too often made to carry the harvest in on their heads, the movement to 'liberate the shoulders': very soon their shoulder-pieces with two baskets were replaced by wheelbarrows[20] or carrier-cycles. This is true socialism, whose first concern is to improve the lot of the humblest and most deprived peasants of the tropical zones (both men and women). The *Can-bo* are veritable socialist monks, whose dedication to the community is quite extraordinary. National unity, consolidated by American aggression, is already making it possible to envisage some kind of wage-suppression – which is considered to be one of the first steps towards communism . . . But that is another matter.

This regime is by no means perfect. North Vietnam, nevertheless, very strikingly confirms the Chinese thesis that men are at least as important as weapons. Peasants armed only with rifles have steadily taken aim at ultra-modern aircraft[21] and sometimes brought them down. Without adequately protesting, we have allowed Vietnam to be devastated by the greatest material power the world has ever known, yet it has shown the world – and especially Latin America – that the North American supremacy is not invincible.

We must, however, establish some more attractive form of socialism, something less monolithic, totalitarian and alienating – more human and efficient[22] to resist imperialism more effectively. In this connection, there is a great deal to be learnt from the Cuban experiment (another setback for the Americans), which I have had the opportunity of studying more fully.

5. The Euphoric Beginnings of Cuban Socialism

Neo-colonialism first reared its head in Cuba in 1901; great strides were taken in the economy during the first twenty years of the American semi-protectorate there. Yet although sugar production passed 4 million tons as early as 1921, thirty-eight years later, in 1959, it was stagnating around 5·5 million, after having reached 7 million in 1952. This represented a much smaller output per head, since in the meantime the Cuban population had more than doubled. Tobacco, tourism, prostitution and associated industries had been added.

The son of an agricultural labourer, who would often be illiterate, could scarcely hope to be more than semi-employed, to cut sugar-cane, or to be a policeman. If his daughter did not care for the peasant grind, she could always go on the streets! Cuba accepted both specializations in this single essential crop and the scaling of sugar production to suit the needs of her great and powerful neighbour. New countries should remember that even if a foreign-dominated economy can get off to a good start by exporting its agricultural produce, there is considerable risk of it stagnating later on.

Castro's revolt was also essentially national in character, directed as much against the American hegemony as against Batista's local dictatorship, abominable as that was. It was primarily led by students – even then – initially with the support of the young urban intelligentsia; the communist party generally remained more or less neutral to the dictatorship. The poor peasants took rather a long time to convince but afterwards, together with the plantation and sugar factory workers, they became the movement's most faithful supporters.

Victory in January 1959 was acclaimed by the great majority of the population in the joyous atmosphere of a National Front. Fidel Castro then tried to define his ideal of humanistic socialism: 'bread and freedom'. In 1959 he made overtures to the United States, not realizing that their political wisdom abruptly waned whenever they heard the word 'socialism' pronounced, or when anyone laid claim to real independence, even if only in the realm of economics. The first agrarian reform law, of May 1960, was reformist; yet its application, entrusted to the army, was distinctly revolutionary. The moderates then quitted the government, while the middle-class progressively fell away from this revolution which was proclaiming itself socialist. The final break with the United States came in the summer of 1960, and most of the technicians, with agriculturalists well to the fore, emigrated to America, lured there by promises that were not always kept.

When the United States stopped buying sugar at preferential prices, a drive of rapid collectivization was triggered off which to a level-headed observer might have seemed too hasty, since it outstripped the possibility of setting up a new and really efficient administration. The Cuban leaders, however, and especially the top one, the *lider maximo* himself, are too ardent always to reason coldly and objectively, or to take account of the actual situation, real possibilities and human limitations. Their reactions are often those of guerrilla fighters, based on emotion. Having been violently rebuffed by the Americans, Fidel Castro naturally turned to their opponents, and even to their ideology. Since the Cuban bourgeoisie were wavering, and even in some cases siding with the Americans, he speeded up collectivization and, on 11 August 1960, announced that instead of mere reforms there would be an agrarian revolution; there was no longer any question of compensating landlords.

The decision, at that time, to set up a socialist state could have started with a fuller and more rational examination of the experiences of other socialist countries – not in order to copy them, but all the same to take them into account. At that time Fidel Castro's overweening confidence led him to say[23] 'Since we started (forty-eight hours after the disembarkation from the *Granma* in December 1956) with only thirteen men, and managed to swell our numbers to 45,000, we shall easily surmount all these present difficulties.' Henri Denis emphasized, in January 1968, how inappropriate he felt guerrilla tactics were for the solution of economic problems.

Recently Mazoyer and Gutelman explained to my pupils that

when a socialist government puts the whole population to work and rapidly achieves full employment, as has been the case in Cuba since 1961, then the amount of wealth created must increase. Now in Cuba, between 1960 and 1963, agricultural production dropped by about a quarter. On the self-managing farms in Algeria, from 1962 onward, it sent down about 30 per cent – while twice as much labour was being employed.[24] Propositions of a purely theoretical character should be distrusted, even if they seem quite logical. Productivity per man-day worked went down about 50 per cent on the Cuban *Granjas* between 1959 and 1963. The blockade and America's attacks had a hand in this of course, but they are certainly not the whole story.

6. *Guerrilla Tactics in the Economy; No Role for Co-operatives*

In 1959 the confiscated estates were handed over to the National Institute of Agrarian Reform (INRA), which, as Gutelman tells us[25] 'was also given the task of applying government policy on all the estates'. The INRA, run by the rebel army, was the only body to have the confidence of the government, which distrusted traditional administration. Its director-general, who had been chosen for political reasons, lacked the slightest preparation or experience necessary for the proper running of such an organization. Gutelman points out that 'the creation of a strong central body, with hierarchical administration' led to very extensive 'compartmentation of the economy. Facts counted less and less, while the "hierarchy" had an increasing tendency to enforce its own point of view.'

Less harm would have been done if this hierarchy had been competent, but instead of putting an agronomist of Alonso Olive's calibre in charge of agricultural production, they chose a 'reliable' man with little understanding of these problems. The technicians began to emigrate in greater numbers and were thus denied the responsibilities which many of them would have been capable of taking on. This led to growing problems in internal and external planning of economic decisions, in the search for an optimum

D

allocation of investments in purchases from abroad and the rational use of producer goods and so on.

These problems would have been surmounted more rapidly if the productive enterprises had been granted financial autonomy. Everyone would have had the maximum interest in better organization if his wages had depended on it. Of their own accord the Cuban leaders decided that the workers would prefer the *Granja del Pueblo*, which was more or less a state farm. This was done without even consulting them at the outset, in 1961, though they asked no more than to be kept informed about what was being decided. The prevailing arguments had a theoretical and textbook character. State property, said to belong 'to the whole people', was *a priori* considered superior (according to the sacred texts, some of them by Stalin) to co-operatives, which were only the property of a group.

Considerations of this sort do not help to fill people's bellies. The dogmatic rejection of any kind of co-operative model for the confiscated estates[26] seemed to me fundamentally mistaken. Gutelman should at least have been able to examine the reasons for this step. The co-operatives would have given rise to many problems, and would undoubtedly have made it necessary to reintroduce land-rent on the state's behalf. It would have been necessary to foresee what was forgotten in 1960 – the need for a minimum level of investment. The co-operatives would, however, have inspired the workers to put twice as much effort into their jobs. In September 1963, the Soviet economist Bondarchuk observed: 'For every peso of wealth the *Granja* worker produces, he gets paid two pesos of wages.' This idea scarcely appealed to him, since the Soviet Union was paying part of the second peso. The natural consequences of such demagogic measures were the earlier onset of inflation and rationing.

Bondarchuk added that, whereas Cuba was making every effort to nationalize the whole commerce in perishable goods, with very limited success, in the Soviet Union 60 per cent of these transactions still took place through private markets and the co-operatives. The curve of agricultural production in Cuba reached rock-bottom in 1963, when only 3·8 million tons of sugar were produced. Something had to be done quickly or the economy would have foundered.

7. Some Improvement Through Decentralization

Gutelman gives a very interesting account of the various measures which were then adopted. By the second agrarian reform the dispersed plots belonging to the *Granjas* were regrouped and, when they became too large, reduced in size. Some decentralization took place, giving greater power and autonomy, not yet to the *Granjas* themselves, but to regional groupings of them, called *Agrupaciones*. Finally 'the singleness of managerial responsibility, together with executive autonomy' was re-established at every level. Yet these improvements did not go far enough. As Gutelman says: 'Judging from the example of other socialist countries, such a rigid conception of the singleness of power seems to entail considerable delay in the taking of decisions.'

Cuba then attempted to make the system of state production work more smoothly, though without wishing to re-examine its basic principles. In order to give the workers a personal interest in increasing their efforts, it would have been very useful if they could have seen concrete results within a short time, in the context of collectives of limited size, whose scale they could grasp. Fidel Castro's discussions with the crowd, interesting as they may be as a means of education, nevertheless still have a paternalistic flavour, and they are really dialogues, for the replies are often prompted.

Even if planning is now essentially established at the base, the very slight part played by material self-interest would seem to call for a host of regenerated men, utterly devoted to the regime. I cannot say that I have come across many Cubans as dedicated as their Chinese or North Vietnamese counterparts – apart from the high-ranking leaders. Even if the latter work themselves to death, they often do so in air-conditioned offices. The sugar-cane harvester, who spends the whole day out in the hot sun, does not have the consolations of gratified vanity open to a man like Che

Guevara; so he cannot react in the same way, and it annoys him to see bureaucrats – even those who do nothing – getting better wages than himself. A drive against bureaucracy has also proved necessary in Cuba, especially since 1966.

In 1959, after a brief hesitation, the Cuban leaders rejected the idea of dividing the large estates up into peasant small holdings; a technician can hardly prove them wrong. Yet in May and August 1960, we found a more widespread desire for property among the Cuban peasants than Havana would admit. Next, those in charge sabotaged the co-operatives for sugar production which were being tried, by giving much greater privileges to the rival *Granjas*. Co-operatives are no longer employed, except when small peasant cultivations are being regrouped.

8. Fidel Castro has no Doubts

Many workers on the *Granjas* felt that they had merely had a change of master, from the owner to the INRA administrator. They did not quite feel 'at home', and it hardly seemed that they were working 'for themselves'. 'Revolution' and 'the State' are abstract ideas, harder to grasp than that of the collective ownership by a small group of producers of the concern for which they work.

Like the Chinese, the Cuban leaders see the economic reforms that have taken place in recent years in the Soviet Union and eastern Europe, making extensive use of material incentives, and a turning away from socialism. The system of state control with which they started is proving very difficult to decentralize effectively. The Che Guevara party are seeking to create through education a new kind of man, utterly devoted to the cause, but it would be dangerous to overestimate the rate at which the average man is able to evolve.

The most serious defect seems to me to lie in the overweening confidence of the Cuban leaders, and especially of their chief. Che Guevara recognized that he had failed as Minister of Cuban Industry and was able to take the consequences by resigning.

Afterwards he was not afraid to give his life for the cause, by going off to fight under almost hopeless conditions – feeling perhaps that he might be of more service to the revolution as a dead martyr than he was alive; or he may have overestimated the revolutionary potential of the Bolivian peasants and miners.

Fidel Castro involves himself in everything, and he is in danger of being swamped under a mass of small details. The Cuban economy is developing thanks to the good sense – but at other times, in spite of the mistakes – of the *Commandante* (or *'caballo'*, as they call him) who, for better or worse, carries the whole country with him. His colleagues understand the danger of his penchant for doing things on a gigantic scale[27] and sometimes try to bring him to his senses. As early as 20 May 1960, however, I had the opportunity of observing that a certain atmosphere of obsequiousness surrounded him – which is very disquieting. Those responsible for the *planes especiales*, better known over there as 'Fidel plans', have priority for all resources of materials, products and manpower. Such a negation of rational planning often ends in disorganizing the work of other enterprises, which are suddenly deprived of essential materials needed for production.

As I have been able to judge, there are many matters upon which Castro is ready to believe that he knows better than the experts; as with the equally rash Khrushchev, this leads him to make very costly errors, which have to be paid for in the end by other socialist countries, or by the privations of the Cuban people.

Using 'selected' seeds bought from the Guineans, plantations were made of the quite valueless wild oil-palm. For the Mayari 'tomato plan' 5,000 hectares of very poor soil, subject to erosion and lacking irrigation, were used. The fuss made about the vineyards and strawberry cultivations seemed to bear no relationship to their actual importance, which was very slight. One must seriously protest against rice-fields being transformed into artificial grazing, in a land where the production of this basic food had fallen by 50 per cent between 1959 and 1964. As for the vaunted 'world record' of thirty-five million pheasants reared when there was a shortage of tubers, another basic food – this seems to suggest that all sense of priorities has been lost.

In 1959 and 1960, some forests growing on very sharp calcareous rocks, economically unsuitable for cultivation, were reclaimed in the extreme west of Cuba and on the island of Turrigano. In 1968–9 the Che Guevara party continued their furious assault on the 'marabu', a tropical legume whose leaves provide valuable fodder. Poor soils were denuded, whereas it would have been better to begin by putting the more fertile pastures under cultivation. At great expense high-yielding Canadian cows were imported, before there was any possibility of feeding them properly. Fidel Castro talks of having earth laid over the rocks in order to cultivate them, 'because man masters nature'. What economic studies have been undertaken to determine which of the mass of possible courses should have first priority? Production could be increased very easily and at very little expense, by putting the best meadows of Camaguey to the plough.

Hundreds of similar examples could be given, but let us halt on this slippery slope before we find ourselves roundly condemning the whole Cuban revolution, which contains so much that is positive. It was greeted with joy at its inception – 'the Cuban festival' as Ania Francos called it. The great mass of workers, until then so despised, regained their dignity with the revolution. This cannot be too highly valued; neither can the really exceptional educational effort. Attainment of literacy on such a massive scale is unique in the world. The production of Cuban cigars has risen considerably and their quality has on the whole been re-established. Industrial output appears to have increased by 50 per cent between 1959 and 1965. One now sees eggs being freely offered for sale. It seems rather hazardous, however, to have staked the Party's honour on reaching an objective of ten million tons of sugar in 1970, when only five and a half million tons were produced in 1968. This shortcoming cannot be entirely attributed to the drought.

In the long run the scarcity of forest products may well prove a decisive factor in holding back the development of the Cuban economy. The priority given to sugar, though certainly deserved, is nevertheless excessive in that it has led to the neglect of food crops, so that the economy has remained colonial in type. It may be that Cuba, formerly dominated by the United States, may be dominated for a long time to come by the Soviet Union. Many controversial problems remain unsolved. The people should be allowed to decide for themselves, with all the facts before them. When I hear that 'Cuba has chosen such-and-such a concept of socialism', I wonder if it was really Cuba, or Castro.

The above was written in June 1968 and confirmed, alas, on 24 August 1968, when Castro justified the Soviet invasion 'by the fact that Czechoslovakia is moving towards capitalism'. This is rather a hasty statement; here again he is being too quick to lay down the law, ignoring nationalism and failing to recognize that the Czechs also might cry: *'Patria O Muerte'*. He does not know the situation in Czechoslovakia well enough to speak out in this fashion.[28]

Until 1967, writers and artists in Cuba were able to work in an atmosphere of cultural freedom such as was then unknown in the Soviet Union. Since 1968 this has become less true.[29] As yet there is no political apparatus through which principles or policies may be challenged, nor any economic structure to enable workers to participate in making the basic decisions. Everybody feels themselves to have some sort of official standing, which often means that they slacken their efforts. Profits are regarded as immoral but disinterested motives are still not capable of taking their place. Militarization is used for promoting socialism.[30]

This rapid survey of socialist phenomena in various parts of the world will seem very open to criticism, and is certainly not exhaustive. However it has enabled me to define the central thesis of this book: that there exists no privileged form of socialism, whose superiority would be self-evident to any impartial observer or sincere revolutionary. The Third World leaders who say they have chosen *the* path of socialism are increasingly coming to understand that there are many paths to choose from, and many socialisms.

What we are trying to do is to help them make their choice, by analysing some of the experiences of those who have made the decision before them – without seeking to conceal their failures, which to date have been more numerous than their successes.

But to begin with we will attempt to brush the cobwebs off some socialist dogmas, first set forth when conditions were very different from today. This will lead us on to state our own ideas of socialism, without presuming to claim any special superiority on their behalf.

NOTES TO CHAPTER 3

1   The official line is nevertheless quite clear: 'The revolutionary party of the proletariat must lead the peasants in the way of co-operation; this thought is always in chairman Mao's mind.' *La Chine*, January, 1968.

2   *La grande révolution prolétarienne chinoise*, by Marthe Engelborghs-Bertels, 'Civilisations', Brussels, vol. XVII, 1967, No. 4 *Bulletin du Centre d'Etude des pays de l'Est* of the Institute of Sociology at the Free University of Brussels.

3   See Han Suyin, *L'Eté sans oiseaux*, Stock, Paris, 1968.

4   At the same time, we should not forget the 800,000 (?) landlords summarily executed. Many deserved it, but certainly not all.

5   'Marx did not recommend people's communes,' said the Russians – as though he could have foreseen everything, for all time. It will soon be the same with Mao's thoughts, whatever the Chinese may say about them now.

6   This proves that the lowering of the birthrate does not depend solely on raising the living standard, but also on education and political conscience. The rate of population growth in China appears to have dropped from 2·3 per cent to about 2 per cent a year, or even less.

7   *L'Afrique peut-elle partir?* Editions du Seuil, Paris, 1966.

8   In France too, May 1968 has shown how dangerous it is to be so dogmatic. 'Some very old-established reflexes, labelled "idealistic", such as a feeling for justice, love and freedom, irritation at the pride and indifference of power, and hatred of savage repression – these reflexes, so long belittled or even ridiculed by scientific analysts, have appeared in full force,' writes Claude Bourdet in *Le Monde*, 5 June 1968, *Prévoir et Voir*.

9   In 1968 they were severely criticized. It would be dangerous to suppress them because 'excessive optimism leads to disenchantment, and to a resistance disproportionately greater than the degree of disappointment. The psychological compensation of a scapegoat is required', says H. de Chaponnay.

10   The issue of *La Chine*, March 1968, quoted above, castigates 'the Chinese Khrushchev' – Liu Chao Chi. It is hard to see why they took so long to denounce such a public malefactor; for as early as 1949, we are informed, 'he hastily threw himself into the unbridled propagation of capitalism, opposing socialism with all his might'. For the Party to nurse such a viper in its bosom for so long, seems to argue a certain lack of vigilance. It is hard to imagine what the secret reaction of Chinese readers with a little education can be.

11   *China in the year 2001*, C. A. Watts & Co., Ltd, London, 1967.

12   Han Suyin adds: 'It makes the city superfluous as a cultural centre and

stronghold of institutions. Cities must not absorb all the brains, talent and know-how. Millions of young educated people have settled in the communes.' Here is food for thought.

13 *Chine surpeuplée, Tiers-Monde affamé*, by René Dumont, Editions du Seuil, Paris, 1965, pp. 155–9. To make out that the little red book and the army's intervention can be the source of all ideas and the basis of all practical solutions, is going a bit too far. From an account of an operation for cancer, it seems that miracles can be performed by referring to this book: one would think one was at Lourdes!

14 Paul Bairoch has calculated that 'according to Western estimates, the income per head in China was approximately the same in 1950 as that of the rest of (undeveloped) Asia; today it is 4 per cent higher. According to the official figures the difference is even greater' (incomes of nearly 300 dollars per head in 1965 – this seems to me exaggerated).

15 The increase in the number of man-days worked per hectare seems to have overtaken the increase in yield per hectare, so that there appears to have been an appreciable reduction in the productivity of the man-day worked, which has been observed in southern China as well.

16 Published in the magazine *France-Asie*, No. 1, 1966.

17 Killed at the front, at the end of 1968.

18 Not to mention the inflexible position adopted by Paul VI in his encyclical *Humanae Vitae* (July 1968), which is content to ignore the dangers of famine in the Third World.

19 *Le Vietnam*, Maspéro, Paris, 1968. See also Le Chau's interesting study *Le Vietnam socialiste*, Maspéro, Paris, 1966. The figures given in this book were out of date even when it was published since they often go up to 1957–60, but seldom to 1961.

20 This was only introduced into South Korea in 1966, several centuries after being generally adopted in near-by China. It seems to me that Korea is the only country in the world where harvests are most often carried on men's backs.

21 'Shumaker (the American pilot) took fright; the peasant of Quang Binh remained cool and fired right at the engine of death that was bearing down on him', writes Dr Nguyen Khae Vien, *L'Epreuve du feu*, Hanoi, 1966.

22 By approving of Czechoslovakia's occupation, in August 1968, North Vietnam weakened its moral position. Silence would have been understandable.

23 Interview with Jacques Chonchol and René Dumont on 26 August 1960, at the Ciénaga de Zapata.

24 M. Mazoyer states that the achievement of full employment is not the cause of the drop in production.

25 *L'Agriculture socialisée à Cuba*, Maspéro, Paris, 1967.

26 See *Cuba, socialisme et développement*, by René Dumont, Editions du Seuil, Paris, 1964.

27 Such as the recent scheme to drain vast polders, or the slap-dash citrus plantations on the Ile des Pins. When Castro announces that agricultural growth will be 15 per cent per *year* for the next twelve years and that within two years milk production will increase fourfold, he must be joking.

28 In this speech, full of contradictions, he criticizes Novotny ('who sold us some old scrap arms taken from the Nazis') just as sharply as Dubcek. It seems to have called forth hundreds of approving telegrams. There were undoubtedly some who had reservations but preferred not to express them.

29 In January 1969, Haydée Santamaria, the heroine of the Sierra Maestra, once more defended freedom of expression.

30 See the postscript written in 1969 for the American translation of my book, *Cuba*. Grove Press, New York, 1970.

CHAPTER FOUR

Socialist Ideas Called into Question by the Facts

1. A Few Reminders from History

Socialist thought, as Henri Denis reminds us,[1] first found expression among 'the French eighteenth-century philosophers, who championed progress and the light of reason', and 'understood that to preach liberalism is to admit the established order, which they opposed'. This struggle against what the Sorbonne students of 1968 aptly called 'the established disorder' was to develop further as social injustices increased, which they did considerably at the start of the industrial revolution. In affirming the 'superiority of the right to work over the right of property' Fichte raised the question of planning; he 'saw very clearly the awkward organizational problems to which socialism gives rise, and realized that their difficulty increases with the division of labour and the diversification of needs'.

Fichte was not a revolutionary, since he looked for 'reform from on high ... by a priestly caste of scientists, who would define social truth with absolute authority', and 'a sovereign animated by the spirit of perfect justice'. It can be seen from my previous remarks that this is unalloyed Utopianism, and I am irresistibly reminded of how Hitler[2] and Stalin managed to interpret these words. Saint-Simon suggested that, instead of engaging in wars and conquests, society should organize work with a view to production (or development as we should say) and to 'improving the moral and physical existence of the weakest class'.

Denis gives Proudhon credit for his penetration in raising the 'problem of reconciling social justice with the preservation of individual freedom'. The Utopian socialists, some of them with primitive Christianity in mind, dreamed of returning to an ideal society. Before the problem could be posed in its entirety, a Hegelian had to learn from the economists that the value of things depends on the work that goes into producing them; he then had to ponder the fact that workers do not enjoy the fruits of their labour, but only receive enough to subsist on. For Marx 'the explanation of history must lie in studying the development of human needs and of man's productive forces ... the basic reality of capitalism is the extortion of surplus value by means of capital'.

For a long time he hesitated to announce his predictions for the future and held up the publication of *Das Kapital*. He declared that the poverty of the working-class would increase until they were driven to revolt. The facts have not borne out this prediction at all, as far as the industries of the more developed countries are concerned. Yet it cannot be denied that there is a *relative* pauperization of the peasant fringe in the rich countries and among the vast majority of the inhabitants of the Three Continents. In some parts of the Andes and in southern India there is even absolute pauperization by precolonial standards. A certain increase in poverty (paralleling the increase in wealth) has therefore occurred, even if it is not quite what Marx predicted, and the recent threat of famine could make it even worse. The danger of famine is more closely connected with the population explosion than with capitalist expansion – though these two phenomena are not unrelated.

Great credit is due to Marx for his efforts to construct a form of socialism, which he called scientific (though this use of the term seems to me improper). 'He anticipated Keynes,' Denis reminds us, 'in showing that the immediate cause of depressions was a lack of investment.' I would add that it is also frequently due to the producers not having enough purchasing power. His most fertile idea, it seems to me, was that the attitudes towards production should evolve at the same rate as the forces of production, or capital equipment and technology as we say now. However, in predicting an inevitable decline in the rate of profit – leading to a situation of under–employment of the factors of production, which would in the long run prove intolerable – he did not foresee that the state would one day possess means of greatly mitigating these depressions.

This cannot be held against him, except by those who still take his writings as holy writ – an attitude which, as André Stawar recalls,[3] was not shared by their author. We may leave such disputes to Marxists and Marxologists, merely referring the curious to the Soviet and Chinese Marxist institutes of the *Institut (Paris) des Sciences économiques appliquées*, or to the reports of the symposium held at the UNESCO headquarters in Paris, from the 8 to the 10 May 1968 to mark the 150th anniversary of Marx's birth. From our point of view, it would be more useful if the basic principles of Marxism–Leninism in action were to be constantly reviewed in the light of what concrete results they have achieved.

2. Ambiguities in the Concept of Worker and Proletarian; the Contempt for the Peasantry

The first mark of the proletarian, according to the Marxist definition, is that he does not possess his own means of production. The word has also acquired a general connotation of suffering and misery. Yet in the developed countries the worker has the benefit of equipment that is continually being perfected and made more productive – and which consequently procures him an ever higher standard of living. He may even buy shares, thus becoming a co-owner.

I am certainly not going to suggest that a socially equitable form of popular capitalism, along the lines advocated in France by Ricard[4] and in the United States, is soon likely to become universal. Workers in America are still being exploited, though to a limited extent; they complain very little, except for the poorest, coloured fringe of Negroes, Puerto-Ricans and Mexicans, whose plight is getting worse. In some respects, however, they are also exploiters, since they profit by the food, raw materials and labour provided too cheaply by the poor countries.

Like 'peasant',[5] the very concept of a 'worker', who does

exhausting physical work, is rapidly declining in the developed countries, in the sense of a manual labourer. Although it is true that the pace of working on a production line may cause undue nervous strain, and that housing and transport conditions contribute to fatigue and so on, the proportion of qualified workers, such as technicians, clerks, draughtsmen, programmers, engineers and administrators, has been rapidly increasing since computers and automation arrived on the scene. Even granting the dubious principle of working-class dictatorship, the ever-shifting boundaries of the 'working-class' would constantly have to be redefined.

One ought to be able to say that it is still this class's destiny to lead mankind, that it is still specifically revolutionary, but, as we saw, there was very little sign of it in the early days of Castroism. In the Richelieu lecture-room at the Sorbonne, on 3 June 1968, an Egyptian student protested vigorously against the assertion, by an African Marxist reciting his catechism, that the working-class were 'in essence revolutionary'. In Egypt, as in black Africa, the workers are relatively privileged compared to the mass of peasants.

According to P. Biarnès,[6] a clerk or worker in Dakar makes as much money in one month as a Senegalese peasant makes in a year. In 1927, Mao had to seek refuge in the hills among peasants to continue his struggle, which had met with failure in the towns. Early in 1968, the Czechoslovak communist party gave us to believe that the workers there were more conservative than the majority of students and the intelligentsia; these two groups have also played a more prominent role in heading revolutions in China as in Cuba and the USSR. Marx and Lenin were of bourgeois extraction.

It seems to me, as an agronomist of rustic origin, that the concept of working-class dictatorship makes the fundamental error of underestimating the role of the peasant. He too is a man who works, with specific civilized values which for the most part are worthy of respect. There were many Russian *moujiks* (in 1905 and 1917), Mexican *peons* (in 1911–20) and Cuban *campesinos* (in 1957–8) who were nevertheless revolutionaries, playing important or even decisive roles. Besides, to rely entirely on the working-class would mean postponing all hope of revolution, and consequently of any decisive social progress, until after the industrialization of the Third World. The real proletariat of today, it seems to me, are the peasants of the non-industrialized tropical countries.[7] This is especially true of the peasant *women*, crushed as they are under the combined burdens of work in the fields, carrying, pounding grain, housework and children – they are the real slaves of the atomic age. Socialist theoreticians – almost all men except Rosa Luxembourg – have largely ignored the exploitation of women by men, which is particularly bad in the Muslim countries, from Pakistan to Senegal and the coastal regions of Tanzania.

Even when the peasants possess their means of production, these are so paltry that they do not disqualify them from the glorious title of 'proletarians', or at least 'semi-proletarians', as Mao called them. A cutting tool or *machete*, one or two hoes (called *daba* or *hilaire* in Africa, *enxada* in Brazil) and sometimes a hatchet make up their weighty capital of a few kilos of crudely fashioned steel for the poorest peasants. Let the 'proletarians' of Detroit, who ride in private cars weighing more than one and a half tons, salute them!

3. Dictatorship of the Proletariat; the Need for Opposition

The proletariat, or even 'the whole of the people', do not in practice have the opportunity of exercising their power themselves, for this could only strictly occur within the context of a city like Athens, or a small Swiss canton. In China, though only during periods of cultural revolution, more direct intervention is possible through the posters and meetings of students in schools and universities. Despite appearances, however, even the cultural revolution was largely directed by the party members closest to chairman Mao who, though a minority within the party, organized a concerted revolt against the majority – an unprecedented and uniquely fascinating event – in the history of communism.

The Russian revolution of 1905 started with the soviets set up by the workers of St Petersburg themselves, without the unions; 1917 began with a libertarian slogan for self-management: 'All power to the soviets'. Yet by 1918 the party dictatorship had worked out its centralized plan for the economy, and the anarchist Makhno had been exterminated by the political police, after having beaten Wrangel in the Ukraine.

From then on the party leaders, with their corrupting appetite for power, were the real dictators. Except in China, North Korea and North Vietnam, a very marked class differentiation has re-appeared in socialist society, this time chiefly based on the exercise of political or economic power, rather than the right of property. I observed in 1962 that between a 'simple *kolkhoz* member' from a poor agricultural producer co-operative, and a driver of the powerful harvesting machines on a 'millionaire' *kolkhoz*, there could be a wage differential of as much as 50:1. (The differential is never more than 4:1 in the Chinese communes.) The Belgrade students in 1968 protested against 'the red bourgeoisie'.

Dictatorship may lead to very dangerous consequences in such an atmosphere, preventing injustices at the root of society from being challenged and hindering the struggle against new forms of exploitation, not unlike the old. Djilas reminds us that the exces-sive privileges of the new ruling class enable it to exploit new kinds of surplus value for its own advantage. There is a great gulf fixed between the Moscow academician and the simple *kolkhoz* labourer of the Oka valley, only forty miles east of the capital. In the capitals of the popular democracies, as in Moscow, 'privi-leged minorities' are to be found, whose arrogance and privileges will always need putting down. The arguments justifying their existence are becoming increasingly difficult to sustain, especially since August 1968; we have seen what scandalous abuses they can cover.

The danger of the former possessors returning in force must be guarded against of course, but popular control should not there-fore be discarded; not only the bureaucracy, but even the top leaders should come within its scope, Fidel Castro and Mao Tse-Tung included! Opposition, criticism and self-criticism will always be indispensable to the progress of a socialist society,[8] and instead of being limited to practical details, as at present, they should have far-reaching powers. Socialism claims to be voluntarist, and wishes to direct the economy. This means that it can make mistakes – which are not automatically rectified, as in a market economy, by 'the invisible hand of profit'. Means must therefore be provided for bringing these mistakes rapidly to light, for delay in recognizing them has been largely responsible so far for the unsatisfactory economic achievement of socialism.

Such freedom can hardly be confined to economics. Socialism would soon have to admit its inferiority at any rate in the developed countries, if efficiency of production was the only battlefront it was defending. Its attraction must lie in its being able to fulfil the people's aspirations better than our 'society of conditioned consumption'. Not without good reason, the 'basic liberties' of the capitalist regimes have come under fire from the socialists. Their shortcomings have been thrown into relief, sometimes almost caricatured by the Gaullist radio and television services, which were at the beck and call of an autocratic regime. What remains of these liberties is none the less precious for all that, especially freedom of speech and access to all information and documents, which are less evident in the socialist states. The criticisms of the socialists would carry more weight if they defended these liberties better in their own countries, as the Czechs tried to do.

Modern mass-media are very expensive to run; the man in the street cannot imagine possessing a television broadcasting station, or printing a national daily at his own expense.[9] His liberty has to some extent been confiscated by the effective custodians of these costly instruments of mass communication, both capitalist and bureaucratic, and cannot be fully exercised unless the ordinary listener or reader has democratic control of the various media, whether it is Prouvost or the Soviet State that owns them.

Sincere socialists must admit that socialism will never be perfect, and will always stand in need of effective opposition, whose nature and scope will themselves always be debatable. The triangle of authority, liberty and justice will never be perfectly equilateral. I am not qualified to examine every aspect of these daunting problems, but elementary common sense leads me to think that if the spirit of tolerance, recommended by the freemasons, were more widespread, then the people's desire for freedom could more easily be satisfied. This tolerance, however, should not be extended to the intolerant, such as those responsible for Santo Domingo, Vietnam, Budapest, Prague and so on.

4. The Simplistic Formula: 'Collectivization of the Means of Production'

Handing over the means of production to the community is said to be the first step towards de-alienating man and putting an end to his exploitation by his fellows. Those who do not do this, ranging from the various 'African socialisms' to the Scandinavian countries, cannot be recognized by the purists as being truly socialist. Among the Scandinavians, however, economic power is controlled in the workers' interests and incomes are to a large extent redistributed by means of taxation. This has enabled them to retain the vitality of capitalism, while reducing social inequalities and giving priority to collective benefits.

It seems rather dogmatic to take collectivization as the only criterion of true socialism; there should be much more latitude.[10] Whether collectivization is practicable depends primarily on the techniques of production and the development of the forces of production. There can be no question of collective ownership for the paltry implements of the African and South American peasants.

Samir Amin goes further and recommends several decades of primitive capital accumulation before socialism should be considered in tropical Africa; modern socialism is very different from a primitive community and cannot seriously be entertained until a certain level of industrialization has been reached. The movement towards socialism in rural Africa would mainly consist in extending the cultivation of cash crops and the use of draught-animals, together with the gradual introduction of an exchange economy. To encourage progress along these lines, Amin believes that forward-looking young farmers should be removed from the patriarchal environment of their family and the village community, which are dominated by old men set in the old ways. The little plough drawn by a pair of small oxen is, he feels, a typically individual implement, quite unsuitable for co-operative agriculture. In Guinea and Mali, the very indifferent results achieved by the co-operative fields, which are generally worked by hand and sown too late in any case, seem to confirm this view.[11]

Yet the Chinese collectivized their agriculture on a massive scale in 1955, before their industry was in a position to equip it properly with machines to 'give free rein to the socialist enthusiasm of the formerly poor or moderately well-off peasants of the lower stratum'.[12]

'Collectivize' is easy to say, but difficult to do properly so that production is increased. What can be collectivized and how it can be done most efficiently at every stage of development still needs to be clarified. A socialist revolution usually starts by collectivizing the large means of production, those which are practically 'socialized' already. Yet the Chinese socialist co-operatives of 1956, and even the people's communes of 1969, only altered the organization of manpower which was essentially still using traditional peasant implements.

For a long time the cowshed on a Soviet *kolkhoz* was (and sometimes still is) no more than a few sheds for looking after cattle, placed side by side, rather like our own industrial workshops during the eighteenth century. One may well doubt the wisdom of measures such as those of Cuba in 1968, by which all businesses were collectivized, including small hairdressers and hot-dog stands. So long as an agricultural, artisan, retail or service enterprise remains within a single family, with perhaps one or two assistants from outside, it seems to me more efficient, and therefore more sensible, to leave it in private hands.

When we come to a shop with more employees, or a small business, the case is more difficult to decide. The problem of the *nature* of collectivization also arises at this point. To whom will the means of production be made over? This is another problem of power, of where the decisions are to be made, and the optimal distance between this centre and the place where the decisions are carried out. Giant hydro-electric power-stations, petrol refineries or harbour steel-works with a capacity of several million tons per annum should obviously be appropriated by the nation.

Light industry, on the other hand, can often be managed better on a regional, provincial or municipal basis – a kind of decentralization which has been carried to great lengths in China. Or it can be run as a mixed economy, like the Niari Sugar Company in Congo-Brazzaville; this arrangement makes it possible to combine high technical standards with effective control by the state – provided the latter does not fall under the influence of private interests. Finally, it may be left to private enterprise, so long as the planning commission is given adequate powers to divert all investment to projects that are really useful to the community.

Self-management might even be considered, as in Yugoslavia and Algeria, where an enterprise is in principle run by the collective producer, whose property it is. The best form of ownership depends on a very large number of factors: the scale of the enterprise, what the producers want, the needs, aims and outlook of society, the level of development, political orientation, and ultimately, skill in choosing. But if socialization is attempted prematurely as in Guinea and Mali (1959–61), it may prejudice development.

The ultimate aim of socialism should be to manage the means of production so that public interests are placed first, while at the same time safeguarding the possibilities of individual fulfilment. This is much harder than simply decreeing collectivization, and will require a constant effort of adaptation. Then there is still the problem as to which investments are to have priority, and through what channels or institutions this is to be determined. The question is not to decide on a particular form of socialism in the abstract, but to carry it out in practice – which is where the whole difficulty lies.

5. Self-management; Clashes and the Limitation of Property Rights

A group of workers will not have all the skills needed for managing the technical side of an enterprise of any size, such as the Yugoslav agro-industrial combines. Qualified technicians, engineers and administrators therefore have to be recruited from outside the group, and often outside the area. This must lead to differences between these managing technicians and the body of workers on matters of conception, organization and demarcation. The workers cannot always be aware of the technological constraints on production, possible outlets, requirements of development, or the overriding necessity for investment – to which they would naturally prefer bonuses.

Everyone is in principle to be paid according to the work he does, but how is it possible to establish beyond all doubt the 'fair price' of goods, or the 'proper value' of work as qualitatively different as scientific research, art, literature, or even politics? A cubic metre of stone broken by hand, or of earth shovelled to a certain distance – these are easier to evaluate. The managers, on their side, often prefer to deal with the workers as if they were employees who were compelled to obey them on pain of being sacked, rather than as participants; whereas under true socialism they would learn to argue with the managing director on terms of equality.[13] When the workers can do this, economic democracy will be established, and the Soviet occupation force in Czechoslovakia will be pitted against the workers' councils.

There are many other areas of conflict, particularly between the interests of the producers and those of the community at large. The latter has the job of carrying out the plan, which has been devised theoretically in the general interest. The workers, however, may prefer to exploit local markets advantageous to themselves, even though this involves satisfying a more or less luxury demand which the plan does not cater for. Moreover, the obligation recently laid on enterprises to pay their way (Belgrade, 1965) cannot always be reconciled easily with planning requirements.

No society will ever be free from conflicts and contradictions, which are the catalysts of change, so the idea of a communist golden age is pure utopianism. Socialism must also find ways of becoming more efficient, since that is its weakest point. No one has yet been able, Séverac says, to draw a judicious line between decentralization of economic administration – so necessary to its efficiency – and certain forms of private ownership. This is a very difficult problem, and one which only revolutionaries in opposition, with no practical experience of administration, would decide out of hand.

Yet socialism is unthinkable, he adds, unless some of the means of production are limited and regulated. Therefore, at every stage of development and in every historical and human situation, we must look for compromises; they will never be perfect, and we shall always have to work at improving them – and to this end we must be free to question them.

Séverac recalled that I had never attempted to construct a theory of socialism, adding that this generally indicates a desire for political power. But such an appetite may be quite legitimate, provided the power is not misused; but we must know its ultimate aim – which is not always to improve the condition of the weak, however loudly this may be proclaimed. There can, of course, be no comparison between Fidel Castro's aims and those of a man like Mussolini.

6. *Other Forms of Exploitation; One Man's Day is Worth Thirty Men's Lifetimes*

Traditional socialism has laid great emphasis on exploitation taking the form of surplus-value extorted by the employer from the wage-earner. Before roundly condemning this,[14] we should first consider what use is made of it; for in a developing society special preference should be given to directly productive investment over luxury consumption. Yet though such investments add to the country's wealth, they also enrich the proprietor at the workers' expense, thus aggravating their social inequality. However, there are many other extortions which are more parasitical in that they also cause wide differences in income, but without raising the general level of production.

The oversimple division between capitalist and proletarian is no longer valid in our modern society, since many other forms of exploitation have evolved. The small proprietor (like my uncle in the Ardennes), who works even harder than his two or three assistants, sometimes finds it very difficult to make ends meet, while providing a valuable service to the community. Yet the lion's share of the national revenue goes to the flourishing tertiary sector. Film-stars, some writers and advertising men, many trades-men and members of the liberal professions – including inter-national experts – are quite disproportionately well-paid.

One has only to see how much doctors fear being forced to work on a salaried basis, and then look at the shoots they rent, to get some idea of the mixture of dedication and self-interest which sometimes goes to make up their profession. It is unreasonable for them to go on strike; and the same goes for airline pilots. An antique dealer on the boulevard Saint-Germain[15] told me recently that he had bought a Rubens for £6,000 and was hoping to sell it for £30,000. By this single transaction he will thus have made as much as an unskilled Renault worker earns in thirty-two years – practically his whole working life, and as much as an agricultural labourer in the poverty-stricken south of India would make in thirty lifetimes, or a thousand years of work, at the rate of £24 a year (200 working days at twelve pence, without board).

7. Enforced Central Planning with Complete Collectivization is not Necessarily the Best Solution

Marxist economists, like Charles Bettelheim, tell us that planning cannot really be carried out without widespread collectivization; otherwise enterprises, instead of following the aforesaid plan, will go after profit. A completely *laissez-faire* economy would be totally ruled by the profit motive. Even though a theoretically pure example of such an economy has never existed, this type of system has for a long time been the predominant one. Strict centralized planning, on pre-1963 Soviet lines, is nevertheless only one of the possible ways in which planning can be carried out. In its time certain people considered it the best in theory. In practice, however, it has been quite unable to demonstrate any real, con-crete superiority, and therefore has finally had to give way to other methods.

As we have seen, especially since 1963, all the economic reforms in progress in the Soviet Union and the people's democracies have in fact involved making planning more flexible, by extending decentralization and allowing greater responsibility and initiative at the base. Profit has been used more extensively as a criterion of economic efficiency, and this has made the physical side of planning less important. Economic facts have proved to be more effective than administrative imperatives. The element of competition, largely responsible for capitalism's vitality, has thus been reintroduced between co-operative or state-run enterprises. The market has an even larger role in Yugoslavia, which is considered a betrayal of socialism by the Chinese, who feel that true socialism ought to be less inegalitarian,[16] though not completely levelling.

For the most part, the new independent states are not yet in a position to collectivize large sections of their economy effectively. They may therefore quite legitimately prefer some form of indicative planning associated with a mixed economy, without having to court excommunication. The movement of prices, with control over investment and foreign trade, make it possible to act with greater flexibility, taking more account of the reasonable desires of the consumers and the needs of the community, these being the two groups which must come first. These priorities are the marks of a true socialism, and they should really be respected.

It seems wrong to condemn all these intermediate forms on dogmatic grounds, for they are certain to produce results if political power is really out of the hands of the monopolies. Nor can it be asserted that these forms will only be adopted provisionally: their social, political and economic efficiency will carry more weight than theoretical considerations when it comes to deciding how useful they are and how long they will continue, and this will depend on how well they are able to evolve and adapt. As the choice of system cannot be based on strictly scientific criteria, it will, in the last analysis, be a political decision.

One may well doubt the common sense, political sense[17] and sincerity of those who glibly lay down the law about such complex problems, by deciding which systems are socialist on *a priori* grounds. The Soviet leaders of 1969 reserve the term for those who enable them to maintain their privileges. I would prefer to try to appraise them by their concrete results, so that my opinions could be discussed, and retracted more easily should the situation change – whereas the USSR cannot afterwards revoke its over-hasty condemnations without losing face. In Hungary it has authorized economic reforms which it condemned in Czechoslovakia, undoubtedly because speech was freer there. Russia claims to be in possession of the truth; when I began teaching in 1936, I reserved the right to make mistakes, otherwise I should have been quickly reduced to silence.

8. The Impossibility of Rigorously Scientific Socialism

Marxism–Leninism claims to be the only scientific form of socialism; we have seen what abuses – horrors even – such a claim may be used to justify. The method of science is to frame laws and then (provisionally) demonstrate their validity by means of experiment. In this way, certain phenomena may legitimately be attributed to certain causes, if the latter are repeatedly followed by the former. Scientific experiments cannot, alas, be performed in the field of history. The conditions under which one revolution takes place, for example, are never duplicated.[18] Besides, there is no clear direction in history, as historians have fairly conclusively shown; no system can pretend to be 'in the mainstream of history', or use this as grounds for condemning all other systems and justifying all its own abuses, by recourse to peremptory, unproven assertions.

Mankind is certainly evolving – by dint of a series of brilliant advances, alternating with setbacks, hesitations, mistakes, downright absurdities and even the most abominable crimes, which cannot at all be said to be indispensable; they are just as questionable as 'the infinite goodness of the Grand Architect of the Revolution'. If only the masses had been better educated, and less infected with the viruses of racism and chauvinism, man might very well have done without his recent wars: Jaurès might have succeeded and decolonization have been peacefully accomplished. We have emerged, as Monod points out, from the Stone Age only to sink back into an age of concrete shelters. Though shelters may not be necessary to it, the atom bomb is still the most perilous of our aberrations no matter who manufactures it – as the *Mouvement contre l'armement atomique*[19] illustrates. The drama of man's situation is that his technical inventiveness has far outstripped his morality, humanity or ability to manage effectively increasingly complex societies.

The multiplicity of current interpretations of Marxism–Leninism is further proof that it is not as scientific as it claims to be. Each school of dogmatists,[20] in the USSR or China, pretends to sole possession of the truth, and since all their vehement claims are quite incompatible, we may well deduce that they are invalid. It would be ridiculous to try to show that one or another of these cliques was either completely right or utterly wrong, since they affirm their revolutionary purity, their possession of the truth and their exclusive ability to give a 'correct' analysis of the situation, without a shred of evidence to support their claims. This enables them to dogmatize without proof, to fabricate the grossest lies, and insult, occupy or excommunicate people as the need arises, for want of being able to convince them.

9. Collective and Individual Self-expression; Foundations of a Self-critical Socialism

The first aim of socialism could be the search for happiness. This quest would justify egotism however and lead to the glorification of economic liberalism, if it were limited to the individual. In February 1959, in New Delhi, a rich Indian told me: 'I have twenty-six servants and I have just come back from the United States, where servants hardly exist any more; so I am not in favour of the American Way of Life.' Many rich men can only appreciate their wealth by contrast. They cannot really enjoy it unless they are surrounded by the poor, whom they turn into beings subject to all their wishes and prostituted to their despotic inclinations. We find the same thing, only worse, in the case of a man like Stalin, in the very heart of a so-called socialist society.

So the quest for happiness cannot justify the right to individual development unless it tends to promote, rather than prevent, the development of others. This collective search means that there must be a system that favours the development of everyone, which is no small requirement. Yet there are certain prerequisites which seem to be indisputable: to begin with, the right of every man to full mental and physical development – to receive the vital minimum, within the limits of productive capacity, that will enable him to live a complete life. All children,[21] for a start, must be entitled from conception, and certainly from birth, to a protein ration adequate to supply everything their brains need for development. During the next decade, at least a hundred million children in the tropics will have their mental growth permanently stunted because of protein deficiency. This is absolutely criminal – and future generations will find it hard to forgive us, if their sense of human solidarity is any greater than ours. For we should be in a position to provide them with this minimum of protein, if only it was not so badly distributed and so often wasted – and if the ending of this criminal neglect were given priority over armaments, or even over the race to the moon. The moon may be of great scientific interest, but there are more urgent problems.

Real socialists are also pacifists, and have a right to peace. This right was forfeited by the social democrats when they ceased to oppose the tide of war by which Europe was submerged in 1914. Afterwards our 'socialists' acquiesced in the Rif war, and other colonial repressions in Indochina after 1936, Algeria in 1945, and Madagascar in 1947. From 1946 they accepted the war in Indochina, and even took a leading part in the Algerian campaign and the infamous Suez expedition. In modern pacifism, the forms of non-violent resistance need to be revised so as to make them more effective (as in Prague, in 1968–9) – not excluding some kinds of guerrilla activity, but at the same time condemning the use of atomic weapons. It must struggle incessantly against the various forms of racism, chauvinism (even of small countries), excessive nationalism, xenophobia and tribalism. Inter-African massacres, from the Sudan to Biafra, are just as abominable as those of the

South African racists; while the Vietnam war is even less excusable than any of the others.

The search for happiness also means that everybody should have the right to as high a level of education as circumstances permit, and one better adapted to the economy's needs.[22] This is a very complex problem; there were some sociology students who demanded that they should all be given positions, even this meant overstaffing. UNESCO now gives priority in advanced functional literacy only to a section of the illiterate adult population, to make it easier for them to master their jobs rapidly, thus increasing the productivity of their work, upon which development depends; that is the primary and essential aim of education.

I would put down the traditional liberties, mentioned above, of expression, communication and the diffusion of ideas, as the fourth priority, without meaning thereby to undervalue them. These imply the possibility of criticizing, even in their own columns, *Pravda, Hong Oi* and *Granma* of Moscow, Peking and Havana respectively, as well as the Springer Press in West Germany, by other means than by printing a careful selection of their readers' letters. For nearly two centuries now, the developed western democracies have placed these freedoms first, and they forget that they can only be enjoyed by well-fed people, living in peace, who have already received a minimum of education. The illiterate peasants of north-east Brazil have an extraordinarily limited vocabulary. The way the rich countries forget this priority is sometimes quite startling, as when we recommended parliamentary democracies before any appreciable development had taken place; though this did not seem absurd to everyone, since this form of government is more susceptible to foreign manipulation.

It is easy to define these priorities, but much harder to suggest ways of achieveing them; the 'socialism in freedom', adumbrated in Prague, is a very difficult undertaking. The attempt would be made to realize these basic priorities in stages, so mistakes and corrections would be inevitable.[23] The aim would be to construct a fairly efficient economy at the service of everyone, forming the basis of a society where every person was free to develop, while serving the prior needs of the community.

A development of this kind, directed towards the common good and carried out by fallible human beings, calls for a society where there is constructive opposition, with everyone participating as far as possible in making the basic decisions. The events of May 1968 caused these ideas to gain ground rapidly within the university;[24] it would be a good thing if they could really be introduced into the factory. However, effective participation in the making of decisions, which is the first step towards self-management, will raise as many problems as self-management itself. In 1969 the employers and the CGT agreed in rejecting it. No one can still pretend that real social progress is an easy thing.

'Take your desires for realities; hand over power to the imagination,' exhorted the free Sorbonne of 1968, adding that henceforth it was 'forbidden to forbid'. It makes one smile to think that the students have not realized that constraints will be necessary in the socialist society which, for want of being able to construct it in the near future, they are going to imagine and specify. They turned France upside-down, but their political analysis seems rather scanty for people who believe a revolution possible in France not long hence.[25] I am not talking here of Stalinist constraints, but of those of all developed societies, from which they will not be able to escape.

They will rediscover the time-honoured conflicts, not only between liberty and power, but also between liberty and the search for greater equality, for which a certain minimum of obligations are required if social injustices are to be reduced. It is a gratuitous act of faith to suppose that the state and sanctions will shortly disappear. But what constraints, even those necessary to economic development, will seem acceptable? An unenforced and unsupported obligation, like unlimited freedom, ends up by being ineffectual; there must therefore be a certain consensus of opinion in its favour – but how is this to be determined?

The plan would naturally have to be established democratically, with as many people participating as possible. Furthermore, to make up efficient works-committees delegates will be required, whose competence and representativeness will always be matters for discussion. As Séverac says, it is impossible to teach everybody everything and make everyone the judge of everything. Communication is not gratuitous and therefore cannot be universal. To believe in absolute equality is to court bitter disappointment.

10. The Protosocialism of National Bureaucracy

Stalinism denied these contradictions within socialist society, though this did not stop it repressing them. It is to Mao's credit that he recognized them in his 1957 study 'On the correct handling of contradictions among the people'. Nevertheless, his classification of the various contradictions, antagonistic or otherwise, might well be questioned, outside China anyway. These contradictions will never be resolved – even provisionally – without the give and take of criticism, self-criticism and opposition, whose scope should be extended to include basic principles and the choice of a political system. Politics is indeed in command, as our Chinese friends proclaim. If the workers', and therefore society's, interests are really to be defended, then the struggle for political power should have priority over a general collectivization of enterprises which the new government would not as yet be in a position to manage properly.

At every step, however, this power is in danger of degenerating and ossifying, to serve the ends of a clique of greedy leaders and of a bureaucracy with petit-bourgeois origins. In 1963, Claude Cadart[26] put the two 'socialist' regimes of Russia and China on the same footing by labelling them both 'protosocialisms of national bureaucracy'. When the socialist states realize, as Cadart does, that in the scale of history they are mere children still (even after fifty years) and that they have, and always will have, a great deal more to learn, then they will be well on the way to making more rapid progress. As a matter of fact the Soviet journalists who were at Hanoi in March 1964 did explain the economic shortcomings there by reference to the youth of socialism as compared with capitalism.

Its maturity should be eased and hastened though, by extending the scope of opposition to deal with political decisions, such as the structure of the government or the economy, or even the very form of the socialist society. The USSR is desperately trying to halt Prague's progress in this direction; its broad principles have gradually been elevated into dogmas, but without any title to divine right. Men have a tendency to perpetuate institutions which once fulfilled a need, and all bureaucracies – whether of the Vatican, Washington, Moscow or Peking – resist reforms which might curtail their privileges.

The establishment of these protosocialisms has done nothing to suppress either national rivalries or ideological conflicts, as Marx had hoped; these are the two factors primarily responsible for the recent Sino-Soviet hostility. In addition there is a very great economic disparity between them, which the Russians, if they were truly internationalist,[27] would have attempted to reduce by sharing out their own resources. On the other hand, the struggles for independence of Czechoslovakia and Rumania in the Soviet bloc, and of France within the Atlantic alliance, seem, for the present, to have a positive aspect – provided that recognition is soon given to other forms of supranationality which do not involve giving way to a stronger power, but rather integration into a true community of equals, in fact as well as in right. Contrary to the wishes of the other Common Market members, who are still too few, de Gaulle refused this kind of integration to the United Kingdom.

Extensive criticism is permitted in scarcely any of the countries where socialism has taken power, especially not in the Soviet Union. The criticism authorized in China is only directed at certain individuals and groups, but they can in no way step outside the framework of the 'Great Helmsman's' thought, without great risk to themselves. Only Yugoslavia and Czechoslovakia (from January to August 1968) have been able to take this opposition further, and even then within rather narrow limits. Some discussion is still possible in Cuba, though always restricted to certain fields, hence the dullness of the Press in this beautiful land. Yet the average level of morality in China and Cuba is higher than in the Soviet Union.

11. Priority of the Three Continents; the Defeat at New Delhi

The disinherited of the earth are the underdeveloped countries; they are as yet scarcely industrialized; the terrible and imminent threat of famine hangs over them unless the birthrate can be rapidly checked and their food production greatly increased. The socialists of the wealthy nations, from the Atlantic to Vladivostock, have the means to reduce the gulf between rich and poor, which has been steadily growing wider in recent years, by giving them more and better aid. Thus the too often purely verbal affirmations of human solidarity could result in concrete action. Those 'socialists' who have still not disowned their intervention in Algeria and Suez shall remain firmly between inverted commas until they admit the error of their ways. There were practically no *Section française de l'internationale ouvrière* members among the insurgent students of May – that is something that will take a long time to live down.

When China began to display greater independence, the Soviet Union refused it further aid. It seems that Soviet aid to the backward countries is sometimes less than France's contribution.[28] A rich nation has no right to call itself socialist as long as it continues to exploit the Three Continents – or the people's democracies. This means, firstly, that the markets of both agricultural and mineral raw materials must be organized on a world-wide basis, so that fairer prices may be agreed on. It is of course impossible to fix an absolutely fair price for each commodity at every moment. However, they could now be raised and stabilized without undue apprehension, for this would certainly diminish the present injustices. Such a rise should be made to depend on increased consumption, rather than merely on reduced production as in the case of the Malthusian international agreement for coffee.

The next step is to give the Three Continents preferential markets for their processed agricultural produce and the products of their young industries. This means increasing aid to these countries for equipment and technical training, with the wealthy nations contributing a net inflow of capital[29] equal to at least I per cent of their gross national product. With Jean Barets (*Technique et Démocratie*) and the Soviet academician Sakharov, I would even suggest raising this rate progressively, within the space of about fifteen years, to 4 per cent of the national product. Sakharov mentions the figure of 20 per cent, but this is unrealistic. Paul Bairoch's more judicious proposal is that 44,000 million dollars should be devoted to aid in 1970. Of course it is not available. The above proposals approximately correspond to those which the governments of the backward countries presented to the United Nations Conference on Trade and Development held at New Delhi in February and March 1968, following the conference of Algiers in 1967. Confronted with the obstinacy of the wealthy nations, both socialist and capitalist, the Delhi conference ended in almost total failure; which showed that the rich countries not only lack all sense of ordinary human solidarity, but are also blind to their own long-term political interests. I no longer try to appeal to their hearts – except when addressing young people who are still idealists – but only to their common sense. Meanwhile, the manufacture of atomic weapons by China may do something towards raising their level of political intelligence.[30]

12. The Stages Towards a World Economy

Industrial development in states which are very small and poor is practically impossible, as we shall see, in the absence of the huge markets necessary to enable large modern factories to pay their way. The United Nations therefore has advised the formation of regional economic federations which would be continually enlarged. The Common Market has shown that such creations raise many political problems: firstly as to the extent of the supranational powers, leading to the progressive abdication of the more injurious forms of national sovereignty involving aggression.[31] In this way, stage by stage and starting from the top, we might set about constructing tomorrow's united world, which is so essential to the survival of the race.

If it could be approached through a common front against

E

imperialism, the first step could be to set up a world-wide economic organization, which would be universal from the start, with China, Korea, Vietnam, East Germany, and the other countries excluded from the United Nations, among its members. If it were given greater powers and was truly supranational, this body could be more vital, active and efficient than the present international organizations. Using funds derived from an international solidarity levy, which would be progressively increased, the development of the backward countries could be undertaken with better chances of success. Its starting-point might be to accept the initial principles described above, which the New Delhi conference rejected. It would also need political powers to enforce its decisions, reached by a majority vote, so that they would be properly carried out in practice. This could mean having armed forces in common one day, if general disarmament does not come about soon enough.

This scheme is not an attempt to conjure up a vision of a heavenly world, in which everyone strolls peacefully about with an olive branch in his hand. All this will never come about through a general consensus of opinion, dragged out of people by moral exhortations. There will be difficulties, sweat, tears; struggles against pressure-groups, imperialism, nationalism, chauvinism; conflicts of interest as well as of ideology. ... Yet peaceful co-existence has already shown us that world wars – which must now inevitably prove suicidal – are not indispensable to progress, whatever Galbraith may say. Future conflicts will not necessarily follow the simple lines of the cold war between socialism and capitalism, since these two blocs are no longer homogeneous.

More to be feared is the possibility of conflict between great nations thirsting for dominion and small countries struggling for independence; or between the bloated rich and the determined poor, the well-provided countries and the proletarian nations. There will always, in any case, be contradictions, tensions, competition and grounds for conflict, as much within countries as between them. The Chinese cultural revolution has shown us one possible way of harmlessly resolving them, by taking calculated risks less dangerous than those of John Foster Dulles. I remember the two factions at Peking University who used catapults to bombard each other from neighbouring buildings, in March 1968. The Czechoslovak resistance of August–September 1968 also introduced some cunning innovations.

13. Socialism Combined with Freedom, at the Lowest Cost

The cost of capitalism in human terms was very great in the early days of industrialization, while the cost of imperialism still weighs heavily on the peasants of most of the backward countries. The human cost of Stalinism was dreadful too, and cannot be shown to have been really necessary. Daniel and Sinyavsky, the Czech people and many others can testify that its burden is still oppressive. The Three Continents are trying to find the best and least costly way out of their underdevelopment, poverty and ignorance – when they are not being betrayed by their privileged minorities. Those who have become aware of the oppression of the United States in Latin America, and who suffer most from it, are seeking to rebel.

The fact that one form of capitalism has proved successful in developed countries does not mean that it is suitable for the backward countries. 'Liberal government and a market economy favoured the West's industrial revolution, but they cannot perform the same function for underdeveloped countries ... since the nineteenth century they have only enabled gross output to increase by 2·2 per cent a year, which is less than the present rate of population growth in the Third World. During the eighteenth and nineteenth centuries the capitalist entrepreneur class had its role to play, but the conditions of those days have now practically disappeared. These conditions were: simplicity of techniques, the small size of the producer units, the existence of a working class, the fact that credit was more important to agriculture than to industry, the absence of social legislation or international agreements, the high level of profits in industry, and so on.'

Paul Bairoch, whom I have summarized above, deduces from this the need for disaggregated planning to promote agricultural and industrial progress (through agrarian reform and investment), as well as a policy of birth-control, which he too rates as a top priority.

Man's great hope of a Free Socialism would seem less difficult to realize in the developed countries. Yet there are several quite different socialist systems vying with one another for the Three Continents' favour. I cannot make the choice for them, since my knowledge of the whole situation is not sufficiently extensive – though most leaders and militant revolutionaries also lack adequate knowledge.

These city-dwellers do not always 'feel' the problems of the peasants very well; they should first go into the country and make a thorough study of actual situations, facts, views and economic and human problems there, so that their political decisions can be based on sounder foundations. A minimum of well-organized effort, and therefore of constraints, appears to be essential for hastening development. These constraints might be made to seem more acceptable by generating enthusiasm for the aims proposed, so that everyone could understand that he is really working for himself and his children.[32]

Already a number of basic principles are emerging. Firstly, there are the perils of fascism, especially the military kind, as well as of unchecked power, dogmatism, bureaucratic abuses, of imperialism with its insidious, lying propaganda, of unjustified constraints, the overestimation of man's capabilities, and of ideological incentives. Secondly, there is the need for dialogue, discussion, a critical sense, wider scope for opposition, initiative, responsibility, general participation in decisions, and sustained efforts to reduce social inequalities, without pretending that a perfectly egalitarian Utopia will soon come about. Thirdly, priority should be given to the basic essentials of development, which, under any regime must be, on the one hand universal education, with growing emphasis on technical training, and the enthusiastic support of those involved, and on the other, productive equipment, which must follow parallel development if maximum efficiency is to be achieved.

In the second part of this book, I shall try to illuminate these rather abstract and general propositions by examining the results achieved by a number of backward countries that have chosen various forms of socialism, not all of which seem to deserve this title. I shall also add some notes on countries that have deliberately preferred non-socialist economies. It is essential, as we shall see, for solutions to correspond more closely to the actual circumstances, which can be extremely various. The way these solutions are put into effect, the general level of organizing ability and the amount of enthusiasm generated are at least as important as the choice of system. No system is universally valid; however, we are anticipating.

One conclusion which stands out more and more, is that it is impossible to tell which is the 'best' solution; so the pursuit of alternatives should never be forbidden, anywhere. Economists often define their aim as the production of the maximum amount of goods and services. It would be both more precisely and more generally true to say that progress leads to increased possibilities and greater freedom of choice in every field. The selection of a marriage-partner, a job, a type of society, community and way of life – these are factors essential to happiness which cannot be expressed in tons, or even in bills from the hairdresser. I would be tempted to reformulate the very concept of value were I not afraid of venturing into the thankless *terra incognita* of philosophy.

NOTES TO CHAPTER 4

1 *Histoire de la pensée économique*, Presses Universitaires de France, Paris, 1966.
2 It seems that fanatics come from the right, since a whole series of liberals were assassinated in Germany in the twenties, and have always been assassinated in the United States. No one assassinated Hitler, though his death would have been even more worthwhile than that of Stalin, since everything depended on him.
3 *Libres essais marxistes*, Editions du Seuil, Paris, 1963.
4 *Nouvel Observateur*, 16 December 1968.
5 Cf. *La France sans paysans*, by Gervais, Servolin and Weill, Editions du Seuil, Paris, 1967.
6 *Le Monde*, 5 June 1968.
7 As well as the unemployed of the slums.

8   In my speech in the big lecture-room at the Free Sorbonne, on 1 June 1968, the vast majority of my 3,000 listeners applauded this sentence.

9   An initial capital of four million pounds would be needed.

10 'Perfected socialism involves more than just public ownership of the means of production; the levels of education and production must be higher than those of capitalism, and the people should really hold the power,' says Hassan Ryad in *l'Egypte nassérienne*. I would add that, in my opinion, socialism will never be perfected.

11 I give further consideration to this point in chapter 6, on Tanzania.

12 *La Chine*, No. 3 of 1968. Twenty years after 1949 it is difficult to understand this continued insistence on the social origins of workers (and often of their parents), since most of the population do not remember the old regime.

13 When de Gaulle, on 8 June 1968, put forward his proposals of participation, it was tempting to reply that he had had every opportunity to practise this himself, in the exercise of power, for a full decade.

14 Séverac considers that the surplus value should not be reckoned as the diminution of the quantity of material goods to which the worker is entitled since the reality of any such deduction cannot be proved. More serious is the fact that the workers forfeit their power of economic management. This new definition, however, is equally hard on the forms of socialism based on centralization.

15 He condemned the students of May 1968.

16 The Russians consider Chinese communism to be too egalitarian, and only appropriate at the very beginning of development, so that it would endanger economic growth if it were artificially prolonged. We shall be in a better position to reply a generation hence, in the light of events in China.

17 Brezhnev, August 1968.

18 Advice to students: the methods of May–June 1968 cannot be successfully repeated during the winter of 1968-9.

19 Now the *Mouvement pour le désarmement, la paix et la liberté*. Its aims are 'to banish violence from the world, to let every nation decide its own destiny and to give each individual the fullest responsibility for his life, his work and the running of the community'. 91, rue du Faubourg-Saint-Denis, Paris, 10e.

20 Fidel Castro has sometimes admitted that he is not in possession of the Truth. Yet here he is laying down the law over the Czechoslovakian affair, without even knowing much about it.

21 In England, which as everyone knows is a highly civilized country, the royal society for the prevention of cruelty to animals was founded a century before the national society for the prevention of cruelty to children. And we are still allowing the children of Vietnam to die – and those of Biafra, the Andes, north-east Brazil, Calcutta, East Pakistan . . .

22 Political education should come first, say my African critics. I quite agree if it is designed to help schoolchildren or students understand the economic and political problems of their day; but if it is to make them recite some political catechism, such as Jules Guesde's socialist catechism in the early years of the century, then I am not so sure . . .

23 With each country having the right to correct its own mistakes *by itself*.

24 I introduced systematic discussion in my 'unpontifical' lessons at the *Institut national agronomique* as early as 1936; it is many years since I suggested that students and assistants should be represented on the Teachers' Council.

25 Written on 25 May 1968.

26 *Revue française de science politique*, October 1963.

27 Khrushchev certainly made a *verbal* promise to share with India.

28 According to the *Financial Times* of 18 January 1968, this aid dropped from 900 to 185 million dollars between 1966 and 1967, while aid from the popular democracies rose from 200 to 400 million dollars.

29 'Net flow' – this means that all the interest, profits, unequal exchange and so on, which go to fatten the wealthy nations, would first of all have to be offset, and then in addition have 1 per cent of our incomes added to it – more for the richer countries, less for those not so well off. The United States would have to offset the $1\frac{1}{2}$ thousand million dollars it extorts, and then add 9,000 million dollars (1 per cent).

30 The United States – and the rest of the so-called civilized bourgeois world – showed more emotion at Robert Kennedy's assassination than at the massacre of hundreds of thousands of Vietnamese – women, children and combatants totalled up each week, under the common heading of *enemy* dead. It took the death of the second Kennedy to make one of his followers exclaim at last: 'We are the most terrifying country in the world.' He would never have thought of saying it before, in connection with the genocide in Vietnam.

31 Such as the French atomic 'defense' which envisages tackling the 'enemy's' big urban centres – obviously the prelude to the almost total destruction of our country.

32 '. . . increase the workers' share in the making of decisions, and bring man closer to free, creative activity . . . the Party should submit a programme bearing on the present development of civilization, without stipulating how citizens should live their lives'. *Rude Pravo*, 10–12 July 1968, translated in the first issue of *Politique aujourd'hui*.

PART TWO

Three Continents in Search of Suitable Forms of Socialism

RENE DUMONT

CHAPTER FIVE

Kenneth Kaunda's Humanist Socialism in Zambia

1. The Colony of a Colony

Until 1963, Northern Rhodesia was in effect a colony of Southern Rhodesia, itself a British colony. Most of the revenue from the copper mined in the North was invested by the privileged white minority in the neighbourhood of Salisbury, the Southern capital. These copper deposits form a southern extension of those in Katanga, and yield twice as much – in recent years about 600,000 tons a year. When Northern Rhodesia became independent on 24 October 1964, under an African government with Kenneth Kaunda as president, it took the name Zambia, from the Zambezi River which crosses the west of the country and forms its southern boundary.

A year later, in November 1965, Southern Rhodesia declared unilateral independence, without the United Kingdom's sanction since it was purely for the benefit of the white minority.[1] This placed Zambia in a very awkward position, for almost all its trade and its one and only railway went through Rhodesia and Portuguese Mozambique to the ports of Beira and Lourenço Marqués. The blockade of Rhodesia also affected Zambia: to obtain petrol it had to improvise an air-lift, then send tankers over an uncompleted stretch of road so rough that dozens of lorry-drivers were killed on it – 'The Wages of Fear' in real life!

At independence, Zambia had about a hundred university students and just over a thousand people with full secondary education. Six years earlier there had been only eleven Africans on the electoral roll. Two years before, neither President Kaunda nor any member of his cabinet had had the slightest experience of government.[2] The country had been 'well' administered by the British, who were much more interested in maintaining law and order than in starting it on the road to development. Its economy was of the dualistic kind typical of underdeveloped countries, with traditional society and the modern sector in violent opposition.

The modern sector consisted first and foremost of the copper mines, which were in the hands of two powerful companies,[3] one controlled by South Africa and the other, the more important, by the United States. Then there was plantation agriculture, with 1,100 white settlers producing maize, beef, cotton, milk – and most important of all 11,000 tons of light Virginia tobacco, for export. When I visited the country in the spring of 1967 only 700 of these settlers remained, and tobacco production had dropped to 4,700 tons. Lastly there was trade, mainly in European or Indian hands, and a few consumer-goods industries.

The traditional sector consisted essentially of subsistence agriculture, only occasionally rising to the level of an exchange economy. The staple foods of the north were manioc and millet, obtained by the shifting cultivation of burnt clearings in the forest (*chitimene*). Maize was becoming more popular everywhere, while some of the Africans, notably in the south and east, were starting to use ox-drawn ploughs, and to grow groundnuts for food, a little tobacco and, more recently, cotton. On the other hand, as in the whole of East Africa, stock-breeding had remained the most backward sector, with a high mortality due to epizootic diseases and a very low growth-rate. From a large stock the yield would only be very mediocre.

In such conditions the first five-year plan was largely justified in seeking to wean the country from its exclusive dependence on copper production – even though the price of copper was high, partly because the Vietnam war, which must end one day let us hope, and partly because of a very prolonged strike in the United States during 1967–8. Yet the money from copper provided many resources, and facilitated the development of an infrastructure, some industry and agricultural modernization. The latter appeared as a necessary complement to industry, since there was a need to increase purchasing power in the rural areas. As the white settlers began to leave or ceased to invest, it became even more necessary to speed up the expansion and modernization of African agriculture. But how?

2. Fifteen Pounds for every Acre of Cleared Land

Zambia is a huge country, one and a half times as large as France, with a population of barely four million. There is a great deal of land which could be brought under cultivation, and to encourage its development the Zambian government offered a bounty of £15 for every acre of land reclaimed. So the Africans set to work, especially in the poorest parts of the country, in the north, where ready money was most scarce. However, they did not always bother to cultivate the land afterwards; some of it was not worth the trouble and was therefore abandoned once the bounty had been earned.

In fact the cost of reclaiming the land with hatchet and machete, expressed in terms of man-days worked, might vary between five and fifty per acre, depending on the density of the vegetation. The fertile land was more densely overgrown, so that poorer land was preferred by those primarily interested in the bounty. Only the sharpest and best-informed Africans heard about this new windfall; so they were able to hire their neighbours to do the reclamation for them. In the far north of the country near Abercorn, I noted that one group of peasants had laid out fifteen shillings in wages – five days at three shillings each – for every acre reclaimed, which enabled them to make twenty times as much in bounty. Chibuku (their millet beer) flowed like water in the village when this was paid.

It is true that much of the land reclaimed was afterwards cultivated, but the choice of land was not always very happy. The reclamation bounty should have been paid only for fertile land, seeing that a soil-map had been published recently that would have allowed the poorest soils to be eliminated straight away. Drinking-water must be available and roads be within easy reach to allow for economic development; only large areas of land should be tackled, since otherwise it is not worthwhile to establish an infrastructure of social and technical services such as agricultural advisers, schools, dispensaries, roads, administration, and so on.

This means that, for each district, development plans must be drawn up by the authorities in consultation with the local population. However, the average standard of technicians has fallen drastically since the massive exodus of the British. Money is therefore not the essential factor in development; comprehensive subsidies encourage people to take the line of least resistance, and do not guarantee real progress. For Gabriel Ardant's benefit, I would repeat that it is not enough simply to set people to work; a certain minimum of technology, organization and thought is now absolutely essential if economic growth is to be proportional to the money and effort put into it.

3. Premature Mechanization: an Obstacle to Complete Transformation

While the reclamation bounty was initiated by the African government, the widespread use of tractors was insisted upon by international experts, white advisers and United Nations reports of around 1963-4.[4] It is true that progress in the traditional method of training the African peasants had already proved very slow because of the lack of knowledge and means, and the shortage of technically-trained men – who were often less competent and dedicated than their Tanzanian colleagues. It was therefore concluded that what was required was nothing less than a complete transformation of agriculture instead of these piecemeal advances. I was reminded of the modernization among the peasantry in Morocco in 1945, whose instigator, Jacques Bergues, declared: 'Modernization will be total, or not at all.' My reply at the time was that modernization was by definition a continuing process, and could never be total.

As a start, small groups of state-owned tractors were set up in each district of Zambia, and hired out to the peasants at the rate of £2 for an hour's work in the field. These tractors enabled some new land to be brought under cultivation, but their use seemed to me bad on the whole in that it tended to demobilize the peasants. Great efforts had been made to spread the use of draught animals, and replace the manual hoe by the plough drawn by a pair of oxen; this long-term educational work has been largely sabotaged by the establishment of the mechanized agricultural service. One minister, seeing a group of agricultural students being taught how to harness oxen to the plough, emerged from his car to launch a vigorous protest against such an old-fashioned approach.

Too many Zambians, when they heard about this service on the radio, decided to wait for the tractors instead of preparing their fields in the usual way. The tractors, however, could not go everywhere, and where they did go they often arrived too late, so that the harvests yielded proportionately less. It was difficult to maintain these tractors properly, dispersed as they were in tiny groups over such an enormous country; the fields to be ploughed were so widely scattered, they had to spend most of their time moving unproductively from place to place. In the most backward western part of the country, on the upper Zambezi, the tractors were not requested by the peasants and in consequence remained practically idle. In this province, Mongu, the actual cost of the official service has been estimated at £50 per hour of productive work, which must be a world record of some kind.

4. Over-subsidized Co-operatives

As soon as a group of farmers had reclaimed a certain amount of land, fixed at a minimum of 64 hectares, the Zambian government would authorize them to form an agricultural co-operative. We have seen that in most countries of Europe and the East great political, economic, administrative and even police pressures had to be applied in order to force the peasants to join such organizations. The communist party in China put all its weight and influence behind this enterprise. In Zambia no pressure whatsoever was required, yet when I visited the country in March–April

1967, more than 200 of these co-operatives had already been established at President Kaunda's request. So I turned my attention to this remarkable development which seemed worth examining more closely.

A co-operative of this kind would usually be formed by a dozen peasants who each contributed ten shillings or occasionally a pound. When the registered capital totalling between £6 and £12 had been amassed, the government would present them with a large tractor on credit, together with its appurtenances – a plough, trailer, cultivator, seeder, manure-spreader and so on. Hybrid maize seed, a large amount of fertilizer, petrol, etc., were also supplied on credit – £6,000 worth in all, about 500 to 1,000 times the amount of the registered capital – a staggering proportion. These peasants, who the day before had been still working the burnt earth with hoes, were suddenly presented with all the means – and responsibilities – of modern cultivation.

But the blockade was still in full force, and in each co-operative at least one piece of equipment arrived too late – here the tractor, there some spare part, the petrol, the seed or the fertilizer. Since the whole success of the operation was compromised by the lack of even one of these elements, yields were very low; though even in normal times they had usually been low. If the land is to be cultivated more intensively, the density of the plants must be increased, but many peasants spread fertilizer on fields that were sown five or ten times too thinly. Such costly equipment should not be put into the hands of peasants who cannot even mend a puncture, also the cost of getting repairs done by a white mechanic who has to drive by jeep from some distant village soon becomes prohibitive.

The Zambian peasants have gone in for co-operative farming not because of their African tradition of mutual help, but because they realized it was the best way of getting money out of the government. One co-operative was set up at the farm of a settler who had left the country; it was near Mufulira, right in the Copper Belt, and had been bought for a good price by the government. The eighteen co-operative members inherited a pedigree pig farm, an orange plantation, a tractor . . . When I visited it eight months later, the orange grove was overrun with couch-grass, the little maize sown had been largely neglected, the tractor had broken down after a fortnight, the sows were without water in the full heat of the sun, and so on. Naturally such fecklessness annoyed the neighbouring peasants, who were well aware that it was their taxes which went to support these layabouts.

When dealing with primitive peasants, agricultural progress cannot be other than slow, except in the case of settlers' plantations, whatever political system may be adopted. Before peasants can make economic use of tractors and modern techniques they must have a thorough knowledge of husbandry and marketing.

5. Three Stages of Agricultural Progress

Our starting-point is the northern peasant with his hoe, cultivating manioc on burnt earth, and millet for his beer. If he wants to change over to maize, he must first of all choose his land carefully, then prepare and sow it *very early*. In a tropical climate with a short rainy season the harvest depends primarily on strict adherence to the agricultural calendar and careful clearing of the fields. If crops are threatened by insects or disease, the struggle against these plant enemies must begin even at this early stage – especially in the case of cotton. So far, however, apart from insecticides and fungicides, with their associated equipment, hardly any external aids to production need be employed. All this would entail very little expense in comparison with the increased harvests. Better seed could also be introduced at this stage. By taking these steps, the traditional Zambian harvests could be doubled, from 5 to 10 or 12 quintals of dry maize per hectare.

Once these simple procedures had been adopted and thoroughly mastered, it would be economic to introduce more expensive and complex techniques, such as the use of chemical fertilizer. Ox-drawn carts and ploughs are more difficult to acquire and maintain. With many implements it would be more economic for several people to buy them in common, which would necessitate a certain minimum of co-operation. Oxen are available in the country; to put them under harness would end the economic absurdity of their being left idle, as at present, once they are full-grown. Fertilizer is still expensive, especially so far from the coast, and its use does not pay except with selected varieties of maize, sown early, protected from pests, in fields ready cleaned, and so on. Yet this second series of improved techniques, in conjunction with the use of maize hybrids, could again double the harvest so that each hectare would yield not 12 but 25 quintals of maize on average land in Zambia. The best land could even produce 35 to 45 quintals.

Only when this second stage has been reached and consolidated (which will take several years) would the peasants be able to spend their savings on tractors – in areas where manpower is scarce. They could be helped with credit; yet unless they pay a considerable proportion of the price in cash, they will not look after the equipment properly; for to their way of thinking it belongs to whoever has paid for it. Thus the tubes of the fertilizer-spreaders *given* to the co-operatives were not washed after use, so that they were corroded by the acid in the fertilizer after the first run.

It would be best to have a unit of five tractors grouped round a service-station staffed by a mechanic; an African mechanic would be less difficult than a white man, though for preference he should be as competent. There would be an official in charge of the technical management of a group of co-operatives, to ensure that their equipment was used to the full. Sound agricultural methods would thus make possible the high yields necessary to pay for the tractor. The director would at first be European, but could soon be replaced by African assistants trained by him on the job. What this boils down to is a new kind of colonization, administrative in origin and capable of being speedily Africanized – provided the Africans make the necessary effort.

Agricultural progress is not easy to spread; it is harder than building a modern factory. Essential though it is, it cannot be hastened by mere subsidies. Before the mass of peasants can be educated they must be made receptive to the idea; there should be propaganda in the countryside to arouse their interest and give them some notion beforehand of the possibilities of technical progress. As for foisting a mechanized *kolkhoz* on a group of peasants who the previous day were toiling away with hoes, the failure of so rash an enterprise could easily have been predicted. In a society completely ignorant of modern techniques, there is absolutely no call for an agrarian system which has already encountered great difficulties in the framework of developed socialist countries.

Finally I would stress the need to improve local food supplies, so that the workers can be better fed on local fruit and vegetables, for the country is being ruined by the great expense of importing them. Flowers from South Africa are still being sold in Lusaka. The home market must be considered first, especially in a country so much off the beaten track.

6. The State Farm: Intensive Training and Commercialization

If one insists on missing out the intervening stages, producer co-operatives under the strict supervision of experienced technicians would still be possible – given adequate resources of capital and cadres – as is shown by the success of the Chombwa scheme, west of the Zambian capital of Lusaka. This form of cultivation resembles a state farm in that all its equipment and know-how are provided by the state. The name 'co-operative' is therefore rather misleading; the labourers are best regarded as workers whose work is sometimes paid for by a share of the harvest. The stock-breeding ranches, which are recognized state concerns, also seem satisfactory.

Yet under this sort of system, even when it is successful economically, the Africans remain merely employees, and progress is controlled from outside. These *sovkhoz* only really seem justifiable to me if they can establish links with the surrounding peasantry, educating and leading them step by step in the way of progress, rather than forming mere enclaves of modernization. They could begin with technical advice, which would be all the more convincing because their own results had been achieved under the same natural conditions.

Equipment for pest control could also be introduced, and selected seed, breeding stock and help in training the oxen could be provided. Yet when the peasants see the performance of the tractors – their speed, power and the fact that they require no feeding or attention – they may become reluctant to avail themselves of the intermediate technique of using draught animals.[5] The problem is a difficult one, and progress may well be slow; it is therefore best, even in depopulated countries, not to let food production lag too far behind the population explosion.

With more intensive training, progress could go faster, especially if technical advisers were more dedicated. At present there is no incentive to produce in excess of subsistence requirements, unless the crops can be properly marketed. Many African peasants have been discouraged by the fact that their efforts to increase production have gone practically unrewarded. In north-west Zambia, north of Mwinilunga near the Angolan border, there were some Angolan refugees who cultivated pineapples with great success. To transport them in good condition to the populous regions of the copper mines and the capital, they needed packing cases; but the Ministry of Agriculture had not budgeted for these, and traders were not anxious to undertake such a risky venture.

In a country like this it would be as well to leave a certain margin for unforeseen expenditure under each heading in the budget. The efficiency of a government with so few members could be increased by decentralization, so that the provinces and districts were accorded greater powers.[6] When all decisions have to pass through the capital, they are slowed down to such an extent that development may be hindered. Also, the uses to which public money is put should be more closely supervised, for African morality condemns a man much more harshly for refusing to help his family than for robbing the state – especially if he does it for his family.

As I had planned to end my tour of one province on a Sunday night, I suggested that a meeting for discussion with the service heads should be held at six o'clock that evening. 'On a Sunday at that time they will all be drunk' was the agricultural official's ingenuous reply. Working on Sundays does not appeal to them at all; there are two big problems here. All this may seem far removed from socialist theories, but we are dealing here with the basic foundations of development, without which neither the elementary welfare of the people as a whole nor the gradual construction of some form of socialism can be envisaged. These notes, referring only to the agricultural sector, may well give a false impression of Zambia's economic development.

Mike Faber stresses the rapid growth of the gross national product – between 13 and 18 per cent a year from 1964 to 1966, dropping to 6 per cent in 1967 due to the blockade. Most of this growth can be explained by the cessation of the flow of capital to the south, the recovery of mining rights, the high price of copper, and the expansion of building, educational services, transport and a few industries. Between 1963 and 1967[7] this growth has enabled imports to be doubled. Buildings and factories are rising rapidly from the earth, and secondary schools are going up everywhere in the country.

Yet most of the country is still in a dangerously backward condition; agriculture, apart from maize, is stagnating. There is a serious risk that the number of paid jobs will not grow in step with the population. High wages have increased costs, and often reduced productivity; while easy profits have not favoured the quest for efficiency. Few Zambians have gone in for producer enterprises, and those who have do not always work hard enough. So qualifications have to be made.

7. Class Differences Brought About by Housing and Education

Urban privileges, especially those of public officials, constitute a formidable barrier to rural development. The racist British settlers kept the African's homes well out of sight; Lusaka therefore has a 'European' quarter, with its villas built in the midst of luxuriant greenery, each one set in the middle of a little park. These are very pleasant to live in, but add greatly to the cost of the infrastructure. Several kilometres away from this 'low density' quarter, as it is now modestly called, are the crowded African suburbs, consisting of round huts and small houses, the modern ones being more attractive and expensive. The distance between these areas increases the costs of roads, public transport, and water and electricity services. What an unproductive burden this class-distinction in town-planning is for such a poor country! Yet the Brazilian cities are an even heavier burden to the peasants.

The rich part of the town is being progressively taken over by the African élite, notably the civil servants, who find themselves rubbing shoulders with the expatriate experts, often British ex-civil-servants, or of other, generally European, origin. The latter, who are too highly paid, are copied by their African neighbours in the neatness of their gardens, the lavishness of their entertaining and the make of their cars. The 'colonial' pay of these experts[8] has an extraordinarily demoralizing effect on the African élite. My personal experience was that many of the features of a colonial society exist here, including the cheapness of goods and frequently the same contempt for servants. The only notable difference is that this society is partly coloured.

The élite send their children to expensive schools (another British legacy) which are distinctly better than those run by the state. Whereas the middle-classes of nineteenth-century Europe tried to leave their children a little money, African class-differentiation is characterized by the level of education, which determines the child's future standard of living. Those with secondary, and especially a university, education are almost certain to belong to the all too familiar privileged minority, so long as they are not tempted into political opposition.

I have already indicated the extent to which the attractions of public office have impeded rural development, by skimming the best brains from the countryside. Industrialization is also being held up for lack of African entrepreneurs, who prefer the security and prestige of public office to the effort and risk of commerce or industry, which are mainly in the hands of Indians or Europeans. President Kaunda's ambition, in this atmosphere, amidst all these difficulties, is to lead his country towards 'Zambian socialism'.[9]

8. *The Socialism of a Christian President, Faced with the Problem of Tribalism*

It would be rash to say that the African peasants want to move towards socialism, because first they need to have a clearer idea of what it is. The Protestant Kaunda calls himself a Christian humanist. Nevertheless, his tolerance, considered excessive by his colleagues, no longer extends to colonization; henceforth, and with reason, he will be less inclined to forgive the past and present exactions of the Christians of Europe. He is no crusader against communism, but at the same time in a true spirit of neutrality maintains friendly relations with Washington.

Yet it is China that is providing the long-term interest-free loan to finance the Dar-es-Salaam railway which, by taking a longer route, will enable Rhodesia and Mozambique to be by-passed. There is a certain tension between the two former Rhodesias, caused by guerrilla activity, which could one day erupt into open warfare. If Harold Wilson had been an international socialist, he would only have had to send in a regiment of paratroopers in November 1965, to re-establish the *Pax Britannica* which would finally have enabled power to be transferred to the African majority. If a race war should one day erupt in southern Africa, a large measure of the responsibility will be his. But he did not wish to deprive the poor pound sterling of the support of the wealthy South African mines.

Kaunda's first intention is to extend political independence by decolonization in the economic and cultural spheres, which he recognizes to be in many ways more difficult than the attainment of political independence. He plans to 'remould society' so as to 'profit from the wisdom and values of [our] forefathers'. Theirs was 'a mutual aid society – a society in which people worked co-operatively and collectively without losing the identity of the individual, for whose benefit and in whose name everything was done'. This is certainly an idealized presentation, but Kaunda is right in stressing the brutal impact on African society of 'the powerful forces from the West which have been aggressively shattering in their individualistic, competitive and possessive approach'.[10] It is certainly true that when the land was communally owned there was – and still would be – enough for everyone; but that was the equilibrium of poor subsistence economy, which does not favour investment.

'Human need was the supreme criterion of behaviour. The hungry stranger could, without penalty, enter the garden of a village and take, say, some peanuts, a bunch of bananas, a mealie cob or a cassava plant root to satisfy his hunger. . . . Life in the bush is hard and dangerous, and a high degree of social cohesion was necessary for survival. . . . Respect for human dignity which is a legacy of our tradition, should not be lost in the new Africa. . . . We in Zambia intend to do everything in our power to keep our society man-centred.'[11]

In response to this definition, independent Zambia is seeking to establish a parliamentary 'democracy', in which political equality is loudly affirmed. This is balanced by the fact that essential power is in the President's hands. The tribalism against which Kaunda has to struggle is much more virulent than in Tanzania. He was able to see how very much alive it was at the congress of Mulungushi, in August 1967, where the delegates were at daggers drawn, and the party leader and Vice-President of the republic were elected on a much more tribal than ideological basis.

Zambia seems to lean towards a one-party system; nevertheless, the opposition who want a *rapprochement* with South Africa (which is a source of money for the Lozis of Barotseland), gained more seats in the December 1968 elections. There is a danger of party struggles degenerating into demagogy, though Kaunda himself does not have this tendency. The chief thing is that the dominant party should be capable of establishing good communications between the bottom and the top, and vice versa. The president is doing his very best to achieve this, but the privileged caste, being primarily concerned with their own interests, will not always co-operate.

9. A Mixed Economy and Clearer Evolution

In the economic sector, this democratic and humanist form of socialism, chosen by the President but depending very much on the level of development attained, has resulted in a kind of mixed economy. In April 1967, Kaunda stated that the land would belong to the state, which could lease it but no longer sell it – especially not to settlers. His journey to China in the summer of 1967 certainly made a great impression on him. The term 'comrades' was frequently heard at the April 1968 congress; the atmosphere had changed. In the agricultural sector, he attached great importance to my report, which I was unfortunately not allowed to circulate, since it criticized certain schemes, such as the ill-fated producer co-operatives,[12] too harshly. Kaunda lays emphasis on the unused human capital, an idea strongly held in China. He stresses the fact that, apart from a few big enterprises requiring a great deal of capital, development has so far been confined to certain areas served by the one and only railway line.

His intention is to decentralize, then maintain a better balance between the various types of occupation and techniques, encouraging small industries and crafts in the rural areas. He emphasizes the need to teach modern techniques to women as well as men, and to make full use of the underemployed resources of human and animal power before buying thousands of tractors. All this is very sensible. Public funds should not continue to be spent on the creation of a class of 'commercial' farmers, though peasants may still rise to this level through their own efforts. Here the *kulak* or progressive farmer is not discouraged, as in Tanzania.

Though Zambia met 65 per cent of its beef requirements in 1963 by slaughtering 65,000 head of cattle, in 1967 the proportion was only 35 per cent from the slaughter of 52,000 cattle, since with the growth of purchasing power the demand had greatly increased. This was also accompanied by a decline in European methods of stock-breeding. Local herds would certainly be capable of producing much more, were it not for the strength of tradition opposing their rational exploitation, which is very difficult to over-come, since there was now a surplus of maize which would be uneconomic to export, in view of freight costs and its price within the country, where it was too highly subsidized. Kaunda also pro-posed the development of dairy-farming (but this has declined since 1966) as well as pig-breeding (which has increased slightly). With his first plan Kaunda had launched the slogan 'An egg[13] and a pint of milk a day for every Zambian, plus a pair of shoes'. In 1968 he realized that this would not be achieved. Tobacco and groundnut production rapidly declined, and cotton lost the ground it had recently gained.

The most important change was the announcement that twenty-six of Zambia's biggest companies,[14] including the *Times of Zambia* were to have at least 51 per cent of their capital purchased by the state. The government intends to control the steel, textile, fertilizer and sack-making industries, which were anyway established on its initiative. As the Zambians have shown little aptitude for business, the state has become the partner and promoter, in the name of the Zambian people as it were, of the traditionally private sector, which hitherto has been run by foreigners. Next it will urge the people to use their savings to buy shares in these national com-panies.[15] However, as Kaunda wishes to avoid creating a Zambian capitalist class, the number of shares that each individual can acquire is limited. And when private companies grow beyond a certain size they are taken under state control.

Copper provides 40 per cent of the national product, 95 per cent of exports and 65 per cent of the state revenue. The copper trusts have been able to adapt themselves to the political change-over better than most of the settlers! They use local fuels and are diversi-fying their activities. Kaunda does not wish to nationalize them yet because his administration would not be able to manage them efficiently. Plans for the trusts' expansion, however, are less ambi-tious than in Chile or Peru, and their 'Zambianization' could well be more far-reaching. In May 1968, Zambia announced that the payment of dividends abroad would be limited to 50 per cent of the profits remaining after tax. In negotiating a new system of royalties, it will consider giving the state an interest in the capital of the mines, which would enable it to push ahead with expanding production. This policy can be compared to the Chileanization of the Chilean copper mines, carried out by Eduardo Frei.[16]

Next there will be a whole series of measures designed to prepare the ground for the Africanization, or Zambianization as they call it, of the economy.[17] Certain categories of jobs will be reserved for Zambians, whether natives or foreigners (Indians or Europeans), who have Zambian nationality. Foreign trade is confined to the smart quarters of the country's ten large towns. Yet Cairo Road, the Champs Elysées of Lusaka, has no Zambian commerce, nor even any Zambians managing its shops; therefore no new foreign businessess will be admitted there in future.

The local banks adjust credit to foreigners according to the amount of their investments from abroad and the priority given to their activities in the plan. Similar measures are to be adopted in future with regard to foreigners who have long been resident in the country, who had hitherto been exempted. These steps clearly differentiate Zambia's economic policy from that of the Ivory Coast, for instance, which is not pushing ahead with the wholesale Africanization of its companies.

Some people may be afraid that Zambia's humanist socialism is rather weak and that the copper trusts may dominate the government. However I do not think this will happen; this presocialism has to take into account the still rather modest level of the Zambians' knowledge, skill, dedication and equipment. President Kaunda does not invest his own money abroad, as do a number of French-speaking African heads of state. His style of life is austere, some would even say puritan. On 7 July 1968 at the ecumenical conference of Upsala, he stressed the moral aspect of development: In the world of today, he said, we give more to the rich; and from the poor we take the little they need in order to pay the rich. The present decade has brought only disappointment and disillusion to the newly independent nations. While life continues to be intolerable for the majority of mankind, peace and security can never be assured. There is no sign of any wish on the part of the developed countries to help fill in the ditch separating the rich from the poor. Kaunda concluded by asking the churches to bring political and moral influence to bear on governments in order to promote justice between the nations.

His insistence on Zambianization – though partly due to pressure by the new African class, the privileged minority who wish to augment their privileges – is also in line with true development. There is a danger that it may aggravate the differences between town and country, unless it is accompanied by a policy of austerity – and may lead to the failure, or even bankruptcy, of prematurely Africanized companies. It would be as well to give posts only to those Africans who are capable of filling them properly and who know how to resist the dreadful spread of alcoholism, which is still one of the most serious threats to the country's future. The white mining experts had improperly defended their privileges by refusing to allow African labourers to acquire any qualifications – an intolerable usurpation which has now been abolished. Nevertheless the average standard of agricultural advisers has clearly fallen since the departure of most of the British staff. Yet if Zambia is to shake off neo-colonialism, progress must continue in this direction. One essential objective is the reinforcement of the state's economic power, without reducing its efficiency.

As we shall see in the next chapter it would be best not to rely too much on co-operatives at this stage of development, even for marketing. In 1967–8, the co-operative which sells the groundnuts from the Fort Jameson area, in east Zambia, had returned no accounts for several years; it underpaid its producers, and the honesty of some of its managers could be seriously called in question. To those who consider Kaunda over-cautious, I would reply that his friendly relations with his neighbour, colleague and friend, President Nyerere, are helping the latter to progress towards socialism, while preserving a respect for man. This criterion of true socialism, as we have seen, is worth any amount of over-hasty plans for collectivization.

Zambia may be advancing slowly towards socialism, but it is taking two precautions which seem to me excellent. In the first place, it is maintaining freedom with regard to information. In the Soviet Union, by contrast, the Central Committee decided to intervene in Czechoslovakia on the basis of erroneous information which the majority of its members had received. Secondly, the state appears to be keeping firm *control* of the economy, and is in a position to do this effectively – without venturing to manage the whole of the economy itself, a task which would be beyond its present powers.

By allowing socialist enterprises greater initiative (which has now been proved necessary to their efficiency), the socialist countries will in practice be giving up the idea of state property, managed by the state. They are handing back the essential attributes of ownership, and responsibility for day-to-day administrative decisions, to the producer units. This is where socialization shows itself preferable to nationalization – provided the overall interests of the national community, as broadly outlined by the plan, are always protected. The general picture is of state control, with management by groups of producers.

Zambia's present evolution, where power is used firmly to defend the people's interests, seems quite satisfactory. The Russians claim to be the only true socialists, while yet introducing, for their own advantage, a special brand of neo-colonialism. They must therefore forfeit any right to condemn other roads to different socialisms. It is often stated that the backward countries, dominated as they are by trusts and imperialism, will not be able to evolve towards socialism. I hope that Zambia and Tanzania are going to prove that it *is* possible.

NOTES TO CHAPTER 5

1 Rather as if the settlers and the OAS had taken power in Algeria in 1961.
2 A notorious difference from French-speaking Africa, which often received a better portion at independence. This is taken from a pamphlet by Mike Faber: *Zambia, the moulding of a nation*, Africa Bureau, London, 1968.
3 Anglo-American Group, with £19 million profits in 1966; and Roan Selection Trust Group, with profits of £10 million in the same year.
4 The joint report of the United Nations' Economic Commission for Africa and the FAO, entitled: *Economic Survey Mission on the Economic Development of Zambia*, suggests, on page 71, that African agriculture requires 'over 3,000 tractors and about 10,000 families of settlers using modern methods'.
5 In December 1968, after my report to the President, the Kafubu group of

co-operatives, south of the Copper Belt, received twenty-five donkeys from the government, to be used chiefly as light pack-animals.

6 Recently there has been progress in this direction: provincial ministers have a place in the cabinet, and have been given greater powers.

7 Foreign currency has been less plentiful since 1968.

8 Their usefulness is greatly diminished by the fact that they stay for such short periods, often no more than two years.

9 *Cf. Esprit*, September 1967, *Kenneth Kaunda et le socialisme zambien*, by R. Dumont.

10 These are rearranged extracts from his speech to the congress UNIP, the party in office, on 26 April 1967, published in *Humanism in Zambia*, Lusaka, April 1968.

11 The words 'man-centred' were stressed by Kaunda.

12 Its suppression was probably due to the Minister of Co-operatives, who felt that the criticisms were aimed at him. He rightly emphasized that the state's spending on agriculture must not continue to favour the settlers; but that is no reason why it should be squandered.

13 While having breakfast in the hotel, surrounded by Englishmen taking their two morning eggs, I did not miss the opportunity of exclaiming to the servant: 'Just one egg for me, one egg for every Zambian', which caused some embarrassment.

14 Breweries, road transport, building materials, two chains of retail stores, the wholesale fish trade, and so on.

15 They should be urged to buy houses on credit, so as to increase their savings and improve their living conditions. As for international tourism, this is aimed too exclusively at the luxury clientele, who are limited in number.

16 Since the above passage was written, the copper companies have been nationalized on the same basis as other industries described above. (Translator.)

17 What it in fact comes down to is very worthwhile jobs for a few privileged people; whereas the aim should be to serve the mass of the peasants with the maximum of efficiency. (G. Belkin.)

CHAPTER SIX

The Strengthening of Tanzanian Socialism through Julius Nyerere's Arusha Declaration

1. Towards a Socialist Non-alignment

At a communist seminar held at Prague in January 1963 it was firmly decided that of all the countries of Tropical Africa, only Ghana (under Nkrumah), Guinea and Mali could be considered as progressing towards the one true scientific socialism, inspired by Marxism–Leninism. Senghor and Nyerere – particularly singled out because of their claim to be constructing some kind of 'African socialism' – were excommunicated. 'If they fail to understand that there is only one form of socialism, we will reject them,' stated the infallible Mr K, still the pope of communism in May 1963, at Bucharest. Yet this same pope, was soon to be dethroned, a fact which ought to have made it possible to doubt his infallibility in 1963 without risking excommunication. Nevertheless, he had made a feeble attempt to destalinize, and his timid thaw was followed by the hard frost of his successors, culminating in Czechoslovakia.

Tanganyika had been a German colony, placed under British mandate by the League of Nations after the First World War. At the 1958 elections for government with internal autonomy, all the seats went to a single party, the TANU. This comparative political maturity, together with the existence of a true national language, enabled it to obtain independence as early as 9 December 1961, even before the associated territories of Kenya and Uganda. With the help of British experts it had drawn up a parliamentary constitution, unsuited to its stage of development, but this was soon offset, as in Zambia, by the power of the president, with his single party. At that time Nyerere's relations with the West were good. He also sang the praises of the African traditions, which formed the basis of the African socialism he was endeavouring to build.

A *coup d'état* against him was planned in January 1964 by the revolutionary wing of the party, dissatisfied by what they considered his too pro-Western alignment. The army mutinied on the same day, and the British paratroopers sent to bring it to heel saved Nyerere from a double peril. Two weeks earlier there had been an anti-Arab revolution in Zanzibar, which soon became very left-wing. Karumé therefore suggested that these two countries should be united under the name of 'Tanzania'. A union with the conservative Kenya was dreaded by the people of Zanzibar, though some of them thought Nyerere was trying to prevent the creation of an African Cuba. All this had the effect of reducing the flow of private investment.

Nyerere was very devoted to the cause of independence for the whole of Africa, but only the USSR and China were willing to supply arms to the guerrillas based in south Tanzania for the freeing of southern Africa: Mozambique, if not Rhodesia and South Africa. Soon China financed a textile factory near Dar-es-Salaam, which was completed in twenty-two months (instead of the expected twenty-four), in the summer of 1968. France started building another near Mwanza, to employ 1,300 workers as against the 3,500 employed in the Chinese one, for the same capacity of production. China, however, then offered an interest-free loan for the construction of a railway from Dar-es-Salaam to serve the Zambian copper-belt, which will ensure Zambia's economic independence and open up the south of Tanzania.

In this atmosphere, Nyerere is gradually approaching a position of non-alignment, anxious to maintain friendly relations with the East and with a certain preference for China, where he was given a splendid reception in June 1968. It was the first occasion for a very long time that a foreign head of state had spent a week in China. West Germany withdrew its aid because of the establishment of an East German embassy in Zanzibar, and the West German ambassador is urging his Western colleagues to take a similar stand. Britain reduced her own aid when diplomatic relations were broken off at the end of 1965, over Rhodesia. While the other African states soon resumed relations with the United Kingdom, despite their pledge in July 1968, Nyerere was still waiting for the latter to make the first move before following their example. The UK, however, will not withdraw her advisers and experts, as de Gaulle did in Guinea in October 1958, in a fit of rancour hardly worthy of a true statesman. The first Tanzanian plan had counted on foreign aid for the bulk of its investment, but the promises were not kept. Moreover, its expenditure was not always very judicious; it would be a good thing to find out who was chiefly responsible for this.

2. The Failure of the Settlement Schemes

In November 1960, the World Bank delivered a report on 'The Economic Development of Tanganyika', in which its experts wrote that 'the promotion of more productive agricultural methods cannot be left entirely to the improvement approach.[1] ... To achieve more rapid progress something more is required, whether through intensive campaigns in settled areas ... or through planned and supervised settlement of areas which are at present uninhabited or thinly inhabited. In fact, the Mission considers that the second of these approaches is in general the more promising in the present conditions in Tanganyika.' They went on to say that the whole arsenal of modern techniques, including mechanization should be introduced at once.

It is true that the scattered population characteristic of the Tanzanian countryside is an obstacle to the spread of technical progress, to the commercialization of crop production and to easy access to schools, dispensaries, mosques and churches. The creation of villages throughout Tanzania would also bring down the cost of community services (such as roads, and later electricity, water and the telephone); it was therefore included in the first plan. Two-thirds of the money set aside for agricultural modernization

F

in this plan was given to the settlement schemes, which involved building modern villages; whereas only one-third went to finance the normal operations of the Ministry of Agriculture.

These settlements have failed almost everywhere, as everyone now recognizes. I have already[2] told the story of the one at Upper Kitete, where a hundred families[3] cultivated 640 hectares of high-altitude corn, with ten tractors and four harvester-threshers, two of them out of action. With equipment like this, two men would have been enough in Canada. At Rwamkona, excessive mechanization combined with an excess of manpower have led to virtual bankruptcy, both in financial and in human terms. Many cotton-growers, obliged to repay their agricultural loans (for clearing, ploughing and insecticides) by having the money deducted from the proceeds of their crops, tried to sell them elsewhere through front-men, so as to avoid payment of their debts. At Karege, near the capital, the coconut plantations were neglected, the official nut harvest was practically nil, and so on.

The basic reasons for this failure were the absence of serious economic studies, lack of effort, and excessive subsidies. In default of 'Chinese-type' political enthusiasm, the settlers were enticed by means of benefits that were exaggerated, not in themselves, but in relation to the country's present resources. They were promised free rations for one, or even two years, whereas it only takes four months to make maize grow; then they were given a little pocket-money and houses that were often finer than present means permit. After the privileged class of city-dwellers, a semi-privileged rural class was thus created. For example, when I visited the Kitete settlement during the summer of 1967, it had already cost 'about' £160,000 or more (outlay and cumulative annual losses). The fact that the figure could not be more precisely specified made me fear that some of the money had been embezzled. Yet in 1967 a dividend of £4·50 per family was again paid to the settlers in this village. A concern showing a deficit, which pays out dividends, should acknowledge them as illusory. However, too much had been promised.

By contrast the relative success of the settlers growing Virginia tobacco in the Tabora region provides confirmation of the fact that these subsidies are quite unnecessary. A centre in Zambia has started a five-year apprenticeship scheme to make African specialists in tobacco; farmers who would have to hire employees. In Tanzania the peasant settlers arrive on an area of land marked out to accord with their capacity; they bring this under cultivation, build their own houses and dryers and settle down, with subsidies only for fertilizer, insecticide, simple tools and drying apparatus – modest sums which are for the most part repaid. From the very first year the harvests have been good, and they have learnt their job as they went along, which is much less expensive for the community. Though those who are illiterate may not be able to read the figures on the thermometer indicating the optimum temperatures in the dryers (which are heated by wood), they soon understand that on such and such a day it must reach the green mark, then the yellow one or the red. The European settlers claimed that they would never learn the job, and kept the valuable monopoly to themselves; for tobacco, like all drugs, is very profitable.

3. The Possible Danger of Reviving Export Crops

The settlement idea has therefore been more or less abandoned, but the losses of the centres already established continue to exceed their gross receipts. On the other hand, production of export crops grown in the traditional way, with help from the agricultural authorities, is rapidly increasing. Sisal was introduced at the beginning of the century by settlers and companies (often German-Swiss), who created some very fine plantations, such as Amboni, near Tanga. But prices have slumped – from £147 a ton in London for the highest quality dry fibre about 1962, to £64 in the autumn of 1967. Before, when the price used to vary cyclically, one could hope to recoup one's losses of the depressions during the periods of inflation. However this can no longer be expected to happen because of the invention of a synthetic fibre, which will make it economic to set up factories as soon as the price rises to about £85, so prices scarcely went up at all during 1968, and most of the plantations showed a loss. In the summer of 1968, an international agreement, rather like the one for coffee, established export quotas for all the big producers, with the aim of maintaining the price at about £85 a ton. The use of the pasture between the rows of coffee bushes for cattle (fed also with sisal-juice) will in future be indispensable in making the plantations pay.

During the boom, in order to profit from this gold mine, the Africans had incautiously been urged to plant small quantities of sisal everywhere. In 1965 the powerful Co-operative Federation of Lake Victoria even built a fibre-brushing and pressing factory to the east of the lake – a much too marginal area. The FAO have since announced that there is likely to be a prolonged slump in hard fibres. The experts were just perfecting a new variety which, by reason of its high yield, would be the only one still capable of holding its own; but it does not flourish at the high altitudes where they had planned to grow it. The co-operatives should go into the technical and economic aspects of the problem more thoroughly before making such investments; yet the agricultural authorities did not attempt to dissuade them. The poorer one is, the less fortunate are one's investments. Of course one can, and must, struggle to improve the terms of trade for primary agricultural and mining products – but is it necessary to stand in the way of progress by continuing to produce dyes, rubber, perfumes and fibres, which are cheaper to manufacture chemically? Especially when there is a prospect of widespread famine?

Coffee has been distinctly successful, thanks to the spread of cupric spraying against the fungus parasite.[4] The price of coffee is protected by an international agreement, which means that the coffee-growers in Tanzania (as in many other countries from Brazil to Madagascar, I have noticed) earn three or four times as much per man-day worked as their maize- or cotton-growing neighbours. The Ministry of Agriculture has gone on too long with its propaganda for coffee, which is still being cultivated, and even planted, in marginal areas which are either too damp or too dry, giving yields and qualities that are often deplorable, thus making inefficient use of good soils.

Other crops are therefore being sought to replace coffee, though ncne are so well protected. I have already done this in France between 1950 and 1956, when I attempted to find a substitute for the vines of the south and west, which were also the most protected crop there. Because of the international agreement, coffee enjoys a kind of monopoly profit very useful to the poor countries whose other commodities are so badly exploited. However, as things are going at present, there is a danger that by 1970 Tanzania will be producing more than 60,000 tons of coffee,[5] whereas it will hardly be able to sell more than 50,000 tons. I therefore suggested that the prices paid to producers should be reduced by means of taxation; this would increase the state's investment potential, and allow it to pay more for food crops.

The case is different with cotton, whose price has been falling slowly but steadily, though the production of Sukumaland, to the south of Lake Victoria, increased much more rapidly up to 1966 than the plan had envisaged.[6] As with coffee, the credit for this is due to the peasants of the region, who are much harder-working than those of the coast – and also to the agricultural authorities for popularizing the use of fertilizers and insecticides. Due to the healthier political atmosphere and the fact that their technicians are better trained, these authorities are more efficient than their opposite numbers in Zambia, yet the 1968 budget put an export duty on cotton, not coffee. Perhaps the pressure-group of the Chagga, who grow most of the coffee on the slopes of the great volcanoes, wields more influence than that of Sukumaland.

Until recent years, the Tanzanian economy rested mainly on the three crops of sisal, coffee and cotton – these are now proving inadequate. With the rapid progress of synthetic fibres it is impossible to say what the long-term future of cotton will be, or if people will still be using it by the end of the century. An interesting attempt to diversify exports has therefore been made with peasant tea plantations, supplementing those of the settlers. Cocoa[7] does not seem indicated, except in a few areas of very limited extent. Pyrethrum, a kind of daisy from which an insecticide can be obtained, gives good returns but has a limited market. For a long time cashew nuts were profitable, but their price has also fallen considerably. Tobacco is the only crop which could be valuable, though its quality needs to be more consistent. Will sanctions continue to stand in the way of Rhodesia selling its tobacco? So far Canada has been the one to profit most from the new markets thus made available.

4. Pounding and Milling: the Exploitation of Women by Men

To the casual visitor it seems that the Tanzanians eat their fill; there are no signs of the hardship visible in India. Yet one needs to take a closer look. Dr Krysler stresses the fact that there is a widespread deficiency of proteins and vitamin A among the poor population. While visiting some farms for the blind, it occurred to me that if a teaspoonful of crude palm-oil, which is rich in carotene, had been given to them from time to time as children, the great majority of these cases could have been avoided. At a wealthy boarding-school with good food, the twelve-year-old girls have an average weight of 34 kg, which is normal, whereas their very much poorer friends at the neighbouring primary school weigh only 25 kg. This discrepancy in their weights emphasizes their nutritional difference, which is bound up with their standard of living and social class.

According to Dr Krysler, the traditional method of pounding maize in a wooden mortar after soaking it in water for a day or two, deprives it of 40 per cent of its nutritive value, 60 per cent of its proteins and 80 per cent of its fats and vitamin A. The diet of the rural population as a whole could be rendered much less deficient merely by grinding the *dry* grain in a small mill so that these losses were avoided. A mixture of two parts of maize to one of beans, together with a little palm-oil, would almost constitute a satisfactory diet. Moreover, the women could be freed from the drudgery of pounding grain. These thoughts first came to me at Bumbuli in the West Usumbura Mountains, in the north-east, where the women have banded together to cultivate a 20-hectare field of maize, on which each of them works one day a week without pay. They were able to buy a mechanized mill – partly on credit – from the proceeds of the harvest. Communal fields like this, undertaken voluntarily, at the prompting of the more public-spirited women, in which their own efforts secure a material liberation, are splendid ventures in practical socialism.[8]

One hears a lot about man's exploitation by man. In my meetings at Dar-es-Salaam I dwelt on the exploitation of women by men, so prevalent in the backward countries, but ignored by African socialism. This caused me to be invited to give a talk on the subject to a Tanzanian women's congress,[9] at which my faulty English was immediately retranslated into Swahili – a language current throughout the whole of East and Central Africa.[10] The Upper Kitete development has cost the state £1,500 per family, thus favouring a small privileged group. I suggested that the more proletarian peasants of the poorer zones should be considered first. As a start, each group of ten families (the country's political organization is based on 'ten-cell units') could have communal means of transport assigned to them: pack-mules in hilly areas, bicycles on the plains.

Pounding grain and carrying[11] can occupy as much as a quarter of a woman's working time. On a bicycle adapted as transport and reserved for the use of the women, 100 to 120 kg could be carried (on roads and level paths) with less trouble than 30 kg. can be carried on the head. Supposing that each bicycle cost £15 wholesale and served five families, it would cost each family no more than £3, which is five hundred times less than it costs to establish one family in a modernized village. It is true that bicycles are already very common in the rich areas, but they are more often used for the men to ride about on than for carrying. True socialism must concern itself, right from the start, with improving the working conditions and lives of the poorest class. The movement for 'liberating the shoulders' has been given priority in North Vietnam.

5. Imports and Food Products

The towns cannot usefully absorb the rural exodus if it escalates too rapidly. Meanwhile agricultural production must be increased.

But if the Three Continents continue to concentrate mostly on export crops, they will be contributing to a slump in prices – a process which it has not been possible to arrest except in the case of coffee. In the meantime, a large part of the population of the backward countries is not being properly fed. As a result of the drought of 1965 there were severe local famines in Tanzania and Kenya, while the irregularity of the rainfall in 1967 brought the amount of maize grown commercially down to 104,000 tons,[12] compared with 123,000 tons during the good year of 1966. Paddy dropped from 42,000 to 27,000 tons, and corn from 33,000 to 14,000. While crops in the commercial sector increased by 7·4 per cent a year[13] between 1960–2 and 1966, in the subsistence sector they only increased at a rate of 2·2 per cent; the population, however, increased by 2·8 per cent a year, reaching 12·5 million towards the end of 1968. Moreover the growing food imports of the Third World as a whole are now almost equivalent to the totality of their agricultural exports – which will make it difficult for them to buy equipment.

In 1966 Tanzania imported foodstuffs to the tune of £9·1 million, which is 15 per cent more than in 1965. Cereals and their derivatives – corn, rice, flour, pasta – were the most important items; then came dairy produce, margarine, fruit and vegetables – all of them commodities which could be produced on the spot under generally quite favourable conditions. The high, watered slopes of the great volcanoes in the north are very suitable for dairy-farming; corn could flourish on the high surrounding plateaux, rice wherever the water-supply was adequate, and small amounts of fruit and vegetables almost anywhere if the soil is fertile. The problem is a complex one. The coconut palms would yield much more if they were better tended, but horticultural and dairy produce demand a high level of technology and costly equipment. As soon as the local requirements for perishable goods are exceeded, their prices slump. Canning and bottling factories might be set up, except that they require large supplies of cheap raw material whose quantity and quality do not fluctuate, and this could not easily be guaranteed at first.

The rich countries protect their own agricultural prices, but not those of the poor countries; by implication, they force the latter to supply them with cheap food, without always realizing that by doing this they are exploiting them.[14] In this general climate of falling prices some distinctions must be made as to the relative importance of various crops. The colonial powers sometimes organized the market for export products, and France even protected their prices, but no such steps were taken with regard to food crops, and as we shall see presently, the marketing of Tanzanian maize was unsatisfactory. In carrying out the much-needed, but very difficult, task of improving the terms of trade, it seems to me that a considerable rise in the relative prices of food products should come first on the agenda. This is all the more urgent in that the prospect of widespread shortage continues to loom on the horizon.

6. Growing Inequalities: 'Colonialism was Better'

In the November 1968 issue of the magazine *East Africa*, Aart van der Laar shows that, between 1960 and 1966, *per capita* consumption only increased by 1 per cent a year; whereas wages had doubled during the six years, taking social benefits into account, and prices had only risen by 15 per cent. Yet the number of paid employees had decreased, especially on the sisal plantations, from 417,000 to 336,000. Many expensive investments had led to the number of jobs being cut down. From 1961-2 to 1967-8, administrative expenditure increased by 90 per cent,[15] and production by one-third. The proportion of primary school leavers entering secondary school dropped from over 30 per cent in 1961 to less than 10 per cent in 1968.

Though primary education is in future to be in Swahili, secondary education is in English. Many children of African leaders are to be found, side by side with foreign children, in the few primary schools that have contrived to remain 'English'. These 'leaders of tomorrow', says van der Laar, 'have only sharpened the sense of indispensability, exclusiveness and power in the selected. . . . Investigations regarding career expectations of pupils and students show that there is a strong preference for well-paid bureaucratic jobs, and that careers with very quick promotion are being expected as a right. . . . Since independence, a process of increasing income inequality has manifested itself, not only between town and countryside, but also between various groups of wage earners. . . . This process of rapidly increasing income inequality has led to a growing dissatisfaction in the countryside *vis-à-vis* the towns . . . those who, largely at public expense, received their education which brought them positions of power in the government, subsequently have the opportunity (by manipulating the selection procedure) to perpetuate an oligarchy.

'Meanwhile, the foreign firms recruit politicians and high civil servants in order to obtain political protection. . . . Up to 50 per cent of these companies' own investments are diverted each year into various people's pockets. Semi-luxury industries are favoured because of the relative proletarianization of the countryside, which makes the market for industrial products limited. The upper echelons of the bureaucratic *élite* (a third of paid employees are in the public sector) are adopting the European habit of consuming imported products, which still further restricts the market. . . . Traffic congestion is resulting from the rapid increase of private cars among the "happy few".'

The students rejected National Labour Service, although this would have been very useful for bringing them into contact with the concrete realities of the country, work and manual workers, which they have too great a tendency to despise. In October 1966, they even went so far as to march in protest behind a placard saying 'Colonialism was better'. This was not wholly negative, because next day Nyerere and his ministers[16] cut their own salaries by 20 per cent. If to all this you add the lack of success of the total modernization model proposed by the white experts, the broken promises of foreign aid and the West's failure to arm the African liberation organizations, it is easy to understand the concern of the brilliant and idealistic socialist Julius Nyerere – also a practising Catholic and a great friend of the Chinese.[17] At the end of the summer of 1966, a friend handed him the English edition of my book *l'Afrique noire est mal partie*,[18] which dealt with similar problems. After reading it, he bought up all the locally available copies for his ministers. Shortly afterwards he set out to take a closer look at the countryside, and found that satisfactory development was not being achieved; then, having retired to Mwanza, near Lake Victoria, he drafted a declaration which was read, in February 1967, to the TANU party assembled for this purpose at Arusha.[19]

7. The Arusha Declaration and Nationalization

Like Kaunda, Nyerere began by declaring that there was no socialism without democracy, but economic justice requires that the principal means of production should be *controlled* by the state. The state must limit the accumulation of wealth in order to attain the objective of a classless society, and root out every kind of exploitation, intimidation[20] and corruption. Declaring that no reliance should be placed on foreign aid, which anyway constituted a threat to independence, he urged the people to depend more on their own efforts. . . . 'The development of a country is brought about by people, not by money.' 'We have put too much emphasis on industry.' 'The largest proportion of the loans will be spent in, or for the benefit of urban areas, but the largest proportion of the repayment will be made through the efforts of the farmers.' He went on to affirm the priority of agricultural development.

This was immediately followed by a decree, on 5 February 1967, nationalizing banks, insurance companies, mills and other large food industries, the big import–export firms, and so on. 'Nationalization' must be understood in the full sense of the word, since it involved foreign companies, which thus reverted to the nation. There was no revolutionary expropriation of these companies; compensations were agreed upon after discussion, payable when they were subsequently handed over. Only the English banks refused for a long time to negotiate over these indemnities, and attempted to sabotage the new policy by abruptly recalling all the higher grade British staff, as they were afraid such measures might spread to the rest of Africa. They did not succeed, because the trained Indian staff proved capable of handling day-to-day business until European and Pakistani replacements arrived; however, it is still hanging in the balance.

Viewed from Paris, however, these measures rather alarmed me, when I remembered the difficulties of Guinea and Mali. So in June 1967, I sent word to President Nyerere that I thought it might be useful if a young Tanzanian economist were sent to Mali to study their chief economic mistakes (which had by then been recognized) and how they were trying to correct them. This advice has not been followed, but Samir Amin, who was economic adviser to the Bamako plan, is to visit Dar-es-Salaam. The investigation I made on the spot, in August–September 1967, at Mwalimu's[21] request, has to some extent allayed my fears.

I then found that the nationalizations had got off to a much better start than in Guinea and Mali between 1959 and 1961. Spiteful voices whisper that they could hardly have done worse. Regrouped under the direction of a first-rate businessman – receiving a royal fee – the import–export trade seems to be functioning more or less normally,[22] as do the insurance companies.

8. The Official Mentality and the Insecurity of Employment

What little I was able to see of the National Development Corporation's state enterprises began to disturb me. I found one ranch manager, on the land, spending the funds allotted to him without the slightest attempt to economize. The accounts were kept in the capital, which meant that they were correct and up to date; but no copy had been sent to the local management, who were completely in the dark as to the prospects of their concern making a profit, its total past and future investments, the returns expected, or its overall policy. They were thus treated merely as executants, deprived of initiative or responsibility and not personally involved in their job.

These men are generally ex-civil servants, educated as such at school and university, who have retained too much of the official's outlook. Every worker in Africa aspires to security of employment, and the unions demand it. The sad part of it is that in the great majority of cases as soon as a Tanzanian worker obtains this security his productivity falls, sometimes by as much as 50 per cent.[23] A Frenchman who was a director of this corporation, gave one final word of advice on the day of his departure: 'You must be able to dismiss anyone at any moment in your state concerns, including the top management.' At a certain stage of development, insecurity seems to be a factor essential to productivity. Mwalimu well understood this; on 7 July 1968, when he opened the textile factory provided by the Chinese, he proclaimed that every factory worker has a responsibility towards Tanzania. The Arusha Declaration demands greater discipline; and if self-discipline is lacking, severe industrial discipline must be imposed by the management.

In another declaration in September 1967, on the subject of 'Socialism and rural development', Nyerere expressed concern over the spread of the capitalist ethic in the countryside, and urged that co-operative village communities should be progressively established on an entirely voluntary basis. One needs to be very cautious here. Parliament was told that some regional commissioners appear to have set up compulsory collectives, sending peasants against their will to the villages they had built. There was a long article in praise of these 'Ujamaa villages', which cited as an example of what can be done by the benefits received by the settlers ... in Upper Kitete. It quite 'forgets' to mention how much they cost the nation. Co-operative villages will only become widespread if they make greater efforts to stand on their own feet financially, and receive fewer advantages. I do not think it is a good policy to try and paper over the failure of the artificial collectives. Nyerere too, in his study *Freedom and Development*,[24] dwells on the absolute necessity of willing co-operation – but also on the need for discipline in work.

9. *Village Communes: Ujamaa Villages*[25]

In 1960, before independence, nine members of the TANU Youth League undertook the collective cultivation of a piece of land.

Today they are known as the Ruvuma Development Association, a group consisting of two hundred families in seventeen villages. This project is one of the few examples of successful socialist agriculture in Africa. 'We began by growing four hectares of cashew nuts; ten ares were grown collectively and from these we harvested three sacks of shelled nuts. From the rest, that is 3·9 hectares, we gathered only two sacks. Our villages have been successful only because they were spontaneous creations in which the people decided to solve their problems themselves and in which all government is local.' – 'At that time we had no ideology; we then realized we must evolve one in order to continue. We have completely modified our methods of primary teaching. We now begin by teaching the children to understand their problems as only then can they grasp that new methods are necessary to solve them. They no longer feel that it is necessary to go to secondary school. Some of the experts sent to us were not "socially involved" ... we sent them back! Mr Ibbott has been with us for six years;[26] he lives in the village and works with us. He is our adviser, but only advises us on what we have decided ourselves.'

In the RDA the work, like the land, is largely collective. There are no salaries. Apart from a little aid from small organizations (War on Want, Development and Partnership in Africa) the only aid received from the government has been essentially 'political'. There is universal education and the agricultural returns are good.[27] Some villages are blessed with running water and motorized windmills. Two hundred families make use of two tractors and one Land-Rover. Decisions are made by committees or general assemblies. Success is also apparent in the degree of specialization achieved in work. In some villages there is a gardener, a driver, a cowherd, a carpenter, a poulterer and a miller – all local people who have been able to specialize as a direct result of the development and diversification of the village economy. The association has built a brick factory and bought a windmill and a sawmill; their future and utility are assured by the members of the group as is the employment of the younger generation. There is no room for new members at Upper Kitete and they do not allow salaried workers to be employed. The children have to leave home when they have finished primary school if they want to find work.

The Tanzanians know as little about this experiment as do the upper levels of the administration.[28] The civil servants on the lower levels, that is to say, those with whom the peasants come into contact did not know what a communal village was. The education of some of those likely to be involved in the future has started so that the experiment may become more widespread, disregarding the lack of any precise ideology among the masses.[29] The confusion is so great that some regional commissioners are trying to bring in socialism by wielding the big stick. However, the Tanzanians are continually being encouraged not to place a blind faith in their leaders and to take part in matters which are of concern to them. Nyerere said 'If you don't exercise power, I, and a few wicked friends, will take it from you.' But this ethic is not always understood by all commissioners, who are appointed by the President and can be recalled by him alone if they commit any offence. Very often before they learnt this, the peasants had time to suffer, because the commissioners control the information, which goes back to the national administration, in proportion to their responsibility to the administration and to the Party in their region. It would be useful to clear the information routes and find a generally acceptable method of covering the activities of the commissioners. Those with nothing to hide see no objections!

Nyerere has created an organization inside the party for the encouragement and spread of Ujamaa villages.[30] The direction of this has been put in the hands of deputy Milinga,[31] one of the nine founders of the RDA. Milinga, himself, has said 'There is no generally accepted form for a socialist village; each group must find from experience what suits it best. Our work consists of encouraging people to understand their situation and to try this experiment, to give them support and to tell them what has been tried elsewhere.'[32] Milinga works 'in the Chinese way'. Although he is a senior member of the Party, having direct access to the President, when he arrives in a village he stays with one of the inhabitants and joins them in their manual work. By the end of the day he has strengthened the feeling of unity among peasants. Socialism fights *with* men. In any case, the credit awarded to him is much too restrained when the importance of the work is taken into account, and it is questionable whether it might not be better if his general officer were installed in a production unit of the Ujamaa type.

On one official visit Mwalimu gave a lorry to the village of Moambara – one lorry in six years is not the best way to encourage the experiment. A method must be found to help natural selection without affecting the determination of the pioneers. Help which is more immediate, more aware of the problems of socialist organization which are attached to every technical change[33] would be more useful and would help to make the traditional surrounding villages understand that Ujamaa is going beyond the ordinary rural life (rural extension) or the idea that God helps those who help themselves (Church and Government) which is perhaps more morally satisfying for the giver but does not produce the necessary awareness of his potential in the peasant, awareness which is at the base of any development.

It is very rare indeed to see people among the disinherited who, simply by organizing themselves differently, in seeing their problems and their relations in a new way come to modify their material universe and open up unhoped for horizons in health, security and thought for their children. Is this an isolated incident, on the sidelines of the new tendencies of the country, or on the other hand, a logical progression – and therefore one from which one can generalize – of nationalism so dear to certain Tanzanians?[34]

10. The Weakness of Co-operatives

The success of these communal villages depends on great efforts being made, and on the existence of a highly-developed co-operative spirit. However, in 1967, out of the twenty-eight Tanzanian co-operatives that were in difficulties, fifteen had their committees suspended and were placed under the supervision of the agricultural authorities. The old co-operatives, such as those handling the Kilimanjaro coffee, flourished for a long time, making comfortable profits from the sale of their produce.

The most powerful of these, the Victoria Federation (of cotton-growers) has put up a magnificent building at Mwanza, within which I searched in vain to find a peasant – who would not have felt much at ease there anyway. The managers' Mercedes, not always used strictly for business purposes, were left with their engines idling. Since then this proud federation has also been placed under government supervision. Its managing director was unduly privileged; it proved possible to dismiss 315 out of 851 employees without impairing its functioning. In the factories for separating the cotton fibres from the seeds, only 395 out of 698 employees were kept on. A number of the co-operatives are too small, with a turnover not large enough to pay the staff or support their general expenses. Their activity is mostly confined to collecting the harvest and supplying a few things such as fertilizers and insecticides.

It is easy to criticize, but the co-operatives would seem to be a useful weapon against the abuses of Indian commerce – though actually these abuses were not very evident except in isolated villages and centres where there was no competition. On the other hand, reliable studies show that in the city the distribution costs of the Indian traders were among the lowest in the world. I was told of one Indian family whose warehouse also saw to the collection of maize; the business was run by the father, while the mother kept the accounts and the son drove the collecting lorry. They have been replaced by a co-operative – concerned only with collecting the maize – which has a manager, a warehouseman, a book-keeper and a lorry-driver: four employees, with four families to support instead of one.

In 1966 the presidential board of inquiry into the co-operative movement received bitter complaints from the peasants, who often found themselves getting less for their produce after the co-operatives had been given the monopoly of marketing it. Though they may call themselves socialists, the co-operative bureaucrats can exploit the peasants more than the traders. Monopolies make for bureaucracy, inefficiency, incompetence and even dishonesty. I have mentioned elsewhere[35] how the Lushoto union of co-operatives paid its producers £11·5[36] per ton of maize which they sold for £23, exactly twice as much, at the National Cereal Board.

This margin included local taxes, which it would have been better to have collected in some other way. But still the general costs, transport, special taxes (counted a second time on delivery at the Cereal Board) seemed distinctly exaggerated. Finally, the accounts mentioned a 'special tax' of £2·5 per ton, a seventh of the price paid to the producer. It turned out, upon inquiry, that this was deducted in order to repair the losses due to an accountant absconding with the cash the previous year – an all too frequent occurrence, especially among the Kilimanjaro coffee co-operatives.

Let us once more repeat that Socialism, Democracy and Co-operation are not magic words which enable miracles to be performed, but are only valid in so far as men practise them. Meister claims that a certain level of development has to be reached before the militancy and dedication required for the success of co-operatives can appear. Meanwhile, in order to correct some of the faults of the Tanzanian co-operatives, I have ventured to suggest that there should be a limited amount[37] of competition with local trade, for some crops, in one or two provinces. In any case the co-operatives, which were so highly favoured, are now under stricter government control, or even management, though there is a danger that this may make them even more bureaucratic.

Any swift, and sometimes even premature, progress towards socialism calls for a very rapid improvement in the general level of morality, if the obvious traps of totalitarianism, and planned terror are to be avoided. I noticed such an improvement in China and Cuba, and it can also be seen in a section of the Tanzanian youth, who in this respect are superior to the rest of the young people of Africa.

11. Discipline in Stock Farming: the First Steps towards Socialism

As in the whole of East Africa, the herdsmen form an ethnic group, a society quite distinct from that of the agricultural farmers. In Ruanda and Burundi the Watutsi herders held the Bantu farmers in a kind of serfdom until recent years. Their opposite numbers in Tanzania, the great Masai nomads, were long regarded as enemies by the Bantu, who were in the process of being conquered by them when the Germans arrived. Since then these herdsmen have fought shy of schools, which has led to their being clearly dominated. In the first place, their cattle are subject to epizootic diseases, of which the most deadly one, East Coast fever, periodically kills off 40 to 75 per cent of their herds. More than 1·2 million calves are lost each year in this way. Their ten million or more cattle hardly provide more than 100,000 tons of meat a year, while their milk yield is proportionally even lower. A large part of the country's total land-area is under-utilized by this vast capital, which in the end produces ridiculously little.

The disease is transmitted by tics, which can only be eliminated by regular parasiticidal baths. Many such baths have been constructed, but the grazing-lands as a whole remain common property. Grass is held to be a gift from God, belonging to all. Since there are no reserves of fodder for the dry season, the herds go off in search of pastures and drinking-water, which become scarcer, and in the process, those who have not had their animals treated infect their more careful neighbours. The amount of dairy produce that Tanzania has to import from near-by Kenya is therefore rapidly increasing (18·5 per cent more in 1966 than in 1965).

Associations of stock-breeders have been formed, who brand each of their animals with a red-hot iron – though they should also mark its age and its owner's name. Then various grazing areas should be marked out, each reserved for some ethnic sub-group, so that this way those who had agreed to have their cattle regularly treated could refuse to let their neighbours' infected animals cross their borders, by killing marauding cattle if necessary. As a technocrat, that is what I suggest, though, however necessary such steps may be, at present they would meet with universal condemnation. Yet population growth is also something quite new, which will make other innovations necessary. Modernization is impossible without changes and constraints.[38]

A second step would be to try and get the greater part of the herds' increase, say about a tenth of the total, slaughtered each year. Otherwise, with too many unproductive animals using the pastures in the absence of fodder reserves, the process of erosion will be intensified and could lead to the Masai territory being turned into a desert, thus destroying the national heritage. A socialist society would be justified in intervening on these grounds, for it ought to show more concern for the lot of future generations than does capitalism. A tax on cattle would provide an inducement to slaughter them, and also finance the technical education of stock-breeders. The tax on four-year-old animals should be made prohibitive, since after this age their value declines. Commercial ranches already produce six to ten times as much meat per hectare as the nomads – but how can the latter be educated when for them such measures would constitute a series of blasphemies, and the crumbling of their whole civilization?

The following course would present fewer psychological difficulties, if it could be arranged. By using artificial fodder, it is possible to feed five good dairy cows per hectare on the slopes of Kilimanjaro – three times as many as in Normandy. With the high prices in this area, milk could be more profitable than coffee. Elsewhere, where prices are absurdly low, the collection of milk could only become economic if costs were cut by intensifying production. The delivery-van of the small dairy opposite Mwanza does 200 km every day and sometimes collects no more than 700 litres of milk! On some rounds in Dutch Friesland a hectolitre of milk is collected per kilometre! Near Mara they only collect the cream. There is soon too much skimmed milk for the family to use, and it is then thrown away – while so many African children are short of protein. It is easier to criticize all this than to find an economic solution.

A socialist Canadian teacher at the business school of Kivukoni, near the capital, asked me what degree of growth I would consider admissible, compared to capitalism, if Africa were to run her economy on socialist lines. 'None at all,' I warmly replied, 'we must try to achieve a socialism of abundance.' By this I meant to reject the implied admission of socialism's congenital and irremediable economic inferiority. Capitalism, however, advances by overturning the established order, and involves severe social and economic constraints. Socialism will not be able to progress if it respects all the traditions which stand in the way of development.

The rejection of Stalinism does not therefore imply that intelligent constraints must also be rejected, but the chief difficulty is that people must be persuaded to accept them without resorting to terror. Some sacrifice of the growth-rate would be worthwhile, provided it were compensated by a better and more humane form of civilization – a socialism creating a society of human solidarity in an atmosphere of freedom and dedication to the community. On this basis, Meister defends self-management, even when it turns out to be slightly inferior in economic terms. Yet it is hard to say where exactly the line should be drawn.

12. *The Traditional Mentality and the Privileged Minorities*

In technical matters we already know a great deal, though further research will always be necessary. But we are more backward in the popularization of modern methods, where we come up against lack of knowledge, trained men, money for buying new equipment and, especially, the traditional outlook. To overcome the latter obstacle, we need African sociologists who have spent their childhood in the society they study, and who belong to it. They will be in a better position than Europeans to discover the reasons why innovation is resisted, and also the motivations of progress[39] where it has already occurred, as in the case of the relatively successful coffee and cotton plantations. Some prefer to increase their leisure rather than their purchasing power; if only they did not have so many children we could simply leave it to them.

By improving the organization of the markets, increased efforts could be made more worthwhile, especially if the peasant were not faced with a widening gulf between himself and the city-dweller. High officials used to leave their offices to go and fetch their children home from school during working hours, using staff cars. They built fine villas thanks to the bank advances which they obtained easily because of their high salaries; these villas they rented to foreign embassies at such high rates that after three years they became rich landlords without having spent anything. Since these abuses led to discontent, members of parliament and party leaders were forbidden, by the Arusha Declaration, to possess either private shares or houses let to others. Some people were so displeased about this that a friend told me Nyerere would do well to look out for his personal safety. Yet such useful local saving should not be discouraged. The saving remains available for use by state or mixed companies in other activities, but in comparison with property speculation such normal profits would appear derisory.

Some of the TANU party officials who visited eastern Europe, including Sofia and Prague, some time ago, are led to assert the leading role of the working class and despise the peasants by their dogmatic Marxist education. The fact that these officials are assigned a jeep, staff and premises soon makes most of them forget that the achievement of socialism in Europe required enormous dedication. The same is true for the union delegates and the managers of co-operatives.

Some young people demonstrated their support for the Arusha Declaration by long marches across the country. I would prefer to have seen them supporting the policy of self-reliance by working harder instead of demonstrating. Nevertheless, through these marches they do demonstrate, educate and emancipate themselves from the old hierarchies and affirm their confidence in themselves; and Nyerere is able, in this way, to maintain direct contact with the peasants, over the heads of the bureaucrats. If he could manage to stir up enthusiasm for development, and put an end to the old ossified habits and profiteering, then there would be room for greater hopes.

Nyerere's proposal to generalize the community villages is the result of his reflections based to some extent on the limited successes I described above – and more from his own desire than from the wishes of the peasants. May there not be a danger of his becoming a visionary one day, if he goes on like this? Out of the 60,000 pupils who in December 1966 finished primary school (where 20 per cent complete the course out of the 50 per cent who enter school) and secondary school, only 13,000 found paid employment or were able to go on to further education. The remaining 47,000 were more or less unsuccessfully retrieved by their families. Very few went back to the land, which they had been taught at school to despise, despite Mwalimu's efforts.[40]

Samir Amin believes that when West Africa reaches the same stage of development as Zambia and Tanzania, the actual construction of socialism should be preceded by a long period of primary capital accumulation.[41] During this transitional period it would be essential to remove forward-looking youngsters from the aegis of their families and the traditional society. It might be dangerous to try to do without the stage of having go-ahead young farmers perfecting the use of modern techniques on their own land, then leading others towards progress.

13. Tanzanian Socialism, a Source of Hope for Africa

If exploitation is condemned to the extent of forbidding the employment of paid workers, there would be a danger of agricultural progress being held up. This point has been stressed by two 'regional agricultural officers', Magani and Lyature, who write: 'A conflict has arisen between the two objectives of growth and the fair distribution of wealth. The most hard-working and enterprising farmers become rich, and their farms increase in size. If growth is to be more rapid, farmers like these must be encouraged. To develop production on a commercial basis, they must be free to take on seasonal hands. If this is labelled exploitation, development will be seriously compromised.' Christian Morrisson[42] even considers unequal incomes a necessary condition for investment, and therefore for growth.

Before the personal profit motive can be reduced, there must be other, equally potent, incentives available. Samir Amin's scheme is based on the European pattern of evolution; if Africa must innovate, it is in Tanzania that a form of socialism starting at the level of a subsistence economy seems to have the best chance of succeeding. For the *kulak* will be against socialism unless he is involved right from the beginning in a communal movement which harnesses the individual's energy to the community's needs. Up to now communal projects, such as India's Community Development, have concentrated on schools and dispensaries, while neglecting the production necessary to cover the costs of maintaining them.

The go-ahead, politically educated young farmer of Tanzania would be more willing to spend his energies within a forward-looking collective village, than he would be in Guinea or Mali. If this can be achieved in the Africa of the seventies, it will be in Tanzania. The wisest course would be to develop the two systems (*kulaks* and co-operatives) in parallel, but without neglecting either co-operation among the *kulaks* on the one hand, or the material interests of the workers in the co-operatives, on the other.

Nyerere displays more impatience than Kaunda in moving towards socialism, but he is making a cautious start. Yet he should guard against building castles in the air, and the rather visionary tone of his speeches, in which he confuses his desires with concrete realities as far as socialism is concerned. He needs to maintain more direct personal contact with the peasant masses, by other means than official tours, when hordes of police-cars create an opaque screen – as I was able to observe myself on the first day of my own tour, which was originally supposed to be official.

Mwalimu must also keep a very careful watch over the management of the public sector, because unless it makes profits it cannot be extended without harming the general development of the country, as happened with the failure of the nationalized companies in Guinea and Mali. Nyerere realizes that he has chosen a bold, though difficult course. He deserves to be commended highly for his courage, because it may provide irreplaceable material for the development of a new society, and not only in Africa. He should not, however, regard himself as a man of destiny, but should always match his theories to the realities of his vast land.[43]

African socialism has to a large extent failed in West Africa: overthrown by the army in Ghana and Mali,[44] and very much watered down in Guinea, where the paper *Horoya* has ceased to mention Vietnam for fear of ruffling the feelings of the 'generous' Americans. Senghor's attempt seems to be growing feebler and feebler. East Africa, then, is taking up the torch of African socialism. Tanzania has taken the first decisive step with the Arusha Declaration, and is preparing other measures. She should be careful to preserve her relatively greater economic independence and consolidate her co-operative foundations. This does not at all mean that Kaunda and Nyerere have come to the end of their difficulties. Meanwhile France is continuing to sell arms to South Africa ...

NOTES TO CHAPTER 6

1 Meaning technical advice mainly, and some supply facilities for the peasants.
2 *Esprit*, May 1968, 'le socialism tanzanien'.
3 Including a score of trained farmers paid by the Ministry for Settlements.
4 Another, and much more serious coffee-berry parasite has appeared in Kenya – where public prayers have been ordained to avert the scourge; however, the phytopathology departments are also working on the problem.
5 55,700 tons in 1968; 48,000 tons in 1967, when there was a drought.
6 It dropped from 435,000 bales in 1966 to 275,000 in 1968.
7 The United States are attempting to produce synthetic coffee and cocoa. Fortunately they are very bad so far.
8 G. Belkin stresses the fact that hundreds of schools, dispensaries and houses have been built collectively; this is a better effort than the rest of Africa has made.
9 *Cf. Newsweek*, October 1967, 'The Ugly Frenchman' (meaning me).
10 It is the second language of Africa, after Arabic.
11 Firewood, water, harvests, fertilizer, etc.
12 The total production of maize seems to vary between 500 and 600 thousand tons. I would not vouch for the accuracy of any of these figures.
13 More or less stagnant from 1966 to 1968.
14 'While saying they want to be friends,' adds Kaunda. Many of them also claim to be Christians.
15 In *le Monde*, 11 January 1969, P. Biarnès states that in Senegal 'the amount spent on administrative personnel has risen by nearly 30 per cent in seven years, the cost of conveyance has increased in the same proportion, while expenditure on equipment has remained stationary and that on public works has gone down by 35 per cent.... The frequent losses of public institutions.... There is no longer anything left over to be put aside for development.'
16 They now earn £2,400 a year, which is less than the white experts.

17   A Canadian nun told me that pro-Chinese Catholics are 'coarse-grained' (*à gros grains* – those who tell their beads [*grains*] quickly).

18   *False Start in Africa*, André Deutsch, London, revised edition, 1969.

19   This town is now the headquarters of the common market organization including Tanzania, Kenya and Uganda, and of which Zambia could well one day become a member.

20   This word is not found in present-day communist manifestos; it seems very important in so far as it concerns the restoration of dignity to the downtrodden. I would like to see this policy adopted in communist countries; by the Russians in Czechoslovakia for a start.

21   The Swahili for 'master', which is what the president is called in Tanzania; it is better than 'His Excellency'. My report is to be published in Tanzania (in English).

22   In the summer of 1968, Jamal, the Minister of Finance, who is a first-rate economist, announced that the State Trading Corporation had made a profit of £530,000 for the first nine months of 1967. It is true that the consumer no longer has a choice between different import companies, but the service provided still seems of a reasonable standard.

23   The ordinary passer-by is struck by the speed of the Zanzibar dockers, who have a very high quota to complete each day, and by the nonchalance of the dockers at Dar-es-Salaam. After allowing their productivity to decline by 30 per cent during recent years, in 1967 the latter demanded a 30 per cent wage increase. However, the Zanzibar dockers err too much the other way.

24   *The Standard*, 18 October 1968, Dar-es-Salaam.

25   This section has been edited (1968) by the Canadian cineaste, Gérald Belkin, who intended to make a film about the Ujamaa movement.

26   Ibbott has obtained remarkable results after six years in the country. He lives in the village with his wife and three children in the utmost simplicity. His principal worry is that he should not take on responsibility that the people themselves are unable to bear. He has come to believe that over and above the increase in the soil's fertility, development rests on new social relations in production.

27   Twelve to fifteen sacks of maize per acre is seven times the amount usually gathered by manual labour.

28   Exception should be made for – among others – the President, who has greatly encouraged the RDA experiment which he cites as an example of his important 'Socialism and Development' scheme.

29   Tanzania has been applying a policy of gradualism, that is to say the new power is prepared to work internally, in the midst of great contradictions and is trying to resolve them by education, persuasion and by making the peasant aware of them. The villages and the President's ideas received a serious setback in September 1969 when the Party's central committee dissolved the RDA following the mixing of local political tensions with personal struggles on a national level. However, as one of the members of the RDA explained, by taking the villagers in hand without specifying exactly what their course is going to be, the Party will henceforth take responsibility for a general policy of social development well adapted to the economic and political realities of the country and aiming at solid results not just in a few

villages but in the whole rural sector. This is what is happening at the moment. The President is trying to prevent the debate spreading into a struggle of factions. Meanwhile numerous Ujamaa experiments have been undertaken: 'There go my people I must catch up with, for I am their leader!' described many a local situation which the author has witnessed. (December 1970.)

30 He knows very well that it is a political problem. At Upper Kitete, the only support which the director has at this level is his Bible, and daily readings from this do not provide sufficient inspiration. He now wants to follow a course to help establish political consciousness.

31 1970: ex-deputy because he did not receive sufficient votes from the Party to represent it (yet another sequel to the dissolution of the RDA).

32 The awakening of the feeling which overcame many European socialists.

33 The introduction of this lorry – quite justifiable on paper – has completely upset the economy of the village. Considerable sums of money and energy have been swallowed up in its maintenance. If one remembers that this village is one of the most developed in the African continent in the field of conscience, experience, co-operation and discipline, one can gather the importance of intermediate technology in practice as well as theory. There is a Swahili proverb: 'Haraka haraka haina baraka!' Hurry, hurry, no luck.

34 In 1971 this question was still unanswered. Ujamaa had made great progress, particularly in numbers, but the capitalist sectors still have a very strong impact on national compatibility. Prudence has been too much in evidence there; for this socialism which is both voluntary and really democratic to grow, a favourable framework and climate of opinion are necessary. The decolonization of institutions and hopes remains to be finally achieved.

35 *Esprit*, May 1968, 'Le Socialisme Tanzanien'.

36 A price which provides very little incentive.

37 Because the economic and technical standard of the Indian traders is higher than that of the African co-operative managers.

38 Belkin thinks that wholesale intervention by the Ministry of Health would be the best way of getting them accepted.

39 The sociology students at Dar-es-Salaam University have just started to make a socio-economic study of their area, for future planning.

40 Shortly after Arusha he published a manifesto *Education for Self-reliance*, partly inspired by my ideas. Fortunately it is beginning to influence educational methods (farm-schools where the pupils earn their keep by manual work).

41 I would also add 'of the increase of knowledge'.

42 *La repartition du revenu dans le Tiers-Monde*, Editions Cujas, 1968. I absolutely deny the validity of this hypothesis once a certain threshold of development has been attained – which is anyway very hard to define exactly. At the outset maybe.

43 My tour of Zanzibar left me rather concerned as to the success of the first plan, which was evolved by East Germans who had very little idea of the situation there. We were denied access to any documents, even though we had been sent by President Nyerere – which goes to show that Tanzanian

unity is still very much a matter of words. As for the Chinese state farm, where Mao's portrait has the place of honour (ousting the local authorities), we were flatly refused entry. The disagreeably 'policed' atmosphere there seems unfavourable to development.

44 'Imperialist and Neo-colonialist machinations', writes J. Vieyra, in connection with Modibo Keita's fall (*Jeune Afrique*, 2 December 1968); 'there may be some truth in this analysis, but it cannot be left at that. . . . In my view there is only one cause: the dictatorship of a single party, aggravated by dogmatism and bureaucracy.' I predicted this fall in the pocket edition of *L'Afrique noire est mal partie*, published in October 1966. (*False start in Africa*, André Deutsch, London, revised edition, 1969.)

CHAPTER SEVEN

Has the 'Liberal' Ivory Coast
Made a False Start?

1. *The Unsatisfactory Situation in West Africa*

I have often been reproached for my haste in proclaiming, so soon after independence, that 'Black Africa had made a False Start'. The new nations, I am told, have not yet had time to get properly under way. Meister even believes that it is impossible for them ever to get started. I wrote that book in 1961–2; seven years later I am very glad to see that, in spite of all their difficulties, the Tanzanian and Zambian 'presocialisms' are making a much better beginning than those of Ghana, Guinea and Mali. Nyerere's and Kaunda's moral calibre, and the stability of their governments, give these two countries a political climate favourable to development. Provided they manage to control the abuses of their privileged minorities effectively, they will soon be able to evolve independent economies, and perhaps socialist villages.

My distressed diagnosis, in which I emphasized the necessity of putting matters right as soon as possible, has been all too fully confirmed by the numerous military takeovers, and by the general economic stagnation of tropical Africa as a whole. When I denounced inter-African racial strife, I had no idea that it would assume such dreadful, genocidal proportions in Southern Sudan and Biafra. Nevertheless, I underestimated the difficulties involved in this much-needed correction of Africa's economic policies. It is no longer appropriate to lay all mistakes and malpractices at the door of the colonial powers. One cannot seriously continue to blame imperialism[1] for everything, or assert that the only course open is a socialist revolution (a rather vague term anyway).

Many different systems can be envisaged, and adaptations must be made to fit every situation. The many factors that have contributed to the failures of Ghana, Guinea and Mali need to be studied in depth before a rational decision can be arrived at; otherwise the same mistakes will be repeated. This job must have first priority for those most responsible and least demagogic African revolutionaries who are struggling to break away from creeds and invective. Osana Afané made a start, before he was killed in Cameroon by the so-called forces of law and order.[2]

Dahomey, with the collapse of its main agricultural exports, is sinking into a state of dependence. In Senegal production has not come up to the planned level; its rate of progress is among the slowest; the expected diversification of agriculture has hardly been achieved; and its industry is stagnant. From Mali to Chad there is very little prospect of development anywhere in the Sahel zone.[3] Niger's uranium deposits will not be enough to get its whole economy off the ground. Colonel Bokassa has done something towards improving cotton production in the Central African Republic,[4] but military regimes, especially African ones, are seldom conducive to development. Only Cameroon, Gabon and above all the Ivory Coast seem actually to be making progress (perhaps Ghana too, though there is room for improvement).

2. Reservations about the 'Ivory Coast Miracle'

The Ivory Coast is not a country that has chosen socialism, not even Senghor's veneer of African socialism,[5] for it proudly aligns itself with *laissez-faire* capitalism. For a long time President Houphouët-Boigny refused to demand independence, resolving to do so only when there was no decent alternative. He then challenged his neighbour Nkrumah, who had adopted socialism and was starting at a distinctly higher economic level, and claimed that in ten years' time he would overtake him. Politically at any rate, Boigny has won. The reasons for this 'Ivory Coast Miracle' are various, and it is hardly possible to assess them all. Samir Amin, however, has made a serious study of them,[6] to which I will refer the reader.

For one thing the natural potential of the forest zone along the Atlantic coast is far superior to that of the inland savannahs. The very fertile volcanic soil of Bas-Mungo in the Cameroons is not to be found in the Ivory Coast, but the Birrimian shale makes good land for cocoa, and the tertiary sands valuable. The soil and climate of a more or less broad coastal strip make it possible for plantations to be highly productive, so long as they are well looked after and fertilized. Robusta coffee long benefited from the strict customs protection[7] given after 1930 to the produce of French colonies – which anyway paid dearly for our manufactured goods. With no such preference or protection, West African cocoa has managed to take the lead from South America, which had a very long start.

This primacy of coffee and cocoa, together with the modern banana plantations and the exploitation of the precious forests, was not without its dangers – to avoid which the Ivory Coast began, even before independence, to diversify its exports with pineapple and rubber plantations (established with capital returning from Indo-China and with compensation paid by us, the tax-payers). The plethora of specialized research institutes (which are more numerous here, and better equipped, than in any of the other ex-colonies) favours new crops, as well as technological progress. The high standards of packaging practised by the Coba-fruit Co-operative of Ivory Coast banana planters assured them better markets than those of the Cameroons, despite the more fertile soil of the latter.

The excellent results obtained with experimental oil-palm plantations by the *Institut de Recherches* (IRHO) have made possible the creation of huge and successful plantations. The plan to plant 32,000 hectares within five years has been considerably exceeded. At the present rate of 10,000 hectares planted a year, the Ivory Coast should have 75,000 hectares of plantations in 1970, and by 1980 should be producing at least 180,000 tons of oil. Despite its *laissez-faire* bias, the state is trying to find ways of accelerating growth, which is the necessary basis for sustained development. The almost total absence of private investors, who were offered pieces of land to plant,[8] caused the system of plantations within the framework of a state company to be adopted; this company also collected in its stores the flow of oil from the peasant plantations which belonged to it. Sodépalm's young trees looked very promising to me; yields of 3 to 4 tons of oil per hectare will certainly be obtained, and will provide serious competition to groundnuts, colza and sunflower.

Yet the price of palm-oil has fallen much more than expected, so that one is inclined to wonder whether the European Development Fund, which financed these plantations, may not be trying to lower the price of oils.[9] However, the growing population of the world will need fresh sources of fats in the future. The soya of the United States and the sunflowers of the Ukraine will not be capable of supplying all the needs of the new nations in the Three Continents. With adequate chemical dressing coconut palms could turn the poor coastal sands to good account. In 1969 a 'coconut-palm plan' was launched, to plant 15,000 hectares by 1971, though the experts would have liked to have held it back until the 'oil-palm plan' had properly matured. It would then have been possible for them to breed sufficient numbers of the new and much higher-yielding varieties of coconut palms; but the Ivory Coast leaders were in a hurry.

As the country's cereal imports were steadily rising, a huge 'operation rice' was finally attempted, guaranteeing a minimum price of 18 CFA francs per kilo throughout the country. This made it possible to cut down imports. Very promising results are being obtained on the revived cocoa plantations. The development of light industry is equally impressive, and industry's[10] share in the national product is rapidly increasing. The proportion of local saving in the total of investment is much higher than in most other tropical African countries. Partisans of socialist development can no longer turn a blind eye to success like this, any more than they can disregard the miracle of Japan.

It appears at first sight that the Ivory Coast is progressively fulfilling the conditions required for its economic 'take-off', the prelude to a self-sustained development. Yet the growth in administrative expenditure since Independence has been quite excessive – though it has slightly abated now. The flow of capital out of the country, chiefly due to the profits of foreign companies and the savings of foreign experts, technicians and teachers, seems to be approaching 25 thousand million CFA francs[11] – which is much too high. It was five to six thousand million in about 1950.[12] The country's debts are increasing at such a rate that soon the bulk of its exports will be swallowed up by debt-servicing payments.

These features show that, despite its rapid growth, the Ivory Coast still bears many of the stigmata of underdevelopment. A great increase in the exploitation of forest products has been achieved by felling the best part of the precious natural timber, which will soon have been used up. Replanting only began in 1966. A high proportion of the timber is still exported in an unprocessed state, so that most of the benefits of its added value are left to European processors. The heritage of the land is rapidly being destroyed by the inefficient cultivation of coffee, which is much more difficult to grow intensively than cocoa. In some areas, such as Gagnoa, there are signs of a shortage of fertile land suitable for new plantations. Meat, vegetable and fruit imports are constantly increasing.

3. The Domination of Foreign Labour Techniques

The coastal environment enables the African peasant to feed himself, without much effort, chiefly on cooking plantains and manioc, even though these foods lack protein. As a result he has no incentive to work hard. On the other hand, in the semi-arid zones nearer the Sahara, especially those which are relatively over-populated, great efforts have to be made in order to survive, at least during periods of heavy work. Samir Amin has clearly shown what a large part of the Ivory Coast's work is done by immigrants, mainly from Upper Volta and Mali, who are generic-ally known as Mossis. Others come down from Niger or even the northern half of the Ivory Coast. The 1971-5 plan predicts that the north will in its turn suffer from a shortage of manpower.[13]

These Mossis provide most of the paid labour on the plantations,

G

whether managed by foreign capitalists or native peasants. This is not to say that the Ivory Coast peasants do nothing; on the whole, however, the southerners do not work as hard as their Senoufos compatriates from the Korhogo region in the north. The credit given to planters makes it possible for some of them simply to hire Mossis and then sit back; in a way this puts a premium on idleness.[14] Moreover, it often happens that communal land, which is now reserved for natives, comes to be sold in various ways at ever higher prices. Property speculation thus provides a considerable amount of unearned income, with a corresponding reduction in the share of earned incomes. Speculation in building land at Abidjan has assumed extravagant proportions.

While the Mossis furnish most of the manual labour, Dahomeans used to provide the civil servants – before they were forced to leave. A section of the small traders are Nigerians, who get plundered from time to time, as happened in March 1968. They were attacked not only by hooligans, as the official explanation at the time implied.[15] The teachers, advisers and technicians are for the most part French. The Ivory Coast is the only French-speaking African state whose European population has more than doubled since independence. It has thus avoided the disasters which often result from rapid and inefficient Africanization carried out chiefly for the benefit of the bureaucracy. On the contrary, Africanization, in the long run absolutely indispensable, has not gone nearly far enough here.

A tendency towards egoistic individualism is observable among the young of the Ivory Coast; this causes them to take little interest in their country's future, and makes them too willing to consign it to the care of foreigners. Some plans envisage a very rapid increase in foreign participation, for instance in education. Too often the Ivory Coast pupils at the Abidjan High School try to go away to foreign universities, which induces many of them afterwards to settle abroad. With 1,500 French teachers in 1968, the Ivory Coast wished to expand its secondary education rapidly, but not enough native teachers were being trained. It therefore demanded 5,000 French teachers by 1975, envisaging a trebling of their numbers in seven years! It is desirable that French cultural co-operation should increase to some extent, but if all their demands grow at this rate it will be impossible to meet them.

4. South Americanization, or 'Better to be Envied than Pitied'

The economic progress of the Ivory Coast is producing rapid growth in the modern sector, in the towns, on the plantations and for a minority of progressive peasants; it is not however accompanied by adequate Africanization, as it or 'Ivorization', now means progress which excludes other Africans. The young Africans still need to discipline themselves to hard work, and become more conscientious at their jobs. Foremen brought up in African villages according to African traditions, having worked their way up, were not too bad in this respect, but this seems less true of young graduates returning from France, many of whom would like to manage mixed-economy companies straight away, in short have a well-paid official position, which does not involve much effort. But this would not be the way to reconcile 'Ivorization' with speedy development.

The bush school has not yet set itself the essential objective of training of peasants in modern techniques; apart from coffee and cocoa planters, the young people who go to school do not return to the land. The government has done all it can, so what remains? Education is necessary to development, provided it is strictly relevant to the country's needs, and does not turn out a lot of unemployed intellectuals to promote economic stagnation and political instability. The second plan set out to develop an educational policy in step with the economy's needs; but it consists mainly of additional courses devised by the Chamber of Commerce. Moreover, educational traditions offer a very strong resistance to this much-needed adaptive process.

Genuinely African culture, indispensable for the development of national sentiment, can never be meted out when the majority of the teachers are French, however well-disposed they may be. As we shall see in connection with India, overall development involves the profound modification of traditional hierarchic structures, such as has taken place in Guinea and Mali. By reforming the system of tenure, the land should be made available to the most enterprising planters, whether native or foreign, so reducing the proportion of public investment. Also, the distribution to some nationals of surplus-values, incomes from property and other unearned revenue, solely on account of their privileged birth, could be avoided.

At the hotel Ivoire in Abidjan, the American tourist has everything to hand, including traditional art, without ever having to stir from its artificial, air-conditioned climate, as foreign as himself. If he is more curious he need only go down on foot, by night, as far as the village of Blokosso[16] 800 yards away, beside the lagoon; there he would see at least a hundred workmen in the main street, who sleep on the ground every night during the dry season. Yet the drawing-rooms of Abidjan lavish all their sympathy on the pavements of Calcutta, where, it is true, poverty is much worse.

I was interviewed on Ivory Coast television (an expensive service for the privileged minority): 'M. Dumont, you criticize us for our fine villas and our Mercedes; but isn't it better to excite envy than pity?' The studio is situated among the beautiful avenues of Cocody, where the Ivory Coast leaders' luxurious villas stand side by side with those of the foreign experts. The interviewer clearly belonged to this privileged minority and was evidently, and understandably, satisfied with his lot. I then asked him how many cases of kwashiorkor (a disease of children caused by protein deficiency) came to the notice of the Abidjan hospitals each month. Thereupon he changed the subject – since the broadcast was live.

The sight of such rapidly widening social inequalities, makes one think that perhaps the 'Ivory Coast Miracle' may end in the all-too-familiar impasse of Latin-Americanization, where an intolerable social situation is perpetuated by the dictatorship of a privileged minority, and may, in its turn, generate an explosion. Corruption and prostitution, typical features of underdeveloped countries who align themselves with the free world, are very prevalent in the Ivory Coast. The photo of a wedding between the families of two Ivory Coast leaders, at Neuilly, showed how some of them regard the customs and costumes of rich Europeans as the hallmarks of certain promotion up the social scale. They fail to see that by acting in this way they repudiate African traditions and conjure up in their stead an image of upstart vulgarity. I did not dare approach the minister Sawadogo, when he paid a visit to the Cocody exhibition, because his whole retinue were dressed in black jackets and ties, whereas I was wearing lighter clothes more in keeping with the April temperature.

5. Real Development Requires More Trained Leaders

If the peasants of the savannahs continue to progress less quickly than the rest, Malinkès and Senoufos will soon become the 'North-East' of the Ivory Coast where, as in Brazil, incomes will lag ever further behind those of the city. The average income over the whole country is considerably more than 200 dollars. If this were calculated after subtracting the incomes of the Europeans and the wealthy minority, it would be apparent that most of the population is still quite poor – which is confirmed by the slums and the average level of nutrition. The country has in fact changed over from a primitive subsistence economy to one, typical of under-development, based on export agriculture from which the wealthy nations profit, as in the banana republics of Central America.

For real development, an independent economy must be achieved, with an adequate agriculture, able to cope with the requirements of the home market. The rice-growing drive is already a step in this direction, and if the northern peasants were better trained, and better helped, they could supply the South with much larger quantities of cereal, meat, dairy and horticultural produce. There should be more concern for the possibilities of inter-African trade, in spite of the problems of starting it. Or many light industries could be developed, such as yarn, hardware, textiles, paper, sacking, pottery, glassware, wooden articles, plywood, rubber and plastic goods, and so on. But these industries presuppose many intermediate products; their production would be costly, in some cases because of French suppliers and always because of the smallness of the market. This stage must therefore be passed; Senegal reached it ten years ago and still seems incapable of getting any further, despite its repeated appeals for foreign capital.[17]

Moreover, tropical Africa is starting out a long way behind the rest of the underdeveloped world. Its natural conditions are distinctly inferior to those of Latin America, for example. Unlike the rich Atlantic countries at the time of the great depression, it cannot afford to make any fundamental errors in its economy, for it would have to pay too dearly for them.

If the wealthy coastal states of the south continue to exploit the poor labour of the savannah, their ethnic and social differences could one day degenerate into political or even military conflict. The poor, who have nothing to lose, make the more courageous fighters, even when they are less well armed, as we have seen in Korea and Vietnam. There would be more room for hope if the *Conseil de l'Entente*[18] were to develop into a real common market tending towards political union; perhaps the neighbouring countries of Ghana and Liberia could one day join it too, first on a confederate, then on a federal basis, if the language-barrier could be surmounted.

Samir Amin stresses the fact that the Ivory Coast's present progress could well ease up in the near future, and there is a possibility of the semi-stagnation which is already pronounced in Ghana. Any extensive development in Africa is unthinkable without heavy industry and a rearrangement of the social structure. Aluminium is now being manufactured in Ghana, and could also be developed in Guinea and the Cameroons. Saharan natural gas and Mauretanian iron-ore might economically go hand in hand. Industry should not be ignored: the production of fertilizer has hardly begun, since consumption is too slight to encourage it.

All this will necessitate sound regional economic planning, with the reorganization of small countries into larger units. The Economic Commission for Africa, part of the United Nations, has already studied this. Before such plans can be realized, however, a whole series of political obstacles, which could stand in the way of

African development for a long time to come, must be removed. Nepotism and tribalism will have to be surmounted by *élites* more dedicated to the nation's welfare. Many people are worried about the future of the country after Houphouët-Boigny.

Unless the privileged minorities wish to lose their dominant position fairly quickly, they should make better use of it and not continue to be indifferent to the lot of the deprived. The students of Abidjan rightly protest against many abuses, but it never occurs to them to denounce the privileges from which they benefit. Like the Tanzanian students, they are quite content to forego austerity for themselves. They are reared in luxury to perpetuate the oligarchy's rule.

I can see Georges Séverac about to criticize me for adopting a moral tone on problems too difficult for a non-sociologist to tackle. All those who believe in man's potential for progress have a tendency to urge him to go much faster, but speed must not be sought at any price, otherwise we shall soon fall back into a neo-Stalinist atmosphere. National unity, once firmly established, should be quickly transcended by the assertion of African solidarity, before it degenerates into chauvinism and endless conflicts. Otherwise Africa could well remain the Cinderella of mankind, easily dominated because of its backwardness and divisions. Where are the young Africans who will make the voice of reason be heard, and compel recognition from their various privileged minorities? Who will have the courage to lead these countries towards true African unity – beginning with economic unity – in spite of the diversity of political systems adopted?

NOTES TO CHAPTER 7

1 Maxime Rodinson in *Israel and the Arabs*, Penguin, London, 1968, talks of this indefinable bogey which, in the oversimple schemas of Marxism, is called imperialism.
2 See his *Economie de l'Ouest Africain*, Maspéro, Paris, 1966.
3 Perhaps this region might benefit more from international aid than from actual development. It should never have been divided politically from the wealthy coast.

4 The country has returned to stagnation since the regional development offices were Africanized.

5 It must be much more clearly distinguished from Nyerere's socialism than was done in January 1963 in Prague.

6 *Le Développement du capitalisme en Côte-d'Ivoire*, Editions de Minuit, Paris, 1967.

7 This has enabled coffee to be grown in marginal areas, which are really too dry.

8 With the single exception of M. Blohorn, who operates a factory in Abidjan.

9 Palm-oil was 240 dollars per ton in 1964; it reached a peak of 300 dollars in mid-1965; by the end of 1968 it was 140 dollars. 'One can hardly expect the markets to become more orderly while Russia and the United States refuse to harmonize their agricultural policies and humanitarian pretensions.' The steps taken by the European community are still 'far removed from any genuine market statistization' – Xavier Torré, *Oléagineux*, January 1969.

10 Between 1960 and 1965 its rate of growth was 20 per cent a year; however, the official figure, calculated in current prices, is optimistic.

11 Four CFA francs are worth one new penny.

12 According to Samir Amin, Senegal seems to be even more exploited; it loses 30 thousand million CFA francs every year.

13 *Cf.* the special issue of *Le Monde*, 15–16 September 1968.

14 *Cf.* R. Dumont, *Guinea, Mali, Côte-d'Ivoire*, 'Tiers-Monde', Presses Universitaires de France, Paris, 1961. My conclusions on the Ivory Coast were too pessimistic, as its subsequent development has shown.

15 Although the Ivory Coast claims to be liberal, its Press and especially its radio and television services are much less free than in Zambia and Tanzania.

16 Europeans write it 'Blockaus'.

17 After Modibo Keita's fall, Mali appealed for foreign capital, but this will in future be forthcoming only for the other savannah countries who have never wavered in their allegiance to the West: Upper Volta, Niger, Chad and the Central African Republic.

18 This is a customs union of Upper Volta, Niger, Togo and Dahomey under the aegis of the Ivory Coast, which takes a minor interest in its satellites' investments; it is disintegrating.

CHAPTER EIGHT

The Effects of the Rising Tide of Population on the Modest Progress of 'Bureaucratic–Military Socialism' in Egypt

1. The Bureaucratic Caste and the Corrupt Landowner

The Nile valley and delta learnt very early in their history that they had to be ready for the rising of the divine river, to make the best use of the flood waters – the only method of cultivation in this desert climate – and lay in reserves against the famous 'seven lean kine'. To this end a caste of priests (wise men, more or less) and scribes was needed, and the administration very quickly became centralized. The high yields resulting from the exceptional natural conditions and an advanced use of intensive cultivation, made it possible to divert a large part of the population into productive labour, such as canal-building, or luxuries such as the construction of the great pyramids,[1] or of temples and tombs like those of Karnak and the Valley of Kings. All this was a heavy burden for the peasants; nevertheless it is the first example in history of a relatively efficient state administration.

After alternating periods of prosperity and decline – the latter being more marked under the Turks – the modernization of agriculture accelerated, first with Muhammad Ali's revival, which made cotton growing compulsory, then under the British Protectorate. To replace basin-flooding, which leaves a fertilizing deposit of alluvium but allows only one harvest a year, a permanent irrigation-system involving dams and canals is gradually being constructed (but is not yet completed); this makes it possible to grow two crops a year, but does not deposit the alluvial mud in the fields; this has to be dredged out of the canals. This irrigation[2] is being developed by British engineers, without adequate compensatory drainage, so that yields are reduced by the permanent underground water-level rising too near the surface; this saturates the soil, and sometimes even brings white patches of salt to the surface – both of which are very bad for orange plantations.

Modernization was confined almost entirely to agriculture, and too exclusively directed towards the production of high-grade long-fibred cotton, most of which was destined for the British mills. Up to 1914, however, production increased more rapidly than the population, even though the latter had started to grow earlier than in most of the other underdeveloped countries. In 1910 the value of cotton exports was four times that of food imports, which were still quite moderate. At the beginning of the nineteenth century the land belonged to the state, but large feudal estates afterwards arose, followed by small holdings. Though some of these large estates were well cultivated, the majority were rented to small *fellaheen*, who became ever more exploited.

Stagnation set in after 1914. It is estimated by economists that until about 1956 overall production just managed to keep pace with population growth, and the gross *per capita* product therefore remained constant. Progress was made in industry and services, but agricultural production declined.[3] With the pressure of population growth, the demand for land increased, and landlords could afford to become more exacting. Their share croppers generally had to hand over the whole of their cotton harvest – which was the most profitable – as well as the greater part of their corn. The farmer had to be left with the maize, and the Alexandrian clover or bersim for his cow or donkey, so that he might survive to be further exploited. As with the paddy-fields of Canton in southern China before 1949, the average land rent rose to 38 per cent of the gross product, and in some cases even reached 60 per cent. The poor *fellaheen* became even poorer. It has been calculated that between 1914 and 1956 their standard of living declined by 40 per cent.

2. The 'Revolution' of 1952, and the 'Reformist' Agrarian Reforms

The 'Free Officers', of middle-class origin, were embittered by the defeat of 1948, to which the corruption of Farouk's regime had contributed. They overthrew this regime with the greatest ease, since it lacked popular support, and concerned themselves to some extent with the workers and development. Though some of the Cairo bourgeoisie may have regarded Nasser as a bandit, they did not lose everything; by the first agrarian reform estates of more than 200 feddan (84 hectares) were expropriated, but the landowners received a considerable compensation. Fortunately though, they were not paid the full market value, which had become quite exorbitant,[4] but only ten times the new legal value of the rent. Full use was not always made of the ousted landowners' technical abilities, because economic considerations were not fully taken into account by this very important reform. Greater attention has been paid to them since 1964, because the backwardness of agriculture has excited more concern.

Ground rents were at the same time fixed at seven times the property tax, yet, especially for the poor share croppers, they are still too high. In 1967-8 the usual rent in the lower delta was between 14 and 19 Egyptian pounds per feddan (42 acres). The Egyptian pound, which is divided into 100 piastres, was then worth about 50 pence on the Beirut market, and more than 75 pence at the official rate of exchange. Its actual purchasing power within the country seemed nearer £1·20 or more. At that rate the rent would be equivalent to about 600 francs per hectare, or 15 quintals of corn!

By a second agrarian reform in 1961, the amount of property that an individual could own was reduced to 42 hectares, but better compensation was given. There has therefore not been a revolution (a word which has too wide a currency here), but an agrarian reform. People were not in a hurry to buy, since the costs were too heavy. It soon became obvious that the peasants to whom the land was allotted could not repay the actual cost of the land to the state, which, as a result, shouldered a large part of the expense, lowered the interest-rate and extended the period of repayment. These measures hastened redistribution of the land.

By 1968, 300,000 families had each received an average of one hectare[5] of more effectively irrigated land, to be paid for in instalments, together with many facilities for cultivating it. Some recipients were so terrified of their landlords that they returned their titles to property with the words 'We are your slaves; we will not accept them'. Landlords often used to advance seed, fertilizer and insecticide to their share croppers and farmers, who were always very poor, so the agrarian reform administration had to take over these functions. Finally, the properties generally remained divided into three large fields, since three-course rotation was practised (cotton, corn-maize, bersim[6]-rice, for example).

Each recipient was therefore given a piece of land in each of the three fields so as to enable individual peasant cultivation to be combined with some of the advantages of large-scale farming, such as the use of tractors and modern machinery; this also simplified irrigation and technical supervision. From the point of view of production, the results obtained by these agrarian reform villages proved quite satisfactory. It was decided that the system of peasants working within a framework of credit, service and selling co-operatives should be extended to the country as a whole, after regrouping the holdings into large units, for purposes of cultivation but not ownership. This means that the individual is no longer free to farm as he pleases.

3. The Mushrif as Village Leader and the Population Explosion

Each village is within the framework of a general co-operative. In 1963–4, this co-operative was in principle managed by an elected administrative council, under the technical direction of a mushrif – an agricultural supervisor appointed by the state. The administrative councils soon fell under the control of the richer peasants, or kulaks, who were the only ones in the village able to read;[7] many of them abused their position. Corruption continued to flourish, and a number of administrators failed to repay their loans. The government, who were on the alert, used these scandals as an occasion for making crushing reprisals, so that today the *mushrifs* are practically masters of the co-operatives.

It is true that they acquire a certain all-round competence at the Agricultural Institute, and hasten the technical progress of their villages; but they will have to be more honest if the countryside is to be truly revolutionized. For they, too, are capable of exploitation – selling off some of their insecticide for profit. Until 1967 the state provided interest-free loans for modern means of production such as seed and fertilizer; since the Six Day War, however, the interest-rate has been 4·5 per cent a year, which merely covers the cost of administering the funds. This help was extended to all farmers, rich and poor, who were in practice obliged to belong to the co-operatives.

The fact that credit is so widely bestowed means that the part played by farmers in financing themselves is reduced – whereas, on the contrary, ways of encouraging saving, or even of making it obligatory, should be found, so as to increase the total of investment. As in India, the co-operatives are not empowered to receive the peasants' deposits, which hardly ever find their way into savings banks. In a number of the villages which I investigated during the winter of 1967-8, the president of the co-operative and the local secretary of the one and only party were still big farmers – not the ex-feudal absentee landlords who live in the cities, but the richer *kulaks*, who employ very badly paid labourers to farm their land. In other villages these *kulaks* had poor relatives of theirs, whom they could twist round their little fingers, appointed as members of the council.[8]

These guided co-operatives allow the *fellaheen* a certain freedom, as well as the stimuli of initiative and personal interest. They make available to them modern means of production, which have consequently been able to spread more rapidly. Statistics from the National Bank of Egypt[9] indicate that between 1950 and 1962 agricultural production increased by 28 per cent; this was not achieved without considerable effort – especially since the yield per hectare was already rather high, while the area of land newly developed was not large. During this period the population increased by about 29 per cent!

Though the production of cotton, which is the country's chief export, had reached 8 million cantars[10] in 1901, it only amounted to 9 million in 1966 and 8·7 million in 1967, two-thirds of a century later. The population has more than trebled, however, so that *per capita* output have been enormously reduced, as happened with Cuban sugar.

From 1960 to 1965, during the first five-year plan, when a certain amount of new land was beginning to bear crops, agricultural production increased by 16·8 per cent, according to official estimates: this is 3·3 per cent a year, against the 5 per cent predicted in the plan. During the same period population growth rose to almost 3 per cent a year. It is therefore uncertain whether there was any *per capita* improvement, for little is known about the amount of crops consumed at home. Since the needs of propaganda must be served, there is a tendency to assume that the increase in crops for home consumption is on a par with that of commercial crops; hence the 3·3 per cent a year is very dubious. In 1910 the exports of raw cotton were worth four times as much as food imports, which at that period were still modest. In 1967–8 food imports absorbed the total earnings from cotton exports, even though the value of some of the latter is now increased because they are already converted into yarn or cloth. From 15,000 tons in 1955 and 300,000 in 1956, corn imports rose to over 3 million tons in 1967, which makes the United Arab Republic dependent on those who supply it with dollars. A hectare of early vegetables, oranges, cotton or rice is much more profitable than a hectare of corn; self-sufficiency in cereals is therefore not a reasonable objective. Yet until industry has taken greater strides, a more balanced development of agriculture would be desirable.

Though the peasants have now been delivered from feudal oppression, they are still in practice at the beck and call of the administration. The condition of the larger tenants, the beneficiaries of the agrarian reform and the small peasants has clearly been improved, but for the very small proprietors and especially the landless labourers there has been hardly any progress until very recently, when their wages were increased. I heard one provincial agricultural director, a typical representative of the privileged class who despise the outcasts, protest against the policies of teaching the peasants to read and of increasing the workers' wages, saying that 'sometimes' it was hard to get hold of any. I was unable to make him understand that these two phenomena represent the beginning of development. In all countries where there is under-employment, landowners complain of a shortage of manpower – but this is only true for a few days in the year, and then only through lack of equipment.

The agrarian reform has destroyed the political influence of the landed aristocracy, and curtailed their economic power, to the advantage of the peasants who farm the land within the frame-work of co-operatives. The landless peasants, whose sad condition continues to deteriorate, do not benefit at all from these measures. The poorest share croppers pay much higher rents than the larger tenants; they derive very little benefit from loans, while the labourers get none at all. These reforms can hardly be termed socialist as most peasants are deprived of their benefits. Feudal liquidation committees were set up, to which the poor peasants could bring their grievances, but the complaints against bureau-cracy and the *kulaks* soon assumed such proportions that most of the files were closed, whilst some murders of *kulaks* and officials, who often richly deserved it, were followed by very stern repres-sive measures. It seems to be a complete misuse of the term 'socialist' to apply it to a regime chiefly advantageous to the minority of rich and moderately well-off peasants, a regime that has overthrown the aristocracy for the benefit of the *kulaks*, who have the administration at their service.

The modern factories which have recently been erected, mainly by the state, have enabled fairly rapid progress to be made in industry. Yet they have a greater need for capital than for labour, and have not created enough employment. Moreover, their management, which is in the hands of bureaucrats who are often of military origin, is not very satisfactory. Illicit profits are mount-ing, production costs are still high, and competition in external markets is very stiff. It is true that some sort of progress and development are dawning, but they are still very far from what they might be, chiefly – as in the case of Algeria – because of exorbitant military[11] and administrative expenditure.

4. *Bureaucratized Co-operatives, or the Friday Boll-worm*

The co-operative may function fairly well when the *mushrif* really has the interests of the *fellaheen* at heart. He is now also responsible for pest-control, since the 1961 disaster when as a result of inadequate precautions a good third of the harvest was destroyed by the boll-worm. The workers who help him with this expensive struggle may not always be very zealous. If waged carelessly this can soon cost as much as 16 Egyptian pounds per feddan. The ex-landlords may gloat over this, for it only used to cost them 8 or 10 Egyptian pounds. The total cost is recovered in the price of the cotton. Other agricultural supervisors exercise their wits by asking each *fellah* family to provide them with one or two children to help with the work so as to keep costs down to a minimum, which they manage to do; for to ask a very poor, under-employed peasant to hire an employee to do work which he can manage with his family, amounts to cutting down both his employment and his earnings, and thus reducing his standard of living.

Some of these agricultural supervisors in the Delta are of city origin; finding 'their' villages very dirty,[12] they leave their families in Cairo or Alexandria. Though work officially stops at 2 p.m., on Thursdays, they reach their homes at about 12 noon or one o'clock. Since insecticide is expensive, it sometimes happens that the staff steal it[13] to sell; so some *mushrifs* carefully lock it up before they leave. However, the wretched boll-worm (*Prodenia litura*) is not very well brought up, and sometimes even takes the liberty of attacking the crops about midday on a Thursday. If it is noticed early in the afternoon its treatment has to be postponed until the *mushrif* returns on Saturday morning. Meanwhile it has had time to do considerable damage. With a staff of eleven for a co-operative of 600 *fellaheen* and about the same number of hectares, one would have thought it would be easy enough to organize a continuous service. Of course this may have been an extreme case of thoughtlessness that was brought to my notice, and one should not generalize from it. Yet the Egyptian civil service is very rapidly increasing the numbers of its staff (160 per cent in five years, which is a world record), in order to avoid at all costs the dangerous situation created by out-of-work intellectuals. Their efficiency, however, has *not* increased. The offices of the Ministry of Agriculture provide an alarming spectacle of inactivity with grubby arrears of work, and old papers and carbons thrown out of the window. One is reminded of India at times. The Ministry of Agrarian Reform seems quite enormous in relation to its task. 'We are at war', I was frequently told, but it was also the fast of Ramadhan, when it was practically impossible for me to get an interpreter or be shown round, except between the hours of 10 a.m. and 2 p.m. Ramadhan was followed by the feast of Little Bairam, when everything stops; officially it began on a Sunday. The offices of one provincial irrigation authority were deserted from the previous Thursday, so that the period of the official holiday was doubled. The gilded youth did not even interrupt their pleasures on the beaches of Alexandria during the Six Day War. Since then the arrival of supplies to the villages has become increasingly unreliable.

It would seem a dangerous step in any case to give such far-reaching management of agricultural production to a government department, unless it has the potential of enthusiasm of the Israelis or Chinese (to be whipped up again with a cultural revolution when it flags). The salaries of the *mushrifs* rise progressively according to their age, but it would be better if they were pegged to the growth of yields and earnings in their villages, and the state of their co-operatives' finances. They would then take more care over selling the members' cotton, and concentrate less exclusively on expensive modern aids such as fertilizer and tractors.[14] It hardly occurs to the *mushrifs* to put their animal power to better use, or improve the techniques of cultivation. The unrepaid credit mounts up, and long periods of repayment (five years) have to be allowed for rural loans; these are mainly given for maize, which is a subsistence crop. The same quantities of fertilizer and water could be used much more efficiently if corn and barley were sown with a drill, nearer the surface, instead of being broadcast and ploughed in. A first move towards progress would be to give the Administrative Councils power to dismiss unsatisfactory *mushrifs*. A decisive step would be for the co-operatives to have to pay all their employees out of their own pocket; then they would try to reduce their numbers. Next the small peasants, and eventually even the employees, would have to be better represented.

5. The Problems of an Irrigation System Dating from the Pharaohs

The Irrigation Ministry has a much longer tradition than the 'genii' of the countryside. Water has always been distributed free of charge, but the cost of bringing it to the edge of each field is mounting (with perennial irrigation, dams, canals, and the drainage for removing excess water) and these expenses are largely met in fact from the heavy tax on land. The *fellaheen* therefore have no interest in economizing with water. Those higher up a canal try to take as much as possible, for fear it may not return soon enough. Regulations exist, but they do not provide any incentive to economize, and so the commodity which limits Egyptian production is largely squandered; moreover, excessive watering harms the crops by bringing the underground water-table too near the surface. Irrigation by sprinkling could halve water-consumption, in the Delta at any rate, but as it is expensive, it would only be economic for groups of farmers. This idea would be much more attractive if water were paid for by volume.

The land tax could be divided into two parts, one of which would become the irrigation tax. Two and a half million Egyptian farmers cannot all be provided with water-meters straight away, but starting with the new irrigation networks, measuring devices could be fitted to record the total volume of water consumed by the members of a village co-operative. The latter would then know that if they cultivate rice, which requires a lot of water, they will have to pay twice as much per feddan as they would for cotton. If a co-operative changed over to sprinkling (which is uneconomic on a small farm) for some of its crops, it would be rewarded by having to pay less water-tax. Those who squandered water would be under closer surveillance by their neighbours, if the latter had to pay a share of it. The second step would be for the co-operative itself to divide the water-tax among its members – at first by estimating, then by properly measuring their consumption. When I held a discussion on these lines at the Irrigation Ministry, I was met with the unanswerable objection that 'It would give us more work!'

If dredging the canals is left to unsupervised companies, it is done badly. This job should be turned over to the co-operatives, who have an interest in being well-supplied with water and it would also give their members more work. More important, however, is the need to improve drainage, lower the water-table, and only plant orange-trees in soil that is well-drained and free of salt (it might be useful if permission had to be obtained before planting).

The growing of two crops a year, which is not even practised everywhere, represents a certain intensity of cultivation: it is quite common to see land left uncultivated for two months or even longer. Many planted-out catch-crops, whether horticultural or forage, do not need longer than this in such a climate. The planting out of soya, which is widely practised in Korea, produces twice as much as by direct sowing, and in a shorter time. Corn and barley could also be planted out as long as there is rural under-employment. Bersim represents a remarkable advance in forage, since nitrate fertilizer is not plentiful.

The whole situation is dominated by the population explosion, which makes it necessary for the United Arab Republic (still called Egypt by almost everybody) to achieve a higher level of useful rural employment. Egyptian agriculturalists, however, who are sometimes lazy and conceited, are too prone to believe that their rotation and cultivation systems are the best ones possible. Two fodder cabbage crops, planted out in succession and well manured, would yield much more than the traditional four cuttings of Bersim, in the same space of time. Four crops of cabbages, and seven vegetable crops, could be harvested from the same field within a single year, by planting them out before each harvest, as is done in Canton. Livestock in Egypt would not then have to fast every summer, for want of forage. Varieties of Sorghum would be equally likely to yield well during the summer. Stock-breeding, however, can only really be improved by reducing the number of animals so that they can be properly fed, and by specializing in dairy or meat production. Yet the aim of the 'Nasser Plan' was to increase their numbers.

Until power-driven cultivators of the Japanese type, which will require more care from the *fellaheen*, arrive, donkeys could still be useful as light draught- or pack-animals – and could free the women from the necessity of carrying loads on their heads. In one village in the northern Delta, I saw a group of donkeys playing with some little urchins, while women filed by with bales of clover on their heads. Socialism will not be a reality, while women continue to be despised like this, as Mao Tse-Tung aptly reminded us.

6. *The Lack of Expertise in Desert Irrigation*

Southern Al Tahrir[15] has been reclaimed since 1953, and northern Al Tahrir since 1960. In these two areas, lying to the west of the Delta, it has cost a considerable amount, estimated at 150 million Egyptian pounds, to supply 73,000 hectares with water and bring 34,000 under cultivation. The traditional agronomist arriving in southern Al Tahrir and letting a handful of the dune sand run through his fingers, will immediately recognize that the ground is unsuitable for cultivation by traditional means. In such excessively porous soils, irrigation by gravity consumes impossible quantities of water and gives very mediocre harvests; the waste would be unjustifiable.

The sand may be improved by adding 150 to 500 cubic metres of alluvium per hectare – provided it is available not far away, since the cost of transporting it any distance is ruinously expensive. In the off-season, it can be distributed more economically by donkey or camel than by modern mechanized processes. However, the alluvium will be held back in 'Lake Nasser' by the Aswan Dam. Then there is irrigation by sprinkling, which avoids wasting water, but involves huge additional expenditure on capital equipment as well as running costs.[16] The sprinkling process employed at Al Tahrir, which uses water at high pressure, is already out of date, since low pressure is less expensive.

Though this type of irrigation has been very successful in the Israeli Negev desert, it requires a certain professional scrupulousness which is everywhere lacking on this huge state farm. Sometimes the pumping station fails to provide the correct pressure or, more often, the sprinkling angle is not changed at regular intervals. Repairs take a long time and are badly done. The state farm system soon proves cripplingly expensive when the staff are incompetent and lacking in *ésprit de corps*. In 1967, I was told, expenses were 3·5 million Egyptian pounds and receipts 1·5 million.

There is a danger that this large state investment, like the Niger Office in Mali, may yield nothing but substantial losses. This is a vital problem, calling in question the whole system of cultivating newly-reclaimed land. Some young Egyptian economists justify the state farm system by claiming, without proof, that this structure allows the maximum commercial surplus to be obtained – this being a prime objective as the lever for development. This maximum surplus could only be achieved if better techniques were used, and the number of jobs considerably reduced; yet the already numerous unemployed still have to be fed. It would be better to give priority to the simultaneous maximization of gross product, employment, and a surplus for export. This could be achieved by cutting down on machinery and other imported factors of production, which use up a great deal of foreign currency.

In a situation like this, which can only be improved slowly, it would be better for the land to be cultivated in small holdings assigned to peasants within a co-operative framework. Though there are several villages in Al Tahrir, no one has dared entrust them with sprinkling equipment, because they squander the water at an appalling rate and still complain of not having enough. If this equipment had been handed over to them, they would have taken more care than hired employees to see that the watering was done correctly, as it would have been directly in their interest. However, two conditions are necessary; that mechanics should be trained to run and repair the motors, pumps, pipes and sprinkling apparatus, and that water should be paid for according to volume consumed – which could easily be measured when it was pumped up for sprinkling.

Until 1965, the government made a great noise about the *new valley* west of the Nile, based on a group of oases in the middle of the desert. It was claimed that these could be enormously extended, thanks to a practically unlimited water-supply far below the surface – the celebrated Gault level, which crops up again in southern Algeria. However, as the first pumpings drastically lowered the water-level so that the small existing oases were endangered, they had to stop. For a long time the regime has lived on a series of mirages, presented as future miracles. But here, even before Egypt's third military defeat in 1967, all these bubbles burst and they had to face up to the difficult reality.

7. The Benefits of the Aswan High Dam and Population Growth

The World Bank and its Western supporters made a major political error in 1956, in refusing to finance the great Aswan Dam,[17] a mistake which was aggravated by the Suez expedition. Another equally serious error was made in 1965, when the Bank refused to help in constructing the railway link between Zambia and Tanzania. Now that the high Aswan Dam has been completed, it will generate ten thousand million kilowatt-hours a year, which will contribute to the country's industrialization. Yet most of the water made available for irrigation will remain in the Sudan.

Yet the United Arab Republic benefits by the control of flooding, which has been effective since 1967, and improved drainage. The newly-available water will make it possible to convert the last 300,000 hectares of basin-flooded land to perennial irrigation. The great advantages of being able to grow two or three crops a year (in the upper valley) may unfortunately be accompanied by the spread of bilharziosis – a dangerous and debilitating parasite disease. The excellent quality of Egyptian onions is the result of cultivation after flooding, carried out entirely in the dry.

There are 550,000 more hectares of land which might be irrigated, at least half of it consisting of good, or even excellent soil, such as the clay made available by draining and de-salting the lakes in the northern Delta, near the Mediterranean. However, if 250,000 hectares of sand are to be watered too, as they intend, it will be absolutely essential to improve on the methods used in Al Tahrir. Let us suppose that in a few years they will be able to do it properly: in 1968, the United Arab Republic fed 32 million inhabitants on 2·5 million hectares, which means thirteen people per hectare under cultivation. This is a record hardly surpassed anywhere in the world: 550,000 new hectares will therefore make it possible to feed 7 million more inhabitants, representing barely eight years growth of a population which is increasing at the rate of nearly a million a year. But the construction of the canals is lagging a long way behind that of the dam; they will not be completed until 1980.

This means first of all that the yield per hectare must also be rapidly increased – which will become more and more difficult to achieve. Subterranean irrigation could be investigated too;[18] this is even more economical of water than sprinkling, but is much more expensive and demands a higher level of technology. These remarks apply with even greater force to cultivation without soil, using nutritive solutions in concrete tanks, a method which is also economical of water. Tobacco, which is at present imported, would grow well under these conditions and would provide maximum employment per hectare. In view of the danger of fraud a military farm might grow it in Al Tahrir.

8. Family Planning and Child Labour

The UAR, at least as much as India, is faced with the necessity of rapidly introducing compulsory birth-control, if it is to survive as an independent nation and give the lie to that sinister prediction by the Paddock brothers, mentioned in the preface to this book. In my report to President Nasser,[19] I stressed the absolute necessity of reducing the annual population growth, well before 1980, to considerably under 2 per cent. Later the rate will have to be lowered even further. One fundamental obstacle to the spread of family planning is child labour, which is more important in Egypt than in most other countries.[20] Progress towards socialism could make a start here by obtaining a more rapid and marked reduction in child labour. Children are responsible for collecting leaves with cotton boll-worm eggs on them, harvesting cotton-bolls, watching cattle, and many other small jobs.

In the villages that I was able to visit, I was told that between 60 and 65 per cent of boys and between 15 and 25 per cent of girls attended school – a differential reflecting the traditional Moslem attitude. However, the poorest children do not spend so long there, or go as regularly as the others, and are often absent when there is an opportunity of doing paid work. I have seen some of them, aged seven or eight, work seven hours at weeding flax or corn fields by hand, for eight piastres, which has a purchasing power of eight pence. If schooling were really made compulsory in the villages (while still allowing long holidays for collecting boll-worms and harvesting cotton) the children, who at present start earning very young, would have to be supported longer by their parents; fewer would then be called 'Désiré'.

In the towns everyone goes to school, since it is free. The desire for education is so strong here that one might limit this free education to the first two children of any one couple.[21] As a beginning, all the privileges traditionally given to large families, such as priority in being allotted land under the agrarian reform, could be abolished. In fact the state ought never to encourage a casual attitude towards producing children. Raising the legal age for marriage and making abortion, along with sterilization and the pill, freely and widely available would be steps in the same direction. Though there are political difficulties involved in the economic penalization of large families, yet, in the absence of deep political convictions, this seems to be the only way of rapidly lowering the birth-rate.

The president of the Arab Socialist Union of Kafr el Cheik told me that Iraq and the Sudan had been disposed to take in Egyptian emigrants – but that 'imperialist pressures' had made them refuse. I protested against the supposition that 'brother Arab countries' could be influenced by imperialist pressures, but forbore to remind him how difficult it had been to transfer excess rural population to the newly-reclaimed land near the Delta, in Liberation Province. At the time of the ephemeral union with Syria, propaganda to go and colonize the newly-irrigated land over there had scant success; the *fellaheen* started to murmur about being 'deported'.

9. Two Wars on their Hands

The Yemen war proved very costly for the UAR, and the Six Day War even more so; they still weigh heavily on the whole Egyptian economy, retarding development. Egypt (rather like France) wishes to indulge in prestige politics as though it were a great nation – which is very expensive. Militarism and liberal socialism do not go together any better in the UAR than they do in the USSR, where information is still subject to very strict controls. The police officer remains the real master in the countryside; the poor *fellaheen* have hardly been freed at all. Though the landlord's influence may be starting to wane, that of the administration is growing stronger.

The best brains are attracted into the army by the high salaries paid to officers; the present impasse and the Soviet influence have embittered them – which does nothing to improve the political climate. As cement is now earmarked for military shelters it is no longer available to provide waterproof linings for irrigation works and seepage of excess water is becoming a problem. Trenches for open drainage take up too much land, but to replace them with underground pipes cement is needed. A great deal is also required for grain silos and other establishments.

The long-term war vital to the future of the UAR is the struggle for development, which will require the mobilization of all its energies. An eventual military victory in the Middle East[22] would be useless if it resulted in a general economic collapse resulting from the fact that the Egyptian economy was no longer in a position to cater for the rising tide of its population. Though the latter must not be allowed to grow too big, development must be given a higher priority; the Egyptians should also show themselves more capable of arousing the people's enthusiasm.

10. Is this a Socialist Road?

The Arab Socialist Union, the single party to which everyone belongs, does not constitute an effective political force in the way the communist parties do. The free officers formed a small group cut off from the masses by the clandestine nature of their activities; the old parties were discredited along with the corrupt monarchy, and the communist party has not managed to take root among the people. The Charter certainly provides for the creation of the party as a vanguard movement, but Nasser's collaborators are more often profiteering bureaucrats than popular leaders or militants sprung from the people. Although Nasser said he wished to exchange his nationalist position for a kind of socialism, his military origins prevented him from having confidence in the masses; instead he made often rather demagogic appeals for an Arab unity intent on conquests, such as was attempted in Syria – but which remained chiefly on a verbal level. While he claimed to be developing an original form of socialism that would gain prestige in the world, his gropings gave the forces of the right a chance to manipulate the situation. He could rely on the people's support until he allowed them greater economic and political rights, and some freedom of expression.

The country was spontaneously up in arms at the announcement, on 9 June 1967, of Nasser's resignation; yet his regime rested on the support of the police, the army and the civil service. Tribalism has been eliminated in this state which has had five thousand years of central government; but what a dead weight its bureaucracy is! The mere act of handing a petition to a high civil servant underlines the degree to which feudal customs still persist. To some extent power takes the place of wealth with these officials, yet the incomes of those who cannot or will not be corrupted are very modest.

The 'revolution' is managed from above; there are no socialist cadres. Some officers, removed from the army as being politically unsound, were made directors of state companies without having the slightest idea what Egyptian socialism might be. The economy is in the hands of men who lack both business experience and belief in the new order. These companies' losses are made up by the government, which enables them to continue; but there is nothing very brilliant about all this. The bureaucracy is simply not capable of forcing the rapid development necessary. Could better results be obtained under a form of welfare capitalism, with the state genuinely in control? The problem of the landless peasants would remain unsolved. There remains China's solution, but is Egypt capable of such efforts?

Workers are not by nature revolutionary; circumstances occasionally make them so. These circumstances do not exist in the UAR because of the very recent peasant origin of the workers, and deeply engrained habits of servitude. Besides, the industrial workers know that they are a semi-privileged group compared with the poor *fellaheen*[23] or the agricultural labourers who earn 15 to 20 piastres (eighteen to twenty-three pence) per day. To judge from the ease with which the Egyptian airforce was destroyed on the morning of 5 June 1967, it really seems possible that there could have been treachery on the part of some military leaders attempting to rid themselves of the government by involving it in disgrace.

The peasants and workers know that the Cairo night-clubs are always open, that the landowners still get comfortable incomes from their real estate, and that property speculation is rife. The ranks of the old bourgeoisie have been swelled by the new privileged class, and their daughters marry officials. They still have a firm grip on the land, for the number of landowners with between 8·4 and 42 hectares seems to have risen from 27,000 in 1952 to

40,000 in 1964. In 1966, their annual *per capita* income was estimated at 718 Egyptian pounds, as against the 13 Egyptian pounds earned by the landless peasants. 'Several hundred million Egyptian pounds have been swallowed up by the production of cars, refrigerators, television sets, washing-machines and heating and air-conditioning apparatus, which only the privileged class can afford to buy . . . at the expense of productive investment', added E. Rouleau in *le Monde*, towards the end of 1967.

A regime of this kind has to respect the forces of tradition, including the most retrograde features of Islam: atheism is still punishable by imprisonment. In such an atmosphere, Egyptian socialism refuses to call itself scientific, but claims to 'rely on science'. In reality it is a bureaucratic-military state that has given rise to 'the parasitic bourgeoisie of public office', the new class of possessors to which I drew attention in black Africa, and which Hassan Ryad calls 'the state bourgeoisie'. This class could only justify itself by halting the population explosion and increasing the rate of investment. For this to occur, Nasser would have to rouse the people – but he was out of contact with them being more concerned with the junta, a clique of profiteers. He could have lifted the country's military mortgage on 9 June 1967; the people would have applauded; they were literally spitting on the officers. But Nasser felt himself responsible for mistakes in foreign policy, since it was his own preserve. This does not at all excuse the Israeli aggression, against which I have taken a stand.

Egypt's political freedom to manoeuvre is limited on the one hand by the subsidies paid by the Arab oil states, to replace the revenue lost through the Suez canal in 1967–9, and on the other hand by the supplies of Soviet arms. The officials' pride of caste and contempt for the *fellaheen*, the filth in the streets, the failure of birth-control, the inefficiency of economic management, the negligence and corruption[24] of a large section of the administration – all this is more reminiscent of the situation in India than of the Chinese revolution. There has been no revolution in Egypt – though, as in Mexico, it is constantly spoken of – only a *coup d'état*. The *fellaheen* are certainly harder-working than their Indian counterparts, and the cadres more numerous and sometimes more effective. The students, who are waking up to the situation, were fired upon at Alexandria in October 1968. Bearing in mind the very moderate progress that has been made, the many abuses and the absence of freedom, Egyptian 'socialism' can hardly be spoken of except in inverted commas.[25]

NOTES TO CHAPTER 8

1 It has been estimated that 200,000 workers spent twenty years building the largest one.

2 Which is being financed by the Egyptians.

3 In his interesting study *l'Egypte nassérienne* (Editions de Minuit, Paris, 1964) Hassan Ryad estimates that in 1960 it was 60 or 70 per cent of what it was in 1870–80. 'The net income per rural inhabitant in agriculture was only £E23 (about 57 dollars) in 1960 – 70 per cent of the corresponding figure for 1882.' I believe this decline must have been overestimated. Bairoch mentions 2 per cent progress in agriculture per annum between 1934–8 and 1961–5, which is slightly lower than the rate of population growth.

4 In 1937 the market value of land, calculated by capitalizing the land rent at current rates of interest, was 4·5 times the cost of replacing works and installations. 'This makes the landlords' monopoly evident,' concludes Hassan Ryad, *op. cit.*

5 This is the average size of an Egyptian farm: in 1962 there were 2·5 million hectares and about the same number of holdings, the great majority of which were very small, less than 1 feddan (42 acres). This reform has not solved the social problem, if it is true there are fourteen million landless peasants, as Hassan Ryad says. However, many of them follow some other calling, or have a small allotment.

6 Alexandrian clover, which is sown in autumn and usually cut between December and June.

7 The old landowners were better educated. However, one of them told me that 'An educated man cannot sit at the same table as a peasant'. Nowhere else in the world have I found poor peasants, especially those without land, held in such contempt. Even after the 'revolution', this attitude persists – hence the inverted commas.

8 The villages are still controlled by the wealthy, the educated and the officials; even the very poorest peasants maintain their solidarity with the richer ones, for fear of the growing mass of landless *fellahs*.

9 More trustworthy than those provided in official propaganda, which give astonishing growth-curves and talk of world records – omitting to point out that their figures refer to the value of production 'at current prices' (which increase fairly steeply), rather than at constant prices.

10 In those days the cantar was equivalent to 44·9 kg (of raw cotton); it is now 50 kg. Recent figures must therefore be increased by about 10 per cent.

11 The latter are mainly paid for out of foreign aid.

12 The Egyptian agriculturalist who showed me round told me he had read that it was very dirty in China too. I agreed that this had been true – before the revolution. Yet even in those days it would have been profitable to remove organic refuse, which is very valuable as fertilizer; it would not have been allowed to accumulate in the village streets, as still happens in the Delta. Before we can speak of there having been a revolution in the United Arab Republic, we should wait for this revolution to manifest itself in greater zeal for work and cleanliness, more respect for women, and less authority in the hands of military officers.

13 An official responsible for agricultural loans told me that there is always embezzlement in the co-operatives, mainly of stores: 'We are doing our best to check it.' That would seem very difficult to do.

14 In one co-operative I visited, near the capital, the hybrid maize seed had been eaten by insects, while there were sacks of insecticide in the very next room. Sacks of superphosphate fertilizer had burst open, and the acidic dust had corroded the metal of threshers standing near by. The tractors were further away, luckily.

15 The Province of the Liberation.

16 Capital of £E160 per feddan and annual expenses of £E25, at the end of 1967.

17 No cost-benefit analysis of the dam or the associated developments was ever carried out. It fills very slowly, and there could be cracks. Its capital co-efficient, in relation to increased production, may well turn out to be very high, when the cost of the new villages is added. Industrial growth could have been presented as an alternative – though in fact both are needed!

18 In René Dumont's Les leçons de l'agriculture américaine, Flammarion, Paris, 1949, p. 255, the subterranean irrigation of early celery at Sanford, Florida, is discussed.

19 I had hoped to receive some corrections and criticisms on this report from the uar before publishing it in Politique Etrangère, No. 263, 1968.

20 In the growing of one feddan of cotton, it is reckoned that 100 to 120 child-days are needed for collecting the masses of insect-eggs, 40 to 50 for harvesting the bolls, and 12 for manure-spreading, a landowner of the lower Delta explained to me. He reckoned the remainder of the work as 35 men-days. Adults are used more for other crops. Another farmer told me that altogether he paid for 70 per cent child-days and 30 per cent men-days, near Kafr el Cheik in the northern Delta.

21 In social terms, this measure would be very open to criticism, since it would not inconvenience the children of the rich; I would hesitate to uphold it.

22 Any solution, if it is to succeed, must first take account of the Palestinian claims.

23 Their diet chiefly consists of bread, Indian meal, and tea, together with a few vegetables; they only have meat about once every two months. At a Cairo dinner-party, I refused the fourth meat course, explaining at the top

of my voice that the peasants did not get enough meat. I am a very ill-mannered guest.

24 The black market is carried on so openly, in the small shops of Cairo, that it must be hand-in-glove with the police. Petty officials do not earn much, it is true. Prostitution, on the other hand, has practically disappeared – which has driven some of the foreign tourists away.

25 This also applies to Destourian 'socialism', especially since the unduly harsh sentences passed on students at Tunis, in September 1968.

CHAPTER NINE

The Military Anti-Communist Regime in South Korea

1. The Growth of Economic Efficiency through the Reduction of American Aid

When Korea recovered its independence as a result of Japan's defeat, it was partitioned like Germany. After Dean Acheson's announcement, in 1950, that the country was no longer to be included within the United States' defence perimeter in the Pacific, the North attempted to reunify it under its own standard.

Perhaps Stalin was not altogether displeased at seeing the young Chinese republic threatened on its flank, when MacArthur drove it to take action by advancing to Yalu on the frontier. In 1960, Syngman Rhee's bland and corrupt dictatorship collapsed at the mere push of a student revolt, during which the old president wept at the bedside of students wounded by the police – a scene unthinkable in Paris.

During the attempt at democracy which followed, the authorized socialist and progressive parties campaigned for the re-establishment of relations with the North, and there was even talk of reunification. This possibility made the Americans and their faithful South Korean allies shudder; General Park Chung Hee had no difficulty in seizing power. He was coolly received by the intellectuals, and at the same time American aid was drastically reduced.[1] This was very useful to him in the end.

Until then American funds had been largely squandered; uncontrolled loans were handed out to enterprises of little utility. Some borrowers found it easy to repay their loans (which were provided at low rates of interest) by lending part of the money at exorbitant rates. The economy was therefore stagnating at a time when North Korea was building factories, modernizing its agriculture and making appreciable advances. Since 1961, there has been an undeniable improvement in South Korea. Loans are better controlled, and remarkable progress has been announced – made possible by the improved scale of priorities established by the first plan for development. The overall growth-rate was 8·5 per cent a year, and even reached 13 per cent in 1966 and 1967. In agriculture it was over 6 per cent.

2. A Darker Side to the Picture; Three Workers per Hectare

Many of the companies which borrowed American funds with state guarantees staged more or less fraudulent bankruptcies so as to keep all the gross profits to themselves. Currency reserves became so depleted that some capital goods could no longer be purchased, though luxuries continued to be imported.

Moreover the industrial development, of a rather neo-colonialist character, is out of step with agriculture, which is relatively stagnant; the successes that have been announced in this field seem the most open to question. Fruit, vegetable and poultry production appear to be rapidly expanding. There has been some progress with fruit, but the production of meat has recently declined. The cereal deficit is only gradually being reduced; it was aggravated by the drought of 1968. In 1966 90 per cent self-sufficiency in cereals was announced, and in 1968 it was predicted that the country would be entirely self-sufficient in them by 1971; however this has not yet been achieved. It is true that the 1948 agrarian reform (reformist, with compensation by the state) made a number of farmers into landowners by limiting the ownership of ricefields to three hectares; yet overpopulation keeps too many labourers on the land – about three per hectare in fact, which is even more than in China!

The average farm size, which in 1930 was only 1·35 hectares, had fallen by a third to 91 ares in 1968. The rural exodus, recently gathering momentum, has reduced the proportion of the population in agriculture to 54 per cent, though there has been no

H

absolute decline in numbers. Seoul, the tentacular capital, whose tentacles stretch into the country, is growing very fast. Its population has just doubled in ten years, reaching 4·3 million in 1968, out of a total population of 30 million. If it continues to expand at this rate of 7 per cent during the next twenty years, it will have reached 17 million by 1988!

The farmer's tiny small holding is not enough to occupy his family, and it is sometimes difficult for him to feed them. He often prefers to become a servant, carrier, small retailer, or bootblack in the city. These disguised forms of unemployment affect perhaps two million of the population, who just manage to scratch a living. The new suburbs climbing the steepest slopes of the hills round the capital and the great harbour of Pusan consist of one-storey houses – which take up too much valuable land in overpopulated countries – with paths only about one metre wide running between them. Cities are being built which, as they grow, will become impossible to live in. Meanwhile, of course, the municipal authorities are making great efforts . . .

The population increased at the rate of 2·9 per cent a year between 1953 and 1960; since then, however, its growth has stabilized, perhaps even dropped slightly, to around 2·8 per cent. Though the gross annual *per capita* income is in the region of 120 collars, the *per capita* value added for those engaged in agriculture is only about 38 dollars – which highlights the enormous, and no doubt swiftly widening gap between town and country. It has been estimated that 51 per cent of expenditure was on food in 1959, and 58 per cent in 1964; if so, then the standard of living of the bulk of the population has not risen – rather the contrary – while social differences have become more marked.

Drought regularly intervenes to reduce production, since irrigation works got off to a much slower start here than in the North. Most of the country's hillsides are still subject to erosion. The important work of reforestation is too much confined to the neighbourhoods of the capital and the large towns; space should also be reserved on these hills for dwellings (which must not be allowed to overrun the plains too much) and orchards. In overpopulated countries, where intensive cultivation is absolutely essential, timber forests are only indicated where no other crop capable of providing more resources or useful employment is possible, or where it is needed to protect the soil, for example. It is most important that hills overlooking irrigation reservoirs should be protected; otherwise the latter rapidly become silted up by erosion.

3. The Financial Problems of the Small Peasant

Let us take the case of a farmer in a village a good hundred kilo-metres south-east of the capital, apparently well-to-do and with a neat little house. He has 1·4 hectares under cultivation (53 per cent more than the national average), half of it rice-fields and half hillside. On the latter he grows corn and barley in the winter and soya in the summer, which give very moderate returns compared with rice. Until a year ago he possessed a fine ox, which was made to work about thirty days a year on his own farm and was hired out to neighbours for fifteen to twenty additional days. This made him quite well off, since over half the farms in Korea have no draught animals.

His son was married last year, and to celebrate this event suit-ably, as custom requires, without derogation or debt – which would be very difficult to get out of – he had to sell his ox. For his daughter's marriage, he would have had to buy new clothes for the son-in-law's family. In the case of a funeral, he would have had to supply the whole village with food and drink for several days, which is a very expensive undertaking. Yet the farmer in question was not compelled, like some of his neighbours, to sell a piece of land: or a piece of his flesh, as Pearl Buck's Chinese peasant expressed it.

Since then, he, in his turn, has had to hire his neighbour's ox; but only for six days a year, so that he is forced to do much more work by hand. It seemed to me that in South Korea the highest proportion of harvests are carried on men's backs of any country in the world. Yet it is true that the *tsigué*, a symmetrical pannier moulded to the shape of the back and with a strap adjusted to the individual shoulder, is a vast improvement on the Sino–Vietnamese shoulder-piece; this is an instrument of torture made of wood or bamboo, consisting of two baskets supported on one shoulder, which is familiar to everyone, at least from photos and films. Yet a large part of the carrying in Chinese fields has for centuries been done by wheelbarrow: why was this method only intro-duced into Korea in 1966, and then only as an experiment? As I have mentioned before, North Vietnam is rapidly freeing the shoulders of her peasants, by means of the bicycle and the wheel-barrow. Hand-carts with a pair of strong bicycle wheels are common in Korea, and prove useful enough on the roads, but as they are at least a metre wide, they cannot go along the dykes between rice-fields which are often no more than 25 cm across. My insistence that this archaic device should be eliminated as soon as possible astounded the Korean agricultural officials, who find it perfectly natural. The higher officials were content to wait by the roadside, and refrained from following me across the fields. Nevertheless, it seemed to me that their activities were more effective and sustained than those of their Indian counter-parts.

As in India,[2] the traditional funeral and wedding festivities are major causes of indebtedness. Added to this is the considerable expense of educating children; secondary schools, and especially the universities[3] to which they try to send them, cost a great deal – and grants are scarce. Official loans consist only of small amounts, often lent at 26 per cent per annum, or even 36 per cent if they are not repaid within the stated period. They are far from adequate to meet all requirements; mainly used for fertilizer, they are largely paid back at the next harvest, at the (subsidized) rate of 8 per cent per annum.

Therefore, if the peasant finds himself in difficulties after a bad harvest, he has to turn to the money-lender, who is always easily accessible, without any fuss or red tape. The latter's services how-ever are expensive; he usually lends at 5 per cent per month – that is 60 per cent per annum. It seemed to me that South Korea was ignoring the fact that usury was the chief recruiting agent for the people's army – or red army, as they prefer to call it – in the Chinese countryside from 1927 onward. Credit may take the most unexpected forms: thus in the vicinity of Taegu there was an old, fairly well-off peasant whose son had been called up; he therefore had to hire men to cultivate his fields for him, though he had no means of paying them. Since these men were less hard up than himself, they agreed not to take their wages until after the harvest, but added a charge for interest. One ten-hour working day is normally paid at 200 won[4] (plus three meals); paid for three months later at harvest-time, it is worth 250 won.

At harvest-time, for thirteen hours' hard work per day, with five meals, the day's work costs 300 won; paid for a fortnight later, when the paddy is sold, it is worth 320 won. The most usual wage (including all meals) on the outskirts of Seoul, for an agricultural labourer regularly employed for nine months of the year, is 100 won for women and 150 for men. In the winter off-season, they can earn 100 won without food. Permanent agricultural labourers, who are fed, housed and clothed, earn about 2,000 won a month (£2·20) in the wealthier areas. A knitter using a machine commonly earns 90 won a day, without food.

For twenty-five working days of eleven or twelve hours, the lowest wages in the rather out-of-date textile factories of Taegu would be about 3,000 won a month for men and 2,000 for women. Strikes are out of the question, as the defaulting worker would quickly be replaced by an unemployed person willing to accept any conditions. Nevertheless, as in Japan, there are two large additional bonuses every year, each equivalent to one or two months' work. In the most modern factories, such as the chemical fertilizer (urea) factory near Gwanju, specialized workers earn 15,000 won a month, and the manager 60,000 won, plus four months' bonus pay. In western Europe the salary differential in a factory of the same type would be 1 to 10 or 15.[5]

4. The Relative Failure of the Co-operatives

Many young peasants see the cities undergoing modernization when they do their national service, and wish to leave the country-side, and their dull village life which offers no distractions. There is always some relation in the city ready to welcome them. Korean hospitality is really extraordinary; they will even deprive themselves, or let their children go short, in order to provide it. Life is very hard for the small peasant. Take the case of another family, in the same village as the one who sold their ox; they cultivate 70 ares of paddy and 10 ares of hillside – which is slightly below the mean, but with a higher proportion of rice.

The woman who answered our questions seemed very frightened in the presence of authority. The government is still dreaded; it fears a peasant revolt (there is incipient guerrilla activity). In 1967 this family harvested 1,080 kg of rice, 550 kg of which were sold for 29,000 won. The remaining 490 kg went to support the nine members of the family: the couple, a grandmother and six children ranging from three to eighteen years of age. Fortunately, in addition to this they had 112 kg of sweet potato, 160 kg of corn and barley and 32 kg of soya, grown on the hillsides, all of which was consumed by the family. If you work out these rations you will see that there is none too much – the equivalent of 700 kg of corn to feed nine mouths. No animal protein, for there is not a single animal on the farm, not even a dog or cat, which would be too expensive to support.

There remains 3,000 won to pay for fertilizer and 45 kg of rice levied as land tax. The husband therefore goes to work for neighbours, though this is chiefly to pay them back for the days they help him with his harvest. He manages to make ends meet by using child labour, and also by converting his rice-straw into cords, which are then woven into sacks; these bring in 550 won a day (ten sacks take thirteen hours' work), of which 250 are the value of the straw. This enables him to buy some fish now and then for the children who – by dint of frugality, austerity and hard work – do not appear to be undernourished . . .

Though he may not say so, General Park is aware of the important role played by the relative success of the agricultural co-
operatives in North Korea – where fertilizer factories were set up
as early as 1946, well before they began in the Soviet Union,
which was still in the coal and steel era.[6] In agricultural progress it
is well in advance of that of the other socialist countries, including
China and North Vietnam. The Koreans have not entirely followed
the advice of their Chinese[7] 'big brothers': they have had the sense
not to set up people's communes, and their producer co-operatives
seem to meet with general approval. Park is eager to develop
credit and selling co-operatives in the South as well, but so far he
has not had much success.

The agricultural co-operatives are ensured a minimum of
activity by the fact that they have been given the monopoly of
supplying fertilizer, which is still rationed, and much in demand
among the peasants. Some of them have opened small general
stores, where the principal item offered for sale is often alcohol.
In many villages the private stores seem better stocked. With a
few exceptions, such as the market-gardening co-operative near
Pusan, the great southern port, there has been a uniform lack of
success in selling agricultural produce. The co-operatives have
marketed only 6 per cent of the rice sold in the villages south of
Seoul, which have been studied in detail by the professor of rural
economy at Suwon.

Moreover, the price of rice is subject to considerable fluctuation.
After the November harvest there is a fall followed by a rather
pronounced rise during the summer, which is often a difficult
period. In the course of a normal year, such as 1966–7, in the
fairly remote villages, the measure of 18 kg of rice would sell at
700 won in November and 900 won during the following summer. To pay his debts, land tax in kind and loans for fertilizer, the
poor peasant is therefore forced to sell the greater part of his rice
at the lower price. Sometimes he has to buy back rice at the higher
price, whereas the big farmers have been able to keep a large part
of their harvests back. If repayment of the loans and taxes could
be spread out over a longer period, the fall in prices would be less
marked.

A Rice Office would make it possible to stabilize the price, as is done in Japan. But, as with the French Corn Office in 1936, this could only be achieved if there existed a dense and efficient network of local co-operatives capable of ensuring that it was always purchased and resold at the official price. To avoid speculative price-increases, food imports all the year round should be made more reliable, for it sometimes happens that there is a shortage of foreign currency for importing rice to maintain consumption during the summer.

Korean rice is, on average, twice as cheap as Japanese, and the land tax takes about 10 per cent of the large farms' harvests – the small farms being partially, and the very small ones completely exempted. Japan's economic development, especially since the last third of the nineteenth century, has been sustained mainly by a much heavier land tax, combined with a much higher price for rice. The only way out for the farmer, under such conditions, was to make his land give high yields – which then became very profitable; for the co-operative would ensure – as it still does – that his produce was disposed of under the most favourable conditions. Professor Yuu confirms that a simultaneous rise in the guaranteed price of rice and in the land tax would be likely to favour development in Korea.

5. The Development of the Hills by Capitalist Enterprise

There are 30 million inhabitants in South Korea, and 2·2 million hectares under cultivation. This represents a much higher density than in Egypt, though there is no general irrigation, the winter is harsh and the possibilities are considerably less. Japan has a greater density, but yields are higher there and in 1968 it was self-sufficient in rice; its industry is also exceptionally well-developed. Yet the possibilities for expanding production in the hills are greater in Korea; one day the area under cultivation could be more than doubled.

Meanwhile this country, so short of land and capital yet teeming with men, must exercise prudence, both in the control of its population and in the economic or even miserly use of its scarce plainlands. Towns, villages and some factories should, whenever possible, be sited in the hills, even if this involves higher costs. Houses should be built in elevated positions. Enormous areas are taken up by cemeteries, yet the dead ought at least to allow their descendants to live. Though the Chinese communists took time over it – seven years – they managed to make their ancestors see reason in the end, and were able to pack them closer together.

There is a motorway under construction between Seoul and Pusan, in which the government takes great pride – but I am afraid that, economically, it is a mistake. If the railway lines were converted into heavy duty double tracks with additional rolling stock, they could be made to carry both more freight and more passengers. Experts consider the motorway a premature expense, mainly designed for the comfort of the privileged minority, but it is they who govern the country.[8]

Though in 1948 the ownership of rice-fields was limited to three hectares per family, now, twenty years later, there is no longer any talk of limitation. On the contrary, entrepreneurs are engaged in reclaiming and planting the hillsides; these are divided into terraces, sometimes too broad – an expensive operation, which leaves wide strips of barren subsoil at the surface. It would be better to plant on narrow ledges, parallel to the contour-lines. Then the planting of new orchards on the plains could be forbidden, so that the latter might be reserved for paddy. The best situation for fruit-trees would be in the still easily irrigable foothills immediately dominating the plains, in light, deep earth.

The most widespread variety of vine is the Noah, a climbing form which gives high yields. It makes atrocious wine, but the fruit is acceptable. Apples, pears and peaches are rapidly spreading. Korea might consider exporting fruit to Japan, though this would necessitate bringing her standards of quality up to those required by this difficult customer. Near Tokyo, on 6 July 1968, I saw peaches rotting under the trees because it was not considered worthwhile to collect them.

There is great emphasis on the mulberry, for Korea wishes to export a hundred million dollars' worth of silk a year after 1975. It would be a good thing if this could be spun and woven as much as possible on the spot, and sold in the form of silk fabric. Having abandoned in turn Provence and Milan, the silkworm is now deserting some parts of the Japanese countryside. It is in search of *very* cheap labour. Our manufacturers may complain about the low wages paid by the Japanese, but they are even more worried about the wages paid in Korea, Formosa and Hong-Kong. Meanwhile, artificial silk is constantly gaining ground.

Reclamation and planting require capital; it is therefore undertaken by the rich. 'Tending silkworms is a job for women, and we pay them at most 100 won (twelve pence) a day', one of them told me. There is no women's union as yet to flourish the demand of 'equal work, equal pay'. At a meeting in Pusan I was told that the spread of large-scale exploitation would reintroduce a form of serfdom. It could mean that social differences, already so great between town and country, may become pronounced even within a single village. Here again there is a prospect of Latin-Americanization.

6. A Special Kind of 'Democracy'[9]

I was invited to attend a conference of university residents mostly from the United States and Korea, which was held at Seoul in June 1968. I had given the secretariat an outline of my address, which contained two brief allusions to the so-called socialist bloc: as examples for the developing countries I mentioned the Chinese schools, half manual work and half study, which develop a taste and respect for manual labour – and also the students for Hanoi, who take the oath of the 'three any's' when they leave university: 'I swear to serve my country anywhere, in any occupation, and for any wage.'

The CIA, which I was told had been well represented in the congress secretariat, then intervened through a Korean interpreter who begged me, to avoid trouble for him, to omit all mention of these 'enemies'. Later a journalist – as their habit is – tried to get me to say that his country was the most beautiful in the world and that my greatest desire was to return very soon. I replied that next time I would just as soon go to North Korea, so as to be able to make comparisons. The interpreter then told me that, in his own interest, he had better not translate that. In their propaganda leaflets, the Prime Minister of North Korea is never referred to except as an assassin, while the propaganda from the North replies in a similar strain about them. It does not seem likely that the divisions of either Germany or Korea will soon be ended.

Though there is an opposition of a sort in South Korea, it is no less ferocious than the government in its hatred of communism. The Press's freedom is very limited. One can hardly speak of democracy when opponents of the regime are kidnapped in France and Germany. The German government, for one, has lodged a strong protest. On the Fourth of July 1968 the officer commanding the American troops in Korea explained more or less that his country was the only motherland and bastion of democracy. All the same, effrontery and impertinence should not be taken this far, either by Washington or Moscow.

The limits of this 'democracy' were made clearly evident when the supreme court of Korea was courageous enough to reconsider its original verdict against certain accused men. Several of its members were then threatened by an extreme right-wing group which has freedom of action since it is believed to have links with the army. The Press may criticize the government provided nothing is said, directly or indirectly, to present the North as anything other than a pack of assassins. Even to talk about the country's eventual reunification lays one open to suspicion.

South Korea's artisan class has not been destroyed as has India's, and its population has reached the critical mass necessary for development; we should not ignore the courage, industry, ingenuity, intelligence and enterprise of the great majority of its inhabitants.

Underdeveloped countries should not be lumped indiscriminately together, for Africa, Central and South America, and the backward parts of Asia have few features in common. Once the dangers of the population explosion and of privileged minorities have been underlined, there are marked differences between the three continents.

Even within these continents differences are apparent. In Asia hard work is the order of the day, at least from Japan to Vietnam and Thailand. In the Philippines, Indonesia and Burma, rather less emphasis is placed on this virtue. The decline culminates in the Indian subcontinent, which I shall make another attempt to grapple with, in the light of my 1958-9 memories and the valuable assistance of recent studies, especially Gunnar Myrdal's outstanding book *Asian Drama*.[10]

NOTES TO CHAPTER 9

1 It was estimated overall at 4 thousand million dollars in 1958; in 1960 it had gone down to 350 million dollars a year, and in 1968 to less than 80 million.

2 Unfortunately, collective weddings, advocated by the Indian authorities since they allow the expense of the celebrations to be shared by several families, have not caught on here.

3 The vice-chancellor of the Confucian university of Gwanju, in the rather backward province of Chollanamdo, told me that professors had also to teach their students what moral attitudes to adopt. As we were discussing May in Paris, I reminded him that this movement had been directed against precisely such paternalistic tendencies, though in a much less pronounced form.

4 In July 1968, 270 won were worth 1 dollar according to the official rate of exchange; the free exchange rate was about 310 won to the dollar.

5 Though the military junta had cancelled the debts of 5 million people and forbidden the lending of money to farmers and fishermen, it had not managed to set up the necessary organization for agricultural loans.

6 'Fertilizer is rice, and rice is socialism,' said Kim Il Sung, who thus gave priority to agriculture and the means for modernizing it well before any other socialist countries. A pity he is too ready to fall in with the personality cult.

7 In 1966 a son of Chiang Kai Shek was visiting his South Korean 'friends'. To please him the Koreans began to make violent criticisms of the 'red' Chinese. After a few sentences he stopped them, purple with rage, saying 'You little Koreans, how can you dare speak ill of the Chinese!' The elect of the Middle Empire will not tolerate criticism, even of their heretics.

8 Professor Yuu told me that, since it is under construction, it should be

turned to good account. If a high toll were charged for private cars, and a lower one for lorries, competition would force the railways to improve. This motorway will provide access to the areas it traverses, and encourage the development of many industries. All the same, if it had not been started, I should have advised against it.

9   This phrase could also be applied to the French 'democracy'.

10   Pantheon Books, New York, 1968 Alan Lane, London, 1968.

CHAPTER TEN

Verbal Socialism and Contempt for Work in India

1. The Long Tradition – Hierarchic, Static, Resigned

Despite its laws, and even in the highest official circles, India is still permeated by the caste system, a system which determines on a hereditary basis the status, the dignity and (for a long time) each individual's role in society. The most highly prized virtue is resignation in the face of the lowliest conditions and to refuse to hope for social advancement, which is the only means of one day bettering oneself. This attitude is a powerful brake to effort and enthusiasm for manual work; the latter is more despised here than anywhere else by many of the castes. As manual work is very badly paid, especially in the country, many fairly well-off people can afford the only luxury that is cheap: leisure. The man who is most respected is the one who does absolutely nothing – not even organize the work of others, because even that detracts from one's dignity!

Though the low castes have the right to eat beef and work cowhide, their untouchable status (Gandhi used to call them *chamars* or *harijans* to remind people that they, too, were 'children of God') makes it more difficult for them to possess land, which is a symbol of dignity rather than of economic independence. Many laws have been passed in their favour since Independence, but, especially in the South, if a foreign expert offers them his hand he is still called to order with the reminder that 'it is not the custom'. In the *panchayats*, or municipal councils, only the humblest and most submissive *harijans* are tolerated, and they do not speak unless the wealthy, high-caste members ask them their opinion.

The fact that cows cannot be slaughtered is often considered in Europe to be the chief obstacle to India's development, but I do not believe it is the most important one. If the cows were well fed, they would provide proper amounts of milk, work and dung (which is more often dried for fuel than used as manure); in that case the fact that their meat was not eaten at the end of their career would represent only a slight waste. What is more serious is that they are too numerous and therefore very badly fed, underproductive, sometimes even destructive to crops, and inevitably, they pose a formidable threat to man.

The Hindu princes often ruled other territories besides their native state, and these they treated as conquered lands, imposing heavy tributes on them – often as much as a third of the harvest – without always giving sufficient consideration to the consequences to the community. While a great deal of work and expenditure should have been devoted to irrigation, roads, and defence against flooding and erosion, the tributes were mainly used for building ramparts, fortresses, palaces and tombs. They also provided much work for craftsmen in luxury goods, splendid jewels, materials and so on. Golconda and the Maharajahs represented fabulous wealth in European literature, which failed to appreciate that it was primarily based on peasant poverty and appalling periodic famines. The community was hardly expected to undertake great public works, as was the case in China in this period.

When the Europeans arrived, these privileged minorities demonstrated their almost total lack of national sense by frequently allying themselves with the conquerors, so as to benefit afterwards from the favours of the new dispensation. In 1793, Cornwallis gave the Zamindars of Bengal full ownership of all the lands upon which until then, they had merely levied land tax. In this way a class of very favoured collaborators was created. The naïve British hoped that, like themselves, they would invest incomes derived from the soil in improving their land. But, they did practically nothing.

2. Corrupt Landowners and Phoney Agrarian Reform

During the nineteenth century there arose a new class of land-owners who benefited both from Eastern feudal privileges and the Western right of full ownership. As noblemen, they had their obedient train of dependents and claimed work and gifts from their sharecroppers and farmers over and above the normal rent. By British law, however, they were freed from their traditional obligations, such as bringing help in times of need, or not dismissing a recognized tenant who had a hereditary and indefeasible right to farm his piece of land. From the Europeans, the land-owners received the right to exploit their tenants, sell them to the highest bidder, or expel them whenever they liked. As the population had long been on the increase, there were hordes of aspiring tenants ready to pay over higher rents. The third of the harvest handed over to the eighteenth-century landowners often became a half, or even more in the fertile paddy-fields where two harvests could be obtained.

Western landowners, who paid land tax and, later, income tax, bore the heavy cost of constructing and maintaining farm build-ings, and often made considerable improvements in their land. The landowners of colonial India, discharged from their tradi-tional public duties, paid less and less tax, and would rent bare fields, devoid of buildings. If they provided capital for farming, it was at an extortionate rate. The only important improvements on the land were carried out by public bodies in the case of major works, or through the corvées of tenants who worked, without pay, to improve a piece of land that did not belong to them, but for which they would afterwards be charged a higher rent.[1]

Before Independence, the Congress Party had greatly raised the hopes of the peasants by promising them a genuine agrarian reform. In point of fact, as Myrdal has shown, the measures actually taken were very weak and chiefly directed towards ending the semi-feudal tenure of the Zamindar 'middle-men'. The latter received substantial compensation, which placed a heavy burden on the state. Since there was no obligation to reinvest the money productively, many continued to spend it on luxuries. Even the Zamindars were allowed to keep the lands which they 'personally cultivated' – which gave plenty of scope for abuses. For land to come in this category, the Zamindar did not have to work it with his own hands or supervise the work, or even reside in the village all the year round. The lands they have retained are usually still farmed by sharecroppers, sometimes passed off as agricultural workers.

While these laws were in preparation, a number of land-holding farmers were expelled from their land so as to increase the extent of the above-mentioned personal estates; the expropriated land was allotted in the first place to 'tenant-farmers'. In India this term implies a caste classification, and a position in the social hierarchy of a village, rather than an economic function. Many of the recipients were therefore the former privileged tenants, who used to sub-let their land to sharecroppers; this they continued to do, so that in the great majority of cases those who actually worked the land merely changed their status from sub-tenant to tenant, and their condition remained very precarious. With rare exceptions, the land has not been 'handed back to those who farm it'. As a consequence of these 'reforms', many landholding farmers were relegated to the status of yearly sharecroppers, who are much too insecure to think of investing.

Finally, it often happened that power in the countryside passed from the big absentee landowners to the middling landowners, merchants and money-lenders in the villages. It is often said in Europe that the Gramdan and Bhovdan movements, started by Vinoba Bhave, a spirited pilgrim disciple of Gandhi's, have achieved an important voluntary agrarian reform. Here, however, the results are even more meagre, since much of the land given in this way to be redistributed is practically worthless, or else the title to it was disputed, or it was about to be affected by the agrarian reform, and so on – so that in 1961 (since when the movement has slackened off considerably, and almost come to a standstill), out of the two million hectares received from 500,000 donors, only 360,000 hectares, amounting to 0·25 per cent of India's arable land, could be redistributed.

3. The Lack of Protection for Farmers and Sharecroppers; Usury and Credit Co-operatives

If farmers could be adequately protected, it would have big repercussions on the agricultural production of India; but farmers and sharecroppers are discouraged from improving their farming methods by the lack of security of tenure, which has never been less. Meanwhile, the many laws that have been passed to limit rents and guarantee security, have often proved less effective than the old customs. There are all sorts of ways of evading the law limiting rents, when the tenant is practically compelled to borrow from his landlord at usurious rates, to sell him his harvest at less than the market price, or give him presents.

Sharecroppers usually pay distinctly higher rents than the farmers, and are often worse off than many employees. Since the limitation of rents does not in general apply to sharecropping, this form of tenure is a fundamental obstacle to any agricultural progress. Gilbert Etienne,[2] relying on dubious official figures, says sharecropping is not widespread. Myrdal, however, emphasizes its importance and adds that, with such a scarcity of land, it seems naïve to fix rents by law at one-sixth of the harvest. It was often said that the state of Bombay had the best legislation on rural rents in the whole of southern Asia – until the day when an inquiry by Dandekar and Khudanpur showed that out of the 1,332 cases investigated, only sixteen paid no more than the legal rent of one-sixth, while in 85 per cent of cases the actual rent was half, or more than half, the gross product.

In the course of my 1958–9 mission, I observed that the sharecroppers near Madras had to shoulder all farming expenses including the purchase of the entire 200 kg of ammonium sulphate per hectare which agriculturalists recommend for paddy-fields. Yet they would only receive half the harvest – only half the increase due to their own fertilizer. It was not worth their while to continue using it, except when an intelligent landlord (the minority) agreed to pay half. Sharecropping really puts a premium on bad farming methods, because the sharecroppers only enjoy half the fruit of their labour and expense; they are therefore inclined to provide as little as they can of both.

The other plague on Indian agriculture is the practice of usury. I myself noticed interest-rates of 15 per cent.[3] – *per week!* – near Hyderabad in December 1958. However, credit co-operatives are becoming more and more widespread. A survey conducted during 1961–2 estimated that they provided 26 per cent of loans to agricultural centres, and this proportion must gradually have increased since then. Myrdal, however, assures us that practically none of these loans have gone to landless workers or sharecroppers, the classes who are unfairly treated. The loans generally remain mortgaged.

The very poor, who sell very little, chiefly require loans for day-to-day expenditure, in case of illness, family celebrations, or even to buy food to bridge the gap. They therefore turn to the money-lender, who is often the trader and landlord as well. 'Credit co-operatives have become mainly the preserves of the upper strata of the village, which include the money-lenders, who often acquire their funds from them', adds Myrdal. An institution founded to combat usury has ended up in the service of the money-lenders. By extending credit to their impecunious clients, they get their really bad debts repaid!

4. *The Failure of Community Development*

It was whispered to me at the United Nations offices in New York, in November 1958, that Community Development was 'the most effective secret weapon against communism, since it would ensure the development of the whole free world'. When a few bands of apostles came to the villages, after Independence, they managed, by their persistent, patient, serene and dedicated efforts, to create several small enclaves of social and agricultural progress. Agricultural Departments' classic propaganda methods, keyed to the slogan 'Produce More Food', had given only mediocre results. It was thought that this was mainly due to the low level of health and education among the mass of Indian peasants.

It was therefore decided in 1952 that within a decade, the whole country should be progressively covered with developmental 'units', each comprising in principle about 70,000 inhabitants. These units were to promote overall progress in the villages, firstly in the field of health and hygiene: public and private latrines, flues in the houses, dispensaries, vaccination, etc. Next they would begin to teach adults to read and write, urge the formation of co-operatives, and try to educate the members of the newly-formed *panchayats*. Last of all came advice to farmers, loans for fertilizer, seed and insecticide, and the popularization of modern agricultural techniques. Yet a great deal of the money was absorbed by administrative buildings, while spectacular and sometimes even luxurious and demagogic, social activities soon took precedence over the promotion of economic progress.

Outstanding progress in agriculture was announced at the end of the first Five-Year Plan in 1956, but those in the know realize that agricultural statistics were systematically underestimated before 1951. This tendency soon ceased when the Ministry of Agriculture became responsible for executing the Plan.[4] Nevertheless, the Indian government, being aware of the true situation and concerned about it, asked the United Nations to send them an international commission of experts; I was in the party, together with the British sociologist Margaret Read and the Canadian, Coldwell. At the Nilokheri training centre, the community development officials tried to make us believe that all was well; but if that were so, what was the point of our mission?

The villages we visited had been scoured clean, though to do this the peasants had sometimes even had to delay their harvests. There was steel equipment for games in the children's parks, though the blades of the ploughs had not always been renewed, for want of metal. The United Kingdom proclaimed itself a welfare state in 1952, when it had 115 kg of iron or steel per inhabitant. India made a similar claim, with only 3 kg per inhabitant – which did not enable it to carry out the same programme. The *Gram Sevak*, or 'village servant', who had a tenth of the unit, or more than 1,500 families in his charge, was supposed to deal with everything by the light of the single plan evolved for the entire country

– which extends from the sub-equatorial plains of Kerala to the alpine climate of the mountains; so the plan was necessarily ill-adapted to most conditions. The apostles of the heroic age were not numerous, and Indian officials had to be called in to spread the movement.

Following our mission, and that of the American agriculturalists from the Ford Foundation during the same period, the Indian government confirmed the policy initiated in 1957 of giving priority to agriculture, which was to make up 75 per cent of the *Gram Sevaks'* activity. The Ford report advised 'pulling out all the stops' in the better watered, irrigated, or more fertile areas, where there was greater potential, and also whenever progressive farming methods were used – these being generally the more important areas and the only ones with any surplus to invest. Economically, this is very sensible; but if the poor areas and subsistence cultivations are more or less abandoned in this way,[5] the social, or even economic and political consequences could one day be very grim. Besides, even when this course was followed, agricultural yields remained very low. Two serious droughts made inroads into the 1966 and 1967 harvests, and would have led to terrible famines but for massive consignments of North American corn: 10·3 and 8·7 million tons – 19 million tons in two years. India has never received as much as this.

Though 1968 brought a favourable monsoon, part of the spring grain harvest could not be properly garnered because not enough storage space had been arranged; the possibility of there being such a good harvest had scarcely been envisaged. Even under the most favourable conditions, as in 1965, a good harvest had not permitted any substantial reserves to be built up for the following years (which there was reason to fear would be lean). In their 1959 report the experts proposed 110 million tons of grain for consumption as a reasonable objective for the end of the third plan in 1966. But two years later, after an exceptionally favourable monsoon, the 1968 harvest yielded 95 million tons[6] for a population of 530 million – 180 kg per head; from which wastage, seed, fodder, the requirements of industry and the reserve for the following years have to be deducted. The majority must still go short. Self-sufficiency is promised within two or three years, but they said the same things at the end of 1958. It is true that more rapid progress is made possible by the Mexican Sonora varieties of corn and especially the Filipino IR8 rices, which are much more productive. However, these selected varieties make greater demands on fertilizer,[7] water, care in cultivation and technical know-how. Meanwhile the rate of population growth is also increasing.

In the *New Statesman* of 19 December 1959, I had already drawn attention to the very clear failure of agriculture in India, in order to emphasize the necessity of rethinking its whole agricultural policy. As a consequence of this article, which stated some of the conclusions in our report to the United Nations,[8] the Indian lobby in the FAO[9] managed to get my work for the latter organization suspended until the summer of 1962. I would have been very happy if such a step could have been useful to India's development! But on the contrary, their only wish was to conceal the defects of their policies – an attitude akin to Stalinism, which could lead to dangerous delay in making the needed corrections.

5. Prestige versus Development; Lack of Solidarity among the Exploited

In the last analysis it was the Europeans who encouraged the spread of usury, by creating individual and transferable titles to property; for this gave money-lenders the certainty of being able to get back their loans by taking possession of the debtor's land, and induced them to offer large sums at exorbitant rates of interest. The collection of the property tax in money, wages for public works and in the plantations, and the larger role played by commercial crops are factors that have accelerated the transition to an exchange economy and upset the whole structure of traditional agriculture, without putting anything better in its stead.

The population explosion has caused the average size of the cultivations to shrink appallingly, so that it has dwindled from about 16 hectares in 1770 to less than 3 hectares in 1915; today it is about 2 hectares in the district of Poona near Bombay. The smaller cultivations make it difficult to support the expense of the traditional ceremonies, which has remained very high. A large section of the Indian peasantry has therefore been greatly impoverished, and the proportion of the rural population without land has greatly increased. Land is constantly falling into the hands of non-farmers, such as traders, officials and non-farming landowners.

Thus the hierarchy in a small Indian village turns out to be much more complex than the stereotyped schemes of the Chinese communists.[10] The proprietors include feudal landowners who have retained positions of power, along with portions of their estates. Then there are the landlords who earn their living by some other calling. These are the two richest groups, who do not usually live in the village; they acquire real estate as an insurance, and because incomes from this source are among the less heavily taxed. The non-farming proprietors who live in the village, on the other hand, tend to be rather poor. Next there are the farming peasant proprietors, who let a part of their land only if they happen to be well off. Their interests are quite distinct from those of the poorer peasants. Yet all these categories of landowners are entitled to a certain consideration, simply because of the fact that they own land.

The other groups include, firstly, those privileged farmers who still have the right of permanent and hereditary occupation, and whose rents are therefore genuinely limited. The interests of the various categories of farmers, subtenants, and more or less precarious sharecroppers are already quite distinct. Next come the agricultural labourers, permanent hands and seasonal day-labourers, who make up at least a third of the population – though some of them may own small pieces of land and/or farm others as sharecroppers. Many individuals fall into two or more of these classes, which does not help to simplify the picture.

Within this complexity, it is possible to schematize a social order in which the landowner who does nothing is placed at the top of the scale – with, slightly below him, his manager, who merely directs the work. Next comes the peasant who works with his hands, but still on his own account; which puts him above the employee, who has to obey others in the course of his daily activity. A peasant can only become more respected by managing to live on the rents from his property, thus becoming a member of the class of non-producers, who merely make others work. Sharecroppers are more respected than employees, even when they earn less, as often happens. Some of the very poor non-workers are on the brink of destitution, but they can only better their condition by becoming labourers, which would mean coming down in the world. Social and economic status may therefore diverge considerably. This hankering for prestige is a much more serious obstacle to the development of Indian agriculture than the sacred cows.

In these circumstances, it hardly seems possible in the near future to stir up a large majority of exploited village peasants against a minority of exploiting landlords and money-lenders. Strong group loyalties would cause the poor members of a caste to defend the interests of their wealthier colleagues. There are too many landowners among the officials for them to promote any real agrarian reform – to which landowning politicians would be even more vigorously opposed. Any increase in effort is checked by the contempt in which physical work is held.

Now, even without a technical revolution, more care in farming could rapidly step up production, provided the workers on the land had a real interest in it. There can therefore be no prospect of a social revolution being successful in the immediate future, until there has been a fundamental change of attitude. Non-economic factors, states Myrdal, tend to unite all the members of the village hierarchy against the aspiration of the landless workers to own a little land.

6. Small Holdings with Employees; Capitalist Producer Co-operatives

Like Dube in his *Indian Village*, I noticed that many Indian land-lords adopt a Malthusian attitude: to maintain ground rents at a high level, they prefer not to reclaim or irrigate much new land. On the outskirts of villages, one often sees large fields suitable for ploughing left undeveloped; these are the property of absentee landlords who fear that to bring more land under the plough would increase the work and thereby contribute to the raising of wages – which are at present absurdly low. Also, higher production would lead to a fall in prices. In this connection, the Indian government would seem to have just as much interest in stabilizing prices, as neighbouring Pakistan. Speculators, however, prefer wide fluctuations. High prices during the times of shortage, especially in 1965–7, reduced fluctuations and made it worthwhile to produce more. A well-marked slump could soon put an end to these advances.

The landlords, who receive the lion's share, live too comfortably, even in times of general shortage, to have much incentive to invest – though they are the only people in a position to do so. They have long preferred to spend their money on luxuries, which bring prestige. Nevertheless, the black market prices of 1966–7 revived interest in the direct cultivation of the land; during this period 24,000 cased wells were sunk in Uttar Pradesh within a single year, compared with the 21,000 sunk during the previous five years.

The farmers or sharecroppers who make improvements on their land do not benefit by them. After paying their exorbitant rents, they often produce hardly enough to live on; however the areas they cultivate are very small. Myrdal's team calculated that on average three times as much money was spent by farming landowners on improving their land, as was spent on the improvement of rented lands. Moreover, most of the latter is paid for by the tenants, who pay 2·5 times as much as their landlords. This is a strong economic argument in favour of agrarian reform.

India's land could be made to give much higher yields by means of irrigation, anti-erosion banks, plantations of fruit-trees, intensive feeding of animals – or, more simply, by better preparation of the ground and by clearing it earlier and more thoroughly. The bad farming which still prevails, exacerbates both seasonal unemployment and the periodic shortages, which in their turn prevent the necessary efforts being made. And the population explosion is making this vicious circle even harder to break.

Even where farms are too small to occupy and support one

family properly, the latter prefer to stint themselves in order to hire employees. On the tiny small holdings of western Bengal, one-third of the total work is done by these labourers. The amount of work done per year per member of a cultivator's family has been estimated at a half that done by each member of a Thai plains family. The proportion of actual workers and the amount of work performed by each one are both much greater in Thailand. With such an outlook, it is hard to see how India can emerge from poverty without far-reaching structural reforms.

After Gandhi, Nehru considered that the only hope for Indian agriculture lay in co-operatives. Producer co-operatives could only reasonably be envisaged after some genuine agrarian reform had occurred, and an effective network of service and credit co-operatives set up. However, as producer co-operatives have long been favoured under Indian law, which grants them large subsidies and loans, landowners passed off as co-operatives enterprises resembling joint-stock companies, which paid exorbitant rents. Thanks to their extremely low wages, these co-operatives were occasionally able to pay out dividends to their shareholders. Recently, some of them were still paying wages of 1 rupee[11] during the season, and half a rupee in the off-season, without food, for a day's work extending from dawn to dusk, with only two hours' break about midday!

The efforts that have been made to mobilize the rural unemployed in the interests of agricultural investment have always failed. Besides, how is one to persuade poor sharecroppers and labourers to do unpaid work which will only benefit the rich landlords? The members of the Chinese collectives are willing to do it, because they benefit directly. Wages must therefore be paid, and the works financed through taxation – but the wealthy custodians of power refuse to pay higher taxes. The cry in India is that a democracy, unlike communism, cannot resort to coercion. They forget, however, that the communists also initially carried out a radical equalization of society, an intensive programme of education and furious propaganda – and that they have at their disposal competent and dedicated trained men to organize their labour. One has only to compare the work of the Chinese or North Vietnamese *can-bo* with that of the Indian *Gram Sevak* to see which is the more dedicated.

7. *The Reinforcement of Social Inequalities by False Socialism*

All the measures taken since Independence, says Myrdal, have ended by strengthening the wealthy strata in the village, and weakening the position of the sharecroppers and landless labourers. City-dwellers who own land support the privileged villagers in their defence of the *status quo*, and furiously oppose any far-reaching reform. The growth of inequality is also partly due to normal economic evolution, since the peasant landowners and privileged farmers are in a better position than the poor to avail themselves of modern techniques. Myrdal concludes that 'As long as working and earning an income jeopardize status, while land-holding and partial or complete abstention from productive work raise it, aggregate output is held well below its potential ... The promotion of social and economic equality[12] is a precondition for attaining substantial long-term increase in production.'

In India socialism was, and still is, the official doctrine of the government and most of the political parties; many businessmen, even, claim to favour a socialist economy. They vie with one another in urging 'the socialist model of society', but are not in a hurry to define it. Some of them simply equate it with social justice, or planning, or understand it as mere ideology of modernization. There is no talk of collectivizing agriculture, the traditional crafts, or light industry. The emphasis is more on the development of the public sector, especially in heavy industry; this was often necessitated, however, by the failure of the private sector, rather than by any ideological motivation. After the wars against China and Pakistan, and the bad harvests of 1966–7, India anxiously tried to raise capital everywhere, for both the public and private sectors. In 1965 industry employed 10 per cent of the population, compared with 11 per cent in 1910: not much of an achievement!

In the villages at any rate, although the exponents of this pseudo-socialism talk a great deal about equality, they have tended rather to move in the opposite direction, which has disheartened the people. Since work is despised, efficiency at work has not been properly recognized or rewarded. Capitalist investment is checked by the constant talk of agrarian reform, but if these reforms are never carried out, the poor become discouraged in their efforts – one loses either way. In the present social climate, which cannot be changed rapidly, any radical redistribution of land (short of a bloody revolution) would meet with insuperable political opposition and would come up against practical difficulties of application and organization; production might well be compromised even more. Myrdal concludes that Communism does not seem capable, even in theory, of providing a viable treatment for the agricultural maladies of southern Asia. This appears to be true of the *present* situation, though one day it may evolve. The eventual explosion could well be all the more dreadful and destructive, as a result of having been too long delayed. Heads will fall – and not all of them to be regretted, when one bears in mind the egotism, avarice, pride and vanity of the great majority of the possessors. This Indian bourgeoisie must now bear most of the responsibility for their country's poverty, for there can no longer be any justification, twenty-two years after Independence, for continuing to put all the blame on colonialism.

8. Reducing the Birth-rate; Giving Dignity to the Oppressed

In these conditions, Myrdal attempts to find some provisional solution to bring about 'an intensification of agriculture through the fuller utilization of a rapidly increasing labour force. At the present time, as in the past, the traditional status hierarchy is an important factor blocking a fuller utilization of labour.' His advice, finally, is that 'it may be preferable to make a deliberate policy choice in favour of capitalist farming by allowing and encouraging the progressive cultivator to reap the full rewards of his enterprise and labour, while approaching the fundamental issues of equality and institutional reforms from a different angle and by different policy means'. In the first place it would be necessary to try to eliminate passive and parasitical forms of ownership, by taxing non-farming landowners heavily and forbidding the sale of land to non-farming or non-resident city-dwellers. The practical application of such laws would presuppose some transfer of power, and that the poor should have a greater say in politics; or else a certain degree of enlightenment among the rich; a highly improbable hypothesis, at least in the immediate future.

As a start in combating the traditional contempt for paid work, I would suggest that most officials and politicians, those physically capable of it, should be obliged to do manual work for, say, half a day each month. Myrdal also proposes that every landless labourer should be allotted a small piece of land; this would give him dignity, a new concept of life, and an independent source of income. A limited redistribution of this kind could begin by sharing out the more valuable uncultivated fields near the villages; expropriated without compensation (following Gandhi), these would bring a minimum of social security, and above all, by eliminating the chief ground for contempt in this way, the traditional basis of status would be attacked at its very root. The employee would then have a prospect of both social and economic advancement before him. J. de Farcy also suggested that a Hindu episcopate should be established in order to adapt the prescriptions of the Sacred Books to the modern age.

If India's ruling classes were to continue to reject any form of genuine social evolution, however moderate, the gap between China and India – even more marked in the field of education than of development, despite China's lack of foreign aid – could well increase. In my book *Terres Vivantes* (1961),[13] I predicted that China would develop better, even though it was in the middle of a serious food-shortage at that time, whereas India had just had a series of very good monsoons but this idea was sceptically received. Since then, India's inferiority[14] has become increasingly apparent, in spite of foreign aid – which has been very great in absolute value, though very modest per head. Of course, one cannot tell how China's proletarian cultural revolution will end, for it demands a great deal of men.

However, unless India can manage to halt her birthrate and speed up her progress in agriculture and industry, she is in for a rude awakening. This country claims to align itself with the so-called free world – but what do our liberties mean to an untouchable family,[15] to the semi-employed and sometimes starving, or to the little beggars on the streets of Calcutta?[16] Indian presocialism should begin with respect for manual labour and the untouchables, the popularization of birth-control, and contempt for parasitic idlers and corrupt money-lending landlords. Even if one accepts this reading of the situation, the remedy does not seem to be to hand. The chances of a revolution are at present diminished by the passivity and resignation of the masses,[17] even though – or especially because – they are so abjectly poor. But then, what would it lead to, in such a context?

NOTES TO CHAPTER 10

1 Yet the British laws did sometimes manage to guarantee security of tenure and a fixed rent. The holders of these privileges frequently became parasites themselves, sub-letting their leases on less advantageous terms.

2 *Les chances de l'Inde*, Editions du Seuil, Paris, 1969. Etienne considers that sharecropping was not an obstacle to development in Japan, but it was, at any rate, in France, and all round the Mediterranean.

3 Even 100 per cent interest per week, for interest in arrears. *Cf.* R. Dumont, *Lands Alive*, Merlin Press, London, 1965.

4 Etienne (*Population*, 1967, No. 2) suggests that in 1952 they were underestimated by 25 per cent, and by 17 per cent in 1958. We were told by those responsible for agricultural statistics at the Ministry of Agriculture in New Delhi, in December 1958, that before 1951 the underestimations had been even greater. It is therefore impossible to be precise about the nutritional improvement due to the first two Plans.

5 Analogous to the landless rural masses in Egypt.

6 8 per cent less in 1968?

7 1,100,000 tons of nitrate fertilizer in 1967–8, which represents considerable progress. Six million tons would be needed as a start, on 120 million hectares.

8 *Community development evaluation mission in India*, New Delhi, 1959.

9 The Food and Agriculture Organization of the United Nations.

10 *Cf.* René Dumont, *Révolution dans les campagnes chinoises*, Editions du Seuil, Paris, 1957.

11 Four pence.

12 'The reduction of social and economic inequalities . . .' is what I would have written.

13 *Lands Alive*, Merlin Press, London, 1965.

14 Government policies are becoming increasingly liberal: 'The Indian government is turning towards liberal formulas, in which the socializing Utopianism of the early years of independence is giving way before the concrete necessity of making the economy pay its way. The public sector suffers from chronic non-profitability, due to its unused productive capacity, bad management, and lack of raw materials and electrical energy. The main burden of investment will be assumed by the private sector.' *Le Monde*, 26 December 1968.

15 'At Kivalur, 300 km from Madras in the district of Tanjore, forty-three people, mostly women and children, were burned alive last Thursday in the huts where they had sought refuge during a pitched battle between 'Marxist' peasants and the employees of a big landowner. . . . The attackers surrounded the huts within which the families, all of whom belonged to the old untouchable caste, had taken refuge, and set fire to them.' *Le Monde*, 28 December 1968. It would be interesting to know what sanctions were applied to this murderer, the 'big landowner'.

16 See Louis Malle's film *Calcutta*.

17 I am generalizing too much here. In India there do exist hardworking peasants, honest and able officials and ardent fighters. But as for the majority of the bourgeoisie. . . . See also J. L. Chambard's *Atlas d'un village indien*, Mouton 1969; also his *Les castes dans l'Inde moderne, leur place dans la vie économique et sociale, Revue economique et sociale*, Lausanne, August 1967.

CHAPTER ELEVEN

The Sabotage of the Mexican Revolution by the Institutional Revolutionary Party

1. A Discontinuous Series of Agrarian Reforms

The paternalism, the abuses and even cruelty of the big land-owners (descendants of those who slaughtered the Indians),[1] who possessed most of the land, amply justified the Mexican revolution of 1911–21. Unfortunately it caused the death of a million people, the vast majority of whom were poor, as well as considerable destruction – much of it avoidable – and a fall in agricultural production. Twenty years later, in 1930, production had still not returned to its 1910 level. By the constitution of 1917, ultimate ownership of the land was handed over to the state, to redistribute it in the nation's interest, and in the interests of a fairer division of the national income. Any group of more than twenty landless Mexicans, living in the same neighbourhood could claim a share of the big estates within 7 km of their village.[2]

The first redistributions, which were more concerned with social justice than production, gave too little land to every villager, regardless of whether or not he was a farmer. The unfortunate result was a lean subsistence cultivation, often inferior to that of the big estate. These distributions were therefore soon discontinued. Dignity had nevertheless been restored to the peons, and progress was being made with the general economy, since capital diverted from the land went into industry, commerce and urban development, while the men freed from semi-serfdom on the big estates could also move to the towns. The victorious factions fought among themselves, massacring each other, until 1926, when they amalgamated in the National Revolutionary Party, now known as the Institutional Revolutionary Party (PRI); this change of name sufficiently indicates its different orientation. The PRI has governed ever since with crushing majorities, which were the envy of de Gaulle when he visited Mexico.

Factions still exist within the party which, though not the only one, is dominant. The left wing, which has less support and is less well organized, has only been in power once in over forty years, between 1935 and 1940. This was under Lazaro Cardenas, who started the redistributions of land once more, on a wider scale, while trying to improve it and increase its yields. He also exerted himself to promote literacy among the peasants and grant them loans. Groups to whom land was distributed, called *ejidos*, were given ownership of the land, and encouraged to farm it collectively. Most of these collective *ejidos* failed, mainly for want of capable, honest and dedicated managers, but also because of the lack of discipline in work among the members. Some of them did well, chiefly with corn in the well-irrigated north-west where land is plentiful, though sometimes they verge on being capitalist companies, which in some cases employ hired labour. It is difficult to graft socialist institutions on to the fabric of a general capitalist economy.

The vast majority of the *ejidos* were divided up into small family lots, on a permanent and hereditary basis, so that they could not be let, sold or mortgaged. Above the group stand the *ejidos* superintendents, who are not always honest. A few rich peasants possess tractors, which they hire out to their neighbours. The allotted parcels of land are generally too small to provide proper occupation and livelihood for the rapidly multiplying families. If a man fails to cultivate his land during two successive years, even if he has carried out improvements, he loses all his rights over it without receiving any compensation. This system discourages investment, prevents full rural employment, and chains the *ejido* worker to his village so that he cannot take advantage of better opportunities for work, which are generally some distance away.

I

2. Rapid Progress in the Troubled Capitalist Sector; a Bad Reform is Better than None

The right-wing of the PRI came to power in 1940, and has remained there ever since; though lately (under presidents Matéos and Ordaz, who have accelerated the distribution of land to the *ejidos*) it has come to be spoken of as the 'centre'. It is a centre which talks left, faces right, and shoots students. One should not allow oneself to be misled by the millions of hectares recently distributed, for most of it consists of arid, stony or steeply sloping land (very predominant in Mexico), which is not suitable for cultivation. The Second World War brought a sharp increase in the amount of work available in the United States; two million *braceros* were much better paid there than at home, even if they earned a good deal less than native Americans. With two million fewer labourers, agricultural production in Mexico has shot ahead – showing that the real trouble had been the excess of manpower.

The demand by the United States for agricultural produce – coffee, sugar, cotton, meat, shrimps, horticultural goods, etc., increased after the war, as did American tourism. There was also an increase in the local population, whose nutritional level rose as well, though much more slowly. The capitalist sector was now certain of being able to keep the best land, which it had selected at the time of the expropriations. Behind men of straw, a certain amount of large estate farming started again, though fortunately on a much smaller scale than hitherto. The landowners wished to live at least as well as before on areas of land greatly diminished by the family allotments; as they had only hundreds of hectares now, instead of tens of thousands, they had to intensify production. The economic situation made it profitable for them to do this, since the terms of trade were at that time favourable to agriculture, and the country was becoming industrialized.

With 8 per cent cumulative progress per year in agriculture between 1946 and 1955, Mexico would seem to have beaten every world record for agricultural growth. It is likely that, as in the case of India's first two plans, the official figures are optimistic, because of earlier harvests having been underestimated. This does not alter the fact that the real growth has been quite remarkable. The new blight resistent varieties of corn, hybrid maize, orchards, up-to-date market gardens and vineyards, and fine pedigree Friesian herds in intensively cultivated lucerne fields near the capital, make an impressive picture on the whole. One essential factor in this progress has been the development of irrigation, which now covers 4 million hectares. About 1949–51, as much as 100,000 hectares a year were being opened up by means of new irrigation.

The other notable factor has been the landlords' anxiety over the agrarian reforms. Therefore, even if progress on the shared-out lands has not been altogether satisfactory, the experiment has shown that in Latin America, even such dubious agrarian reforms as Mexico's are very much better than no reform at all. No other Latin American country has achieved such an expansion of its agriculture. Yet Brazil's potential is far greater than that of Mexico.

3. A General Deceleration; Least Progress in the Ejidos

Between 1956 and 1965 agricultural growth went down by half[3] to 4 per cent, though it was still quite considerable. During this time population growth became more pronounced. The greatest progress continued to be made in the private sector, which still possessed half the arable land – the best half, including 70 per cent of the irrigated land. It is therefore not surprising that it accounts for two-thirds of total production. In any event, agriculture, though employing half the active population, provides no more than one-fifth of the national revenue; whereas industry, in which 15 per cent of the active population are engaged, provides nearly a half.

The *ejidos* generally progress more slowly than the capitalist farms because most of their cultivations are much too small; other contributing factors to this slow progress are the peasants' lack of knowledge and, in some cases, lack of effort[4] – and above all their lack of loans. The *Banco de ejidal*, founded to provide credit for *ejidos* members, often only gets back three-quarters of its loans. The size of the loans is based on the costs of cultivation and on the area cultivated. But in the first place, the very poor farmers must live, which takes up almost all their gross receipts, so that they are hardly in a position to repay their borrowings. Thus the capitalist farms are slowly reabsorbing a section of the *ejidos*, whose lands and labour services they rent. Since this is illegal, they make very little lasting investment. Mexican agriculture needs to be freed of its 30 per cent or more surplus manpower, which is holding up progress. In this connection, it is interesting to observe that in 1910 Mexican industry, undeveloped and badly equipped as it was, already employed 16 per cent of the active population – which is a higher proportion than in 1968.

Despite its recent modernization, achieved through heavy investment, industry is incapable of taking up all the available manpower. This makes it impossible to relieve the rural congestion rapidly, as was done in the United States; especially as the constantly rising rate of annual population growth is approaching 3·8 per cent. On the other hand, in 1966 and 1967, growth in agriculture fell to 2·7 per cent a year. The possibility of the food situation becoming more serious in the near future cannot therefore be dismissed.

Mexican development is still of the colonial type, in which the two sectors, modern and traditional, are perpetuated. Industrial growth is restrained by the inadequate purchasing power of the rural population. Since 1960, Mexican factories as a whole have only been working at half their capacity. *Laissez-faire* development has not given enough consideration to priorities, or to the possible effects of enthusiasm; here, more than anywhere else, it is solely governed by the quest for profit. It has certainly proved successful in the United States, where social differences were less marked, the privileges of the 'happy few' less excessive, and there was a good possibility of exploiting the rest of the world. But as I have already shown, none of the Third World countries can hope to repeat the 'American miracle'.

During a meeting held in Mexico in August 1966, I was asked whether it was advisable for the country to accept investments from abroad – which have made up about 35 per cent of the country's total investment in recent years. This question cannot be answered without reservations, as I shall show by means of two different examples. The Coca-Cola bottling factories may well pay for themselves within two or three years, and once this has been achieved, they will continue to pump the poor peasants' savings to the United States. After drinking two or three bottles a day, these peasants can no longer afford to buy fruit, an egg, or a glass of milk for their children. Hence the sales of local produce suffer, as well as the health of the population and the supply of foreign currency; the balance for the country is therefore wholly negative.

If Nestlé, on the other hand, open a factory for the processing of milk, the enterprise will be amortized over ten years and will also teach the peasants modern stock-breeding techniques, organize the sale of concentrated food, and introduce artificial insemination, intensive forage growing and so on. It would thus create a focus of development, benefiting health with its milk and promoting the growth of agriculture and of the country as a whole. Moreover a European trust would be much less dangerous politically for Mexico, than an American one. One must therefore be wary of taking any dogmatic stand on this matter, or of trying to stereotype such a complex situation.

The earliest irrigation works were, naturally enough, the most economical. They were sometimes skimped – since the contractors found it easier to buy the inspector than the requisite quantities of iron and concrete. Now they need reinforcing. The new works cost three times as much per hectare, so three times less of them are carried out. Moreover the monoculture of corn or cotton over much of the irrigated areas does not give maximum profits, or provide the maximum amount of work. If the Mexicans are to be better fed, a larger share of land should be devoted to stock and horticultural produce. More forage is also required for the protection of the soil.

4. Poverty, Alcoholism, Corruption, Usury, Erosion

Undeniably progress has taken place, for the country which used to be a big importer of cereals, has recently begun to export them. As in France, this costs a lot in subsidies. Yet large areas of under-nourishment and poverty persist, especially among the over-populated mountain *ejidos*. When the *ejidos* are near towns or big farms, paid work is available, in which case the small patch of land provides extra employment and a minimum of subsistence. It gives the security and dignity which, as we saw just now, is lacking in the landless peasants of India.

For those who live off the beaten track, the situation quickly deteriorates when their allotments become too small, for the population of the village may have doubled or trebled since the first distributions were made. The remarkable evidence, collected on tape by Oscar Lewis in his book *Pedro Martinez*,[5] shows how serious the rural situation often is. Poverty also persists in the towns. Mexico City is growing much too fast, creating overt and concealed unemployment, pedlars, boot-blacks,[6] prostitution, juvenile delinquency, slums and alcoholism. A very vivid and accurate picture is given in *The Children of Sanchez*, by the same author.[7]

The Mexican government dislikes having its sores probed in this way, and the director of the cultural organization which allowed these books to be distributed in the country soon lost his job. The PRI is content to be patient; the revolution is permanent because the Institutional Revolutionary Party is always in power. It keeps its hand firmly in the till for the benefit of the privileged minority: 2 per cent of the population receive about 40 per cent of the total of personal incomes. The party has shown a capacity for absorbing its most active and vocal opponents by offering them a small slice of the cake. Some people claim that one can make a political career for oneself more rapidly by starting in the opposition, and then going over to the PRI for an agreed con-sideration. The ravages of alcoholism are also taking on alarming proportions. Illiteracy still persists despite the vigorous efforts that have been made to eradicate it.

Various forms of usury still flourish in the villages, since the official loans do not cover all the peasants' financial needs. Unsecured loans for consumption often involve interest of 5 per cent or more per month – the same rate as in South Korea. A commoner practice is to sell crops in the blade; they are paid for two or three months before harvesting, but at a full third below the normal price. Nothing is done by the National Peasants' Confederation, associated with the PRI, which continues to carry on rather demagogic propaganda about the new land distributions.

In order to subsist, the poorest peasants in this mountainous country have to till ever steeper slopes, which quickly succumb to erosion after a few meagre harvests of maize. If they had been planted with orchards, forage trees, or nopal (the non-spiny cactus of North Africa), it would have been possible to protect the soil and at the same time make it yield more employment and greater resources. Agave juice when fermented provides maguey, the wine of Mexico, and when distilled, its liquor, tequila. Pasteurized before being fermented, it forms a delicious and very nutritious juice, rich in sugar, vitamins and even protein. Under intensive cultivation, the agave gives higher yields than any other plant on stony, semi-arid slopes.

Capital must be available to create these plantations and for buying stock and supporting life until the harvests materialize, which would not be for several years. The state must take a hand in financing these investments, which would seem to be on a par with irrigation in importance. Yet it is not in this sphere that the Mexican revolutionaries, heirs of the agrarian revolutionary tradition of the murdered Emiliano Zapata, expend their energies.

5. 'Land to the Tiller'

This was the cry in 1911; others were 'Land and Liberty' and 'Land and Books'. In that pre-capitalist era, the principal factor of production and means of subsistence was still the land, and to share it out more fairly seemed to be the foundation of social justice. Since then its importance has continually waned, because more and more capital and technical knowledge are now required. If the large estates, which are at present the best cultivated, though many of them are very extensive, were divided up into small near-subsistence allotments, their yields would soon shrink by as much as 40 per cent. Since there are only 15 million hectares under cultivation, for an agricultural population of nearly 25 million, it would be impossible to give each agricultural family 10 hectares for dry cultivation, or four hectares of irrigated land like that in the Laguna de Torreon; yet this is what would be needed to create small farms nearly paying their way but not susceptible of modernization.

The Mexican Marxists are not unaware of these facts, and they know that Castro did not divide up the large estates in Cuba, but preferred to transform them directly into state farms. They nevertheless claim that the redistributions should continue; with greater justice, they also demand increased loans for the peasants, especially the *ejidos* workers. More effort should, at the same time, be devoted to improving the rate of repayment, for to have a quarter still unpaid, after so many years, can hardly be favourable to development, or to the renewal of loans. The independent Peasant Confederation, associated with the left-wing opposition, has begun a very courageous struggle against usury. At its instigation, the peasants try to halt and unload lorries carrying harvests bought (at a very low price, before they had ripened) by usurious traders. Mechanized farming co-operatives rent the small peasants 'poor man's tractors', acquired cheaply in Czechoslovakia in exchange for Mexican tobacco.

The militant peasants who carry on this struggle risk their lives every day, for killings of all kinds are still all too frequent in Mexico; the privileged minority will not easily allow itself to be dispossessed. The United States did not turn a hair in August 1968, and some people even believe that they secretly encouraged the Russians to occupy Czechoslovakia. Ph. Ben suggested this in *Le Monde*, at the end of August 1968. Thus they have tacitly assumed the right to intervene militarily if there were a Mexican revolt. If this should happen, they already know that the Russians would not go beyond the same verbal level of protest as America in August 1968. Yet Johnson's warnings on the subject of Rumania, shortly afterwards, unquestionably had an effect.

6. 'Land to the Good Tiller'

I was recently invited to two agricultural symposia in Mexico (August 1966 and February 1968), organized respectively by the Centre for Agricultural Research and the Employers' Confederation of the Mexican Republic. I tried to make my proposals at these conferences realistic, bearing in mind the unlikelihood of a revolutionary solution in the near future – despite the courage of some of the students, young workers and young peasants. Mexican agriculture would soon be in a position to provide full employment for the rural population, if only it was granted the loans necessary to finance all the works which are so badly needed.

Irrigation canals, roads, plantations, anti-erosion works, the opening-up of the hot coastal regions (where the most land is to be won, provided proper sanitary precautions are taken) – the list is not exhaustive. Mexico could have over 12 million hectares under irrigation one day, which is three times as much as at present – and farm over 30 million, which is more than double the present area. Here as everywhere, the state lacks resources. Nevertheless, the French budget takes a good quarter of the national revenue – 27 per cent in 1969. Hardly more than 8 per cent[8] goes on the Mexican budget, while in many less developed countries the proportion may be 15 per cent or more. A group of Mexican bankers pointed out to me that when the United States was at a stage of development 'analogous' to Mexico's in 1968,[9] her taxes were very much lower. But they underestimated the role of local taxation, the vast natural resources per head, the massive influx of men and capital from Europe, the very much higher rate of private investment and so on. They are always haunted by the same dream of this utterly unreproducible American model.

'Land to the good tiller' might be a slogan more conducive to agricultural modernization. Some degree of mobility in the ownership of land needs to be reintroduced, so that it may more easily fall into the hands of those who show themselves capable of making the best use of it. In the collective sector, usufructuary rights in the *ejidos* could be withdrawn, and the value of any improvements reimbursed – which would provide an incentive to carry out more of them. In the private sector, similar encouragements could be given in the case of tenancy. These measures are not without their dangers, because high concentrations of cultivations could lead to abuses and favour the new large estate method of farming which has already reared its head to some extent.

If the government really wished to defend the people's interests with more than just words, they could easily do so. A heavy tax on land would compel proprietors either to farm more efficiently or relinquish ownership, and if the tax was made progressively heavier as the area of land owned increased, large estate farming would soon be checked, especially where cultivation was too extensive. The second step would be for all farms of more than 25 hectares of irrigated land, or 100 hectares of dry cultivation, to make a standing agreement with the agricultural authorities to expand their investments in step with a regular 4 per cent increase in production; this would be the condition for their retaining their use of the land. The stockbreeders of the arid northern zones would then be compelled to plant non-spiny cacti, capable of tripling the yield of meat per hectare. Plantations would be created and anti-erosion works constructed on the slopes, while the irrigated areas would have to include a certain minimum of intensive forage and modern stock-breeding, etc. For its practical application this plan would require an honest administration, dedicated to the poor. The state is destined to take a larger share in directing the economy and if far-reaching modernization is to take place, it will have to exercise this control in the national interest, which means including the interests of the oppressed.

Instead of pseudo-revolutionary verbiage designed to mask, and therefore help protect, the interests of the privileged minority, it would be better for the time being to have the competition of a welfare neo-capitalism, combined with social protection. This is feasible on account of the considerable development that has already taken place (65 per cent of investments originate within the country); it would also offer more scope for hard workers – who deserve more help in the form of loans. As in India, the oppressed could then be given better protection than that afforded by the operation of a static agrarian right. Economic and social progress could be reconciled by a more rapid expansion of industry, an increase in the number of jobs, the protection of the poorest employees (at present the interests of the better-off come first), the enforcement of a minimum wage, and the granting of more loans and technical aid to the peasants. The protection of the oppressed workers, and above all peasants, needs to be better organized, with unions truly independent of the party in power, so that they can genuinely represent the interests of their members.

None of these measures will prove adequate if the pressure of the population on the land and in urban employment continues to grow at its present rate. Two basic preconditions for the modernization of rural Mexico, and for eventually steering it towards socialism, are birth-control (without which the country will have a population of one and a half thousand million within a century) and a more rapid exodus from the land. A third precondition would be to remove power from the hands of the privileged minority, should they be foolish enough to oppose reforms necessary for economic progress. To this end a reorganization of the left-wing of the PRI is required, as well as a new Cardenas with a better knowledge of economic problems than the old guard of the revolution, or their direct heirs, possessed.

When Pope Paul VI condemned the violence in Bogota, during the summer of 1968, he did not dwell on the violence perpetrated by the rich against the poor which represents the actual situation in Latin America. He freely condemned the guerrilla movement, while neglecting to criticize the big landowners who continue to have squatters and union leaders massacred – or the Brazilian[10] Indian Protection Service, which is killing its protégés in order to take their land. So long as the Church leaders leave these 'i's undotted, they will continue to be suspected of hypocrisy.

Between 1926 and 1929 the Mexican Church, openly opposing the genuinely reformist government of the time, refused Communion to the wives of poor *ejidos* members, as being guilty of complicity in the 'theft of land from its rightful owners' represented by the agrarian reforms! Every human-being has the right to respect and a minimum of consideration, and if this is not forthcoming, then, in all conscience, he has the right to revolt. Though those who do not share their struggle may hardly be entitled to incite them to revolt, I cannot see that they have any right to condemn it. The more intelligent Americans of the Peace Corps in Quito are attempting to promote a legal revolution. Events will show us whether this is possible, but the Brazilian army is making it increasingly unlikely.

The future of the Latin American countries therefore lies in their freeing themselves from imperialism and achieving solidarity, at least in the economic sphere, in the face of the powerful northern neighbour which has taken them under its tutelage. This is why I suggested in Mexico that a national union should be formed of all who are devoted to the cause of economic independence. Yet the privileged minority feels itself threatened by the student revolts. It therefore arranged the premeditated massacre in the Plaza de las Tres Culturas in Mexico City, on 2 October 1968, when at least two hundred people were killed. This could well hasten the coming of the revolution. Meanwhile the subcontinent must develop by its own resources, evolving economic unions independent of Washington and in a position to bargain with it, if not as equals, then at least from a less inferior position.

NOTES TO CHAPTER II

1 There are a number of films which help one to get a better understanding of Mexico, including Eisenstein's *Thunder over Mexico*, Reichenbach's *Mexico, Mexico, Viva Zapata* and many others.

2 See especially René Dumont's *Lands Alive*, Ch. VI, Merlin Press, London, 1965.

3 Or by nearly half; because this growth-rate is probably nearer the truth than the 8 per cent announced for the previous decade.

4 It is astonishing to see *ejido* members, short of land, under-employed and obtaining inadequate harvests, who nevertheless allow their fields and gardens to be overrun by weeds.

5 NRF, Paris 1966, Gallimard, Panther Books, London, 1969.

6 It is particularly shocking to see an adult polishing the shoes of a young schoolboy who despises him.

7 Gallimard, Paris, 1963. The Mexican Tourist Office's propaganda for the Olympics mentions nothing but fiestas, luxury, paradises and other splendours.

8 'There has been a fairly general decline in the rates of capital formation in Latin America since 1957,' notes Paul Bairoch.

9 No analogy is possible, since Mexico cannot conquer or exploit the United States.

10 The share of national education in Brazil's federal budget has dropped from 11 per cent in 1965 to 7 per cent in 1969, whereas military spending has increased – according to Serge Lafaurie in the *Nouvel Observateur*, 13 January 1969.

PART THREE

The Structure and Forms of 'Underdevelopment'[1] in Algeria: the Search for an Algerian Solution

MARCEL MAZOYER

CHAPTER TWELVE

Independence: Algeria on the Edge of an Abyss

In November 1954, one hundred and twenty-seven years after the Bey of Algiers struck the French ambassador with his fan, thus precipitating the French occupation of Algeria, the decisive armed struggle in Algeria began. For seven years the National Liberation Army (ALN) was to hold its own against a French army 500,000 strong. In 1962, independence consecrated the political victory of the National Liberation Front (NLF) over the forces who were waging one of the last struggles for the preservation of the Empire in France and Algeria.

At the close of this long and devastating war, Algeria was on the edge of an abyss. Military and civilian casualties were nearly a million, not counting the wounded. The peasants had been uprooted wholesale and two million of them emerged from the transit camps. On their return they found their villages razed to the ground, the *mechtas* (farms) destroyed, their fields overgrown and their herds annihilated. Some 500,000 refugees crossed the Moroccan and Tunisian frontiers to return to Algeria; there were nearly two million unemployed and nearly half the population stood in need of help.

Within a few months, 800,000 people left Algeria – about 80 per cent of the French and other Europeans, whose material and moral interests suffered by the settlement of the war. The country thus lost nearly all the trained men who had been working there before independence. Businesses, the administration, and over a million hectares of the best land were in a state of utter neglect.

In fact, the Europeans in Algeria, of whom there were more than a million, owned the essential means of production in agriculture, industry, transport, wholesale trade, the banks and so on. About 40 per cent of the country's cultivated areas, that is 2,800,000 hectares, was owned by about 22,000 colonials. They also controlled 5,500 out of 7,000 (or 80 per cent) of industry. Of the more highly qualified men, 15,000 out of 16,300 (90 per cent) were European, and in the liberal professions 9,200 out of 11,300 (80 per cent).

Independence was accompanied by a widespread upheaval of the economic and social structures.[2] The war was to a large extent responsible for Algeria's unhealthy situation, the desolate countryside, the urban poverty which was aggravated by the recession, and the disorganization and paralysis of the economic and administrative machinery. We should not forget that this catastrophic conjunction of circumstances occurred in the context of 'underdevelopment', which left little room for hope of a miracle.

Algeria's 'underdevelopment' was very marked: her industry was very weak and her agricultural population large. Her under-employment, unemployment, illiteracy and shortage of trained men were the outcome of an essentially dependent and dominated economy. Algeria's exports to France, and those controlled by French interests, amounted to 80 per cent of the mineral raw materials and agricultural produce: wine, fruit and vegetables. France provided the bulk of her industrial products, consumer and capital goods. This dependent economy lacked coherence and it was particularly vulnerable because the trade between Algeria and France was more important than internal trade.

In this exceptional situation, the worst – which some hoped for and others dreaded – did not happen. Production fell, it is true – it could hardly do otherwise – but it did not completely founder, because this deprived race discovered the energy and the men to develop an original economic and political experiment. When a system is completely overthrown in a context of acute under-development, the situation seems chaotic; yet a nation, a state, an economy, and new relationships within society have sprung from it. The Algerian people managed to survive and have begun to develop and transform their economy.

Algeria shows the common characteristics of 'underdevelopment', as well as situations and forms inherited from her unique past. The path of her emergence will likewise be her own, though in many ways the projects of the New Algeria are of more than purely national interest.

Bearing some of these points in mind, I shall set forth the ideas which they suggest to me, with particular emphasis on the agricultural problems that I have had the opportunity of studying.

The first necessity was to ensure that the twelve million Algerians threatened by famine had enough to live on. The peasants and workers of the abandoned farms busied themselves with getting the sowing done.

There were immense difficulties and they had to fight to prevent the abandoned lands being cornered by speculators. The FLN (the party) and the ALN (the army) supported the struggle of the workers and peasants.

The administration was disrupted, skilled workers and craftsmen in short supply, and tractors and machinery dispersed, broken down or sabotaged. In the worst-hit areas the means of production had disappeared. The 'regrouped' peasants' lands were lying waste, and the level of production of the land left vacant was threatened.

To repair this catastrophic situation the ploughing campaign was launched; all the country's available resources had to be mobilised to crop three million hectares of cereals. This mobilization was carried out by the government, the party and the army, with the help of the peasants and agricultural workers. It was a genuine campaign of the masses, of a socialist character, for men and equipment were thrown into the common task regardless of their economic origins. The participation of every authority was obtained, from the lowest to the highest.

Seed, which was to be returned after the harvest, was requisitioned wherever available.[3] The 700 tractors of the *Société agricole de prévoyance*, together with 500 imported from Yugoslavia and 300 from France, took part in the operation, moving from region to region, as they were needed.

This campaign was a resounding success: the 3 million hectares were cropped, and 1963 was a good year. With 23 million quintals (of hard wheat, soft wheat and barley), it was one of the best harvests for ten years (the previous average was less than 20 million quintals). The ploughing campaign was repeated during the next two years, to give time for agriculture to get reorganized.

Socialist Sundays were organised: railwaymen and mechanics from the agricultural workers, to get their tractors and equipment working again. The 'tree days', in the course of which thousands of hectares were reforested, were an expression of the same concern.

Independent Algeria has scored another promising success in education. National education, which has 21 per cent of the budget, is the biggest item of state expenditure. With 8,000 certificated teachers, 10,000 instructors and 13,000 monitors with primary training, Algeria has been able to give 55 per cent of her children a primary education, as against the mere 12 per cent who received it during the colonial era. There are 7,000 students at university, 90 per cent of them Algerians, as against 5,000 students before, of whom only 10 per cent were Algerian.

During the months following Independence, Algeria took over the greater part of the machinery of production, both in agriculture and industry. A predominantly socialist sector was created by first taking over ownerless property and then by nationalization.

What are the structures and forms of Algeria's economy and society after Independence? To what processes are they due, and what constraints follow from them? What strategy should be adopted in order to overcome these constraints? These are the problems I shall tackle, relying on a general analysis of the situation, but also upon a more careful study of some of its typical aspects.

NOTES TO CHAPTER 12

1 For lack of a better expression I shall continue to use this, taking care to bring out its real meaning.
2 Samir Amin, *L'Economie du Maghreb*, Editions de Minuit, Paris, 1966.
3 H. Bourges, *L'Algérie à l'épreuve du pouvoir*, Grasset, Paris, 1967.

CHAPTER THIRTEEN

'Resisting Fate but Facing the Facts': a line of Development for Algeria

1. *Distortion and Disequilibrium in the Algerian Economy*

The modern sector of agriculture, which mostly belonged to the European colonists, is now included within the 2·5 million hectares under self-management. It evolved on the most fertile land – littoral plains, hill-slopes, wadis and the better-watered, cereal-growing plateaux. Meanwhile, Algerian agriculture, forming what is known as the traditional sector, was driven back to the ravaged hill-slopes, high steppe-like plains and the mountains.

The modern sector, with its 2·5 million hectares of fertile land, provides work for only 250,000 labourers – 200,000 of them permanent and less than 50,000 seasonal – in the production of commercial crops chiefly destined for the market for export. Traditional agriculture, on the other hand, with less than 6 million hectares of poor or deteriorated agricultural land, has to support 650,000 farming families and 600,000 families of landless peasants.

With nearly a third of the land – the best land – for one-sixth of the agricultural population, the potential productivity of the worker in the modern sector is five times that of the traditional sector. This distortion in the allocation of resources, in the distribution of available land, and in incomes, has resulted in massive unemployment and the pauperization of the most deprived class of peasants.

The underemployment and unemployment stemmed from the fact that external imperatives guided the market and technology of the modern sector. The traditional sector, driven back to the

less fertile lands and left to its own devices, can hardly offer its
1·3 million male labourers more than fifty days' work a year. The
work actually done is equivalent to less than 300,000 permanent
jobs, and the under-employment to more than a million.

In this sector, the effort of day-to-day subsistence on the most
marginal land, which is threatened by erosion, is made at a cost
to the fertility of the land. The over-cultivated land is literally
'consumed' by non-intensive and anarchic cereal-growing and
stock-breeding. Incomes are often catastrophically low, barely
adequate to buy a survival-ration of cereal: less than two quintals
per person per year.[1] This extreme pauperization has led to a
massive rural exodus chiefly towards the coastal towns, and to
the development of slums.

The underemployment and unemployment cannot be absorbed
by industry. Algeria depended mainly on France for her supplies
of industrial products. With the inclusion of mining, building and
public works, Algerian industry represented only 27 per cent of
the national product. Before Independence, it provided no more
than 125,000 jobs. This means that trade and the services, as well
as the administration, are still very overdeveloped. Another
consequence has been the emigration of 500,000 labourers to
France.

Independence and the departure of the Europeans have created
450,000 jobs for Algerians to fill; 180,000 in the urban economy,
150,000 officials, and 120,000 in the army. However, this is not
enough to absorb the rural unemployment, which remains at the
same order of magnitude (equivalent to a million jobs). Between
150,000 and 200,000 workers remain affected by urban unemployment.

An effort can and must be made, through simultaneous industrialization and agricultural development (by intensifying the
modern sector, and getting the traditional sector started), to create
jobs and wealth, in order to provide both incomes for the unemployed and their families, and a corresponding increase in the
national revenue.

2. *The Reliance on Unsuitable and Costly Modern Techniques*

In quest for a strategy of development, Algeria cannot reckon without the distortion and disequilibrium that have resulted from her former dependent status and economic domination. She must also take account of the fact that this distorted and dependent economy has considerable potential.

Independent Algeria has inherited some important assets established during the colonial period; urban infrastructure: transport, relatively modern towns, railways, roads, ports, aerodromes; social infrastructure: hospitals, schools; industrial infrastructure: extractive industries connected with mining and mineral oil, food and agricultural industries, light engineering, water-works, steam-generating stations, etc.

If the resources used to create there infrastructures were available today, it is quite certain that the productive capacity installed under the new economic and social conditions would be different from that conceived within, and for the benefit of, the institutional framework of colonialism.

For one thing, this capacity is not adapted to the country's needs, and does not conform to its requirements for development; it costs more, in some instances, than it brings in.

The vineyards, which cover 350,000 hectares, are the most typical example. France was the privileged outlet for Algerian wine, but this outlet is now subject to heavy restrictions. Were it not for the special links which existed between France and Algeria, these vineyards would never have assumed such proportions; they must now be adapted to the new conditions of the market. This kind of conversion, as we shall see later, is not easy, and meanwhile the vines, which cost a considerable amount to establish, continue to take up land, machinery and various supplies. A section of these vines cost more than can be recovered in receipts.

Even the road network and some of the urban infrastructures do not always answer the real needs of the Algerian people, and these investments are beyond the means of the nation's economy.

The maintenance and management costs to which this productive capacity gives rise are all the heavier in that the technological criteria used in planning it were those of a developed country. It requires a great many trained men and technicians, and in this way helps to exacerbate the shortage of them.

Getting started again was no simple matter. Previous levels of production could not be fully re-established. A considerable amount of re-conversion was necessary from the outset, as in the case of the vineyards. The production of some goods and services, designed mainly for Europeans, had to be heavily cut. In spite of these drawbacks, it would have been unthinkable not to have made use of this potential; getting the modern sector functioning again was a basic objective.

On the grounds of expense, partial unsuitability, the shortage of trained men, and the difficulties of management, opinion has been gaining ground in favour of the severance of traditional commercial links and the immediate, radical re-conversion of the economy towards internal objectives. Such an economic policy, taken to any lengths, would cause Algeria to fall back on a basically subsistence economy, incapable of satisfying her growing needs, and would involve a considerable setback in her civilization and technology.

After the United States ceased to import sugar from Cuba, or supply her with petrol, the island was cut off from its traditional outlets and sources of supply by blockade. At first the Cubans thought that, by rapidly diversifying and industrializing, they could soon surmount the constraints resulting from the historical distortions in their economy. They quickly realized, however, that the 'line of least resistance' for development[2] must be to rely on specialized production corresponding to the natural conditions on the island, and upon the machinery of production carried over from the earlier period.

This policy has nevertheless been accompanied by a certain amount of diversification, in keeping with the country's needs and with the improvement of the productive machinery (food and agricultural industries). It is possible only in so far as Cuba can find stable markets and sources of supply within the socialist camp, and terms of trade that will enable it to accumulate the capital needed for development.

The task of getting the Algerian economy moving again was made easier by the fact that, due to her links with France, Algeria was not severed abruptly from her markets or sources of supply. Moreover, the international division of labour shaped by colonization was not wholly irrational. Algeria is, for instance, well placed for growing citrus fruits, and she can find certain outlets for her wine.

3. Beginning of a Strategy for Economic Recovery

From the outset, however, it was not enough simply to get the economy working again. Not only was it necessary 'to take the facts into account', but also 'to reject the inevitabilities'. At the same time, Algeria had to inaugurate some strategy for correcting the distorted structure of her economy. She could increase productive employment and raise incomes through industrialization, the intensification of agriculture in the modern sector, and by getting traditional agriculture under way. No long-term policy of development can be based solely on agriculture,[3] for geographical factors limit its productivity. In any case, means of production of industrial origin, such as fertilizer, machinery and implements are necessary for development. Yet industrialization is a relatively lengthy process, incapable of providing rapid answers to the problems posed.

It is therefore necessary in the short term to rely on agriculture as well, for this is the broadest sector, and there is a margin for considerable progress. Moreover, to a large extent, progress in agriculture is a precondition for industrial progress. Agriculture provides the food to support the population of the cities and the workers in industry; it supplies produce for export, and earns the foreign currency needed for purchasing equipment and modern technology. In addition, it furnishes raw materials for light and, in part, for heavy industry.

Algeria is fortunate in having a fairly large oil revenue,[4] which can help finance her industry; however, the rest will have to come from agriculture, which must therefore develop and achieve a surplus. Her population, after all, is predominantly rural. The amelioration of the subsistence, working and living conditions of this population must provide a growing market for industry, both in consumer and capital goods – the latter providing the basis for agricultural modernization.

Thus agriculture forms the starting-point for the nation's economic development, and must advance before industry can come into its own as the dominant factor and driving force.

Industrialization will provide productive employment, but it cannot play its part to the full except in so far as it becomes integrated into the country's economy, transforming its raw materials and helping to modernize it. The value of industrialization therefore depends to a large extent on the links it can establish with the agricultural sector.

Gérard Destanne de Bernis has shown[5] that the four industries which come nearest to fulfilling these conditions are: heavy industry, plastics, fertilizer, and cement. However, there should also be emphasis on light industry and the agricultural and food industries, to pave the way for agricultural development.

According to Tidafi[6] 'the first step in the process of industrialization could be made in processing, through the development of industrial crops and agricultural industries. During the transition period, this primary industrialization would create new jobs, reduce imports of processed agricultural produce, and save foreign currency for purchasing the basic means of production.' Nevertheless, this does not diminish the importance of the fundamental groups mentioned above.

The Bône iron and steel plant (*Société nationale de sidérurgie d'Annaba*), which aims to produce 500,000 tons in 1969–70 and a million tons in 1973–4, will have the desired multiple effects on metal manufacturing industries. So it must foster other industrial nuclei in its wake: shipbuilding, car building, pipes, and especially agricultural equipment. Tractors and agricultural equipment will be manufactured at Constantine, and there is to be a phosphate fertilizer factory in Annaba (formerly Bône).

From 1969, the petrochemical complex of Arzew (near Oran) will produce ammonia and the nitrate fertilizers needed in increasing agricultural production. The national oil company is preparing to build another petrochemical complex consisting of a gas liquifying plant with a capacity of six thousand million cubic metres, an ammonia factory with a capacity of one million tons, and ethylene and polyethylene units. Algeria's basic industry is thus being extended in the directions most in keeping with the national interest. In 1969, her budget for capital expenditure came to 6 thousand million DA[7] – nearly double the figure for 1968 – 4 thousand million of which came from the treasury. The current budget was only 3·9 thousand million DA. All this goes to show that considerable efforts are being made towards development.

Yet it will be many years before industry can create a million new jobs. Attempts must be made to mobilize manpower resources in the other sectors of production.

NOTES TO CHAPTER 13

1   This is roughly equivalent to £8 per head per year.
2   *Cf.* Michel Gutelman, *L' Agriculture socialisée à Cuba*; Maspéro, Paris, 1967.
3   *Cf.* Tidafi: *L'Agriculture algérienne et ses perspectives de développement*, Thèse, E.P. H.E.X, Paris, 1968.
4   Oil provides 20 per cent of tax revenue (*cf. Le Monde*, 2 February 1969).
5   G. de Bernis: '*L'Industrialisation en Algérie*', in *Problèmes de l'Algérie indépendante*; Tiers-Monde, Presses Universitaires de France, Paris.
6   *ibid.*, p. 367.
7   The dinar is worth seven pence.

CHAPTER FOURTEEN

The Search for Full Employment by Making Best Use of Land, Algeria's Scarcest Resource

Michel Gutelman[1] has shown that 'the classic formulation of the theory of underdevelopment, according to which capital is scarce and manpower correspondingly "over-abundant", no longer holds true when the existing structures have been overthrown by a genuine and far-reaching socio-political revolution'. Referring to C. R. Rodriguez, he adds: 'capital is not scarce, it is merely misappropriated by the controllers of the large estates, sterilized by the hoarding of rich speculative businessmen, and finally diverted to the imperialist metropolis'. Indeed, most of the Latin American countries clearly do export capital to the United States.

However, it is not the capital misused during the period previous to Independence that has to be reckoned up, but that which is available for rational investment at the present stage. And such capital is relatively scarce in Algeria, because the massive exodus of the Europeans and the almost total lack of trained men and technicians, makes it very difficult to reorganize production.

A big share of the capital and foreign currency will go towards ndustrial development. The possibilities for investing money or capital goods in agriculture will therefore be limited, while trained men and technicians will also be scarce.

The most must be made of these limited resources. Besides, unlike Cuba and many Latin American countries, Algeria has no large reserves of fertile land which could be rapidly brought into use by agrarian reforms and the abolition of latifundism, to give full rural employment. Agrarian reform is certainly a prerequisite for Algeria, but full productive employment is much more difficult to achieve in her countryside.

1. *The Arable Land*

Of the 237 million hectares of land in Algeria, 208 – about 90 per cent – belong to the desert or semi-desert areas of the south. Northern Algeria represents only twenty-nine million hectares. A large proportion of this land is still very bare – hilly, salty, badly watered, or badly drained. When ploughed and sown, in most cases it hardly yields more, and frequently yields less, than the amount of seed put in. Profitable agriculture, even subsistence agriculture, is impossible here, and the land is occupied by forests (2·4 million hectares), esparto grass (3 million hectares), and common grazing (5·3 million hectares); 10 or 11 million hectares are unproductive.

There are barely 7 million hectares under cultivation, which represents less than 30 per cent of northern Algeria, and less than 3·5 per cent of the whole country. These seven million hectares include 600,000 hectares of vineyards and orchards, and slightly more than 250,000 hectares of irrigated land, of which 50,000 are watered by major, and the rest by minor, irrigation works.

Hence the area devoted to cereals – which form the basis of the population's diet – is of the order of 6 million hectares, nearly half of which is laid fallow as a result of rotation. This works out at an average of 0.25 hectares of cereals per inhabitant.

Every year this area is diminished by erosion: it is calculated that Algeria loses 38,000 hectares a year from this cause – a hundred hectares a day.

Rainfall is the principal limiting factor. Some perennial crops, such as vines and olives, are better adapted to inadequate or irregular rainfall. Irrigation makes it possible to develop the more exacting crops: market-gardening, industrial crops, forage and fruit (citrus). In the south, where the rainfall drops below 350 mm, cereal-growing becomes marginal and gives way to pasture. The forests, esparto-steppes and common grazing represent forms of exploitation less intensive than farming.

Thus these various ways of turning the land to account compete within an agricultural space that is not only inelastic, but is being still further diminished every year by erosion.

2. The Prime Problem of Algerian Agriculture: Raising the Productivity of Arable Land

Algerian agriculture is characterized by the scarcity of two essential factors of production, land and water – and by an abundance of manpower. These features are accentuated by the instability inherited from the earlier period. The distortion between the modern sector (mostly under self-management now) and the 'traditional' sector (which dominates the private sector) comes from the fact that the best-watered land, which is most suitable for cultivation, has been earmarked primarily for export production adapted to the requirements of the French market. The agriculture which supplies the needs of the growing population has therefore been driven back to the increasingly marginal zones, which are difficult to cultivate, unproductive, and subject to erosion – thus contributing to the degradation of the nation's heritage of land.

The development of a profitable agriculture in the areas producing for the external market, which had the monopoly of the best land, led to the establishment of speculative monocultures, or near-monocultures, which drew on the vast reserves of under-employed manpower according to its seasonal labour requirements. The mass of labourers, the main work-force of the country, is therefore relegated to the territories least suitable for production. Manpower is only admitted to the best land, which is reserved and monopolized, in so far as the highly profitable productions for the external market require it. A massive economic distortion is thus formed, with men too numerous on the poor, over-exploited land, and less numerous on the fertile land. There is no longer a correspondence between men and land, between the peasants and their principal means of production.

To achieve the best economic situation, arable land must be allocated in the best way possible. The work-force must therefore be redistributed according to the potentialities of the various regions, allocating to each region the work and production which would achieve the optimum use of its arable land.

Under present economic conditions, Algeria is more or less committed to an exchange economy, which can be converted but not abolished. What then does 'utilization of the arable land in the best possible way' involve?

All agricultural produce is either exported, or else goes to satisfy internal needs, replacing some potential (or actual) import. For the Algerian economy, the equivalent in foreign currency of the 'produce', or the import-saving corresponding to it, constitutes a gain. From this must be deducted the cost of imported supplies necessary to the production.

This 'foreign exchange balance' is the best yardstick at present for the growth of the country's wealth. The country has to put its own resources to productive use, which involves higher business profits, and higher incomes from work.[2]

From the point of view of the community as a whole, the most valuable production is not merely that which makes the biggest profits, but above all the one which also produces the largest increase in productive employment.

Until full employment is obtained, high gross output is more important than net profits.

According to the criterion we have adopted, Algeria has every interest in developing a more intensive system which will secure the highest level of employment whenever possible. Fruit-growing, vineyards, market gardening, and irrigated industrial, vegetable and fodder crops associated with stock-breeding must be developed at the expense of cereal crops and non-intensive stock-breeding.

Unfortunately, there are numerous factors restraining the spread of these crops – market constraints to begin with; the produce must be either consumed by the producer, saleable on the rather limited home market, or else exportable. It is by no means always possible to export, as the market for wine serves to remind us. Finally, fruit-tree plantations, the construction of dams and systems of canals for irrigation, factories for processing industrial crops, livestock and stockfarming buildings – all these require those other scarce resources: capital and technology. The desirable development of systems of intensive exploitation will therefore, of necessity, be limited.

3. The Calculated Conversion of the Vineyards

The problem with regard to the vineyards is that far from being extended, they must be reduced, or partially concerted.

Before Independence, they occupied 350,000 hectares, providing over a quarter of the gross agricultural production, and the overwhelming majority of exports. France used to pay the Algerian vine-growers preferential prices that were well above world prices. Outside the protected French market (which has the largest production, and the largest consumption), the world market for wine is one of the worst there is, for it has to absorb all the excess production of Portugal, Greece and southern Spain, where wages are even lower than in Algeria. Wine, and the vine, provide the best illustration[3] of the Algerian economy's dependence and vulnerability. France did not abruptly cut off her imports, but has reduced them progressively. From over 10 million hectolitres before Independence, they fell to 7.5 million hectolitres in 1965–6, and to less than 4 million hectolitres in 1967–8. On the other hand, the USSR has increased her imports; after buying 1 million hectolitres in 1968, an agreement has been signed by which the Soviet Union will buy 5 million hectolitres of wine a year, during the next seven years. These sales[4] come within the framework of a bilateral agreement governing the trade between these two countries. The USSR provides capital goods for industry, agriculture, aviation (aeroplanes and helicopters), shipping (oil-tankers and fishing vessels) and public works, as well as consumer goods; she also loans Algeria experts and technicians.

The price of this wine appears to be lower than the price paid by France, which is forty-two to forty-five pence per degree/hectolitre (*cf. Le Monde*, 31 December 1968). However, this observation is of limited significance because, in a bilateral agreement of this kind, the price of the wine can only be evaluated in relation to the price of the goods and services provided in return, which may also be lower than on the world market. The USSR has become the principal outlet for Algerian wine, just as it became the main outlet for Cuban sugar.

The vine is a very important crop for Algeria, so long as she can find a reliable partner willing to guarantee quantities and prices which will cover the cost of production. The product brings in a large amount of value-added tax, and a considerable quantity of foreign currency. The products capable of surpassing, or even merely equalling, wine in this respect all require intensive cultivation and in any case are limited, either by the market or by the country's capacity for investment.

The vine, on the other hand, is already established, and the techniques associated with it are among those which the peasants and self-management workers are best at mastering. The 'balance of payments' of the *already established* vine is hard to beat, taking into account the cost of establishing other crops to replace it; unless the price of exported wine falls too low, it cannot be improved upon.

The reduction in vineyards, as René Dumont[5] wrote as early as 1963, must be done cautiously; I would even go so far as to say that it should be calculated, since there are numerous parameters involved which cannot be understood without careful study.

The reduction of the vineyards seems less urgent and important than might have been envisaged, because the ageing of the vines, due to insufficient replanting during the years before and after Independence, limits their productive capacity (it has been estimated that 35 per cent of them are over twenty-five years old). This cessation of replanting has led to the decline of the nurseries. Though the planned level of production can be attained even with

K

old vineyards, one must ensure that the gap will be bridged, and provide for their renewal, on a smaller scale perhaps, but rejuvenated in the right proportion.

There should be a technological conversion of wine vineyards to the production of table grapes and grape-juice. In 1963, René Dumont indicated the following possible lines of development: early table grapes could be grown on the Sahel dunes, provided varieties were chosen that were acceptable to Scandinavian and Central European consumers; late table grapes (December, January and February); also products destined for home consumption. Algeria imports raisins. Table grapes could be consumed on a large scale, if an economic network such as Italy possesses were established. In a land where little alcohol is drunk, grape-juice could advantageously replace fizzy lemonade and other unhealthy drinks. The normal methods of preparation, bottling and distribution are too expensive (seven pence per twenty centilitres!) for it to be consumed on a large scale in Algeria, but economical processes of manufacture and distribution exist which would make it possible for this fruit-juice to be sold at the same price as wine, or even less.[6]

The geographical conversion that would lead to the release of the highly potential plainlands, because the vineyards are either abandoned or moved to the hillsides, should be carried out primarily in those regions where it will be possible to establish market-gardening, fruit, or even prime vegetable production economically. Of these areas, the first claim to conversion must go to those with hybrid vines producing wine unfit for consumption, or to those with the oldest and most 'depreciated' vines, the uprooting of which represents a smaller capital loss. In the irrigated zones, the vines will give way to industrial and forage crops.

Using such simple criteria, several tens of thousands of hectares can be picked out for priority in conversion. Similarly, a section of the vineyards can be delimited, which produces superior quality wines (VDQS, about half a million hectolitres) or wines which are widely known (1 million hectolitres); these would not in any circumstances be considered for conversion. The Committee for the Conversion of the Vineyards is already busy with these preparations. For the mass of intermediate vineyards, however, the exact level of production, and the choice of regions to be replanted or converted, are very delicate matters. Careful economic and technical research have to be carried out; there is no cadastral survey of the wine industry!

One cannot afford to wait for the Algerian wine industry, most of which is in the self-management sector, to adapt to the new economic conditions of its own accord. Like vine-growers the world over, the self-management workers are attached to their product. On the Annaba plain (Bône), they were not even to be won over by the prospect of receiving water for irrigation; 'Vines give more work', they told us in 1965, adding: 'We like vines round here.'

Overall planning will be necessary. The department of Crop Production and the Wine and Vine Office are initiating research efficiently directed and co-ordinated by means of planning; the latter has a primary role to play, as we shall see from other examples.

At all events, vine-growing is not a field in which we can expect any increase of productive employment or agricultural income.

4. *Irrigation: A Powerful Way of Raising the Potential of the Land, but Expensive, Limited and Hard to Control*

In a Mediterranean climate, if water is made available the principal factor limiting agricultural potential is removed. With irrigation, the possibilities of development are of quite a different order to those of dry agriculture. One hectare of irrigated cultivation (fruit-trees, market garden, or industrial mixed farming with vegetables and forage associated with stock-breeding) is worth five to ten times as much as one hectare of cereals or dry mixed farming, in terms of productive employment and value-added receipts. Irrigation is therefore a potent means of 'multiplying' the productive capacity of cultivated land – a scarce and 'inelastic' resource.

Irrigation works (dams, channels, etc.) cost a considerable amount in dinars and foreign currency. It is difficult to make these investments profitable. They must be followed up by a rapid and intensive exploitation of the new potentialities created by irrigation, and such development presupposes a very considerable technological, economic and social break. A high concentration of technically-trained men is required. Even so, the rate of return on the capital invested in irrigation-works will hardly come to more than 5 or 10 per cent.

On the other hand, the increase in the nation's wealth due to irrigation, related to the expenditure of foreign currency, is of greater importance. The interest-rate of such a national investment, evaluated at conservative estimates for buying, constructing or replacing the works in question, is generally in excess of 20 per cent. It may therefore be a worthwhile investment.

Algeria is not, however, in a position to obtain a massive and speedy increase in the agricultural potential of her land by means of major irrigation. Possibilities of investment are slight. The civil engineering firms, who construct dams and distribution networks, have a restricted productive capacity. The authorities responsible for preparing the projects, supervising the sites, and development, constitute another limitation.

In Algeria, something in the neighbourhood of 100,000 hectares are supplied with large-scale irrigation works, while the surface actually irrigated amounts to less than 50,000 hectares. Priority, during the next fifteen years, must go to the development of 40,000 hectares in the areas where the irrigation works already constructed are not being fully utilized (about 5,000 hectares at Maghnia, 15,000 at Bou Namoussa, 5,000 in the middle Cheliff, and 10,000 on the upper Cheliff).

Besides, it will hardly be possible to build more than one large dam every four or five years, making three in fifteen years; these could be situated in the Oran area, in the Cheliff valley and on the Mitidja – representing say 20,000 additional hectares. Altogether, in fifteen years, the irrigated surface could be increased by about 60,000 hectares.

Supposing that irrigation multiplies the soil's productive

capacity by six, one might say that the irrigation of one hectare 'creates' the equivalent of five more hectares of arable land. 60,000 hectares under irrigation are therefore equivalent to 300,000 more hectares of dry cultivation, or 5 per cent of Algeria's agricultural land.

An increase of this order would obviously not be capable of absorbing the unemployed and underemployed rural labour-force. Yet it would be wrong to neglect large-scale irrigation; for with the 50,000 hectares already irrigated, the 60,000 possible during the next fifteen years, and the almost equally great unexploited potential of the Mitidja, the Cheliff, the Oran area and the Bône plain, it represents a long-term possibility of growth equivalent to nearly a million hectares of arable land – 15 to 20 per cent of the present productive capacity of Algeria's soil.

These large irrigation complexes are difficult to design and manage properly. Increased productive capacity is of little interest unless it is followed by the rapid development of irrigated cultivations. This real problem is often rendered twice as difficult by extraordinary contradictions, and the unco-ordinated be-haviour of opposed economic agents and interests. The world's largest irrigation works are rarely successful at an economic level.

Algeria is no exception; the situation she inherited at Independence is quite scandalous, with 100,000 hectares supplied with facilities for irrigation and only 50,000 actually using them, with unprotected reservoir dams which silt up, and so on. Before analysing this situation in greater detail, we shall try to get a better idea of how such conditions may arise when co-ordinated management of the works and of the development is lacking.

5. The Cumulative Process of 'Underdevelopment' in the Irrigated Areas of Southern Portugal

As an example, I shall consider the irrigation works of Alentejo in Portugal, which shed light on the situation in Algeria. Large-scale irrigation works have been initiated in Alentejo by the

Portuguese government. The costly civil engineering operations in the irrigated perimeters have not been followed up by development to bring in revenue. Investments authorized by the community have failed to bear the economic and social fruit which one would expect.

Yet in Alentejo too, the potential made available by irrigation is immense, enabling the possible range of crops to be extended, and allowing yields to be doubled, or even quadrupled. Apart from the inadequate and inconveniently distributed rainfall, which is the main limiting factor, the other physical characteristics of the region, climate, soil, etc., permit a wide range of temperate, mediterranean or even sub-tropical crops: industrial crops (sugarbeet, cotton, tomatoes, tobacco . . .), forage crops (lucerne, bersim, sorghum and maize for fodder), a very varied selection of vegetables (cabbage, cauliflower, artichokes, gherkins, melons, etc.), flower and fruit crops (citrus, peaches, pears, etc.).

The non-intensive growing of cereals in dry cultivation, which predominates in the big estates, provides small gross yields of between five and fifteen quintals per hectare. Fallow still occupies an important place, and vegetable crops for food or forage form the basis of the not very widespread beginnings of crop-rotation. On the stubble and fallow land, herds of Alentejan cattle and the local breed of sheep utilize several hundred more units of forage per hectare. Black rootling pigs are reared in the open, in the traditional way, thus making use of the acorns from the cork oak and ilex plantations. For dry crops, except for the vineyards and some plantations, the gross yield is usually less than £75 per hectare.

The present development of the irrigated land is still non-intensive. Traditionally, it was based on the growing of rice and, to some extent, maize. In recent years there has been an astonishing development of tomato cultivation and the manufacture of crude tomato concentrate, the latter being exported to undustrialized countries, especially Great Britain, where it is very profitably used by the big food combines. The market prices are very low. Even with high yields of sixty tons per hectare, and a good organization in the Portuguese factories, one should be able to cut production costs still further thanks to the low wages (5 to 10 francs a day).

These monocultures, or near-monocultures, by no means exploit all of the above-mentioned potential.

In terms of agro-technics, the present methods of development are rapidly degrading the irrigated soils. The complementary earth-works for rice-growing have not been carried out properly. Due to the precariousness of his tenure (five to six years), investments made by the cultivator have to be amortized within a few years. At the conclusion of his period of tenure, the land abandoned by the entrepreneur has been damaged by bad drainage; if this treatment is repeated, it may gradually make the soil unfit for cultivation, and sterilize both the valuable capital of land, and the costly infrastructure of irrigation-works.

The increased cultivation of the industrial tomato is giving rise to uninterrupted successions of this crop, which are harmful to the structure of the soil. In the end, the infestation of the land by the plant's specific enemies makes the crop practically impossible, so that the capital of land and irrigation-works created at great expense, are wasted.

The scarce and expensive commodity, water, is wasted no less than land. Submerged rice crops use 15,000 to 25,000 cubic metres of water per hectare in a year (which is equivalent to 1·5 to 2·5 metres of rainfall); in relation to the 50 quintals of grain obtained per hectare, this is enormous. Though the grain is good, it consumes three to four times as much water per hectare as maize (which uses 6,300 cubic metres per hectare a year, for yields exceeding 60 quintals). Yet even maize does not use water very efficiently. Vegetables, fruit or forage only require between 5,000 and 8,000 cubic metres of water per hectare a year, and give gross yields, value added, and rates of employment all much higher than those provided by rice or maize.

In fact, these near-monocultures of rice or tomatoes, in a region of chronic underemployment and unemployment, only employ a fraction of the available manpower. They require seasonal labour without the advantage of staggered crops to provide productive work during the off-season. Stock-breeding, which involves working all the year round, is also practically absent. On the whole the available manpower is largely under-utilized, unemployment persists and emigration from the area, though so far slight, is beginning to occur.

The negative aspect of development at present cannot be referred to any technical shortcomings in the entrepreneurs or workers of Portugal. Both the latter, on the contrary, are capable of putting up a very good performance. Nor is lack of economic initiative to blame; quite the reverse – as is shown by the explosive development of tomato cultivation as soon as the concentrate factories and commercial market had been established, and also of vegetable-growing around the cities, within the rather narrow limits of the market. When the market for some profitable production appears and gets organized, the cultivators' economic response is relatively speedy and effective, provided it does not involve too heavy an investment with deferred profitability. The negative characteristics are not therefore due to any lack of technical ability or enterprise.

A large amount of capital has to be invested in order to establish balance rotations of industrial, vegetable and forage crops, and develop production systems which make a high contribution to gross output, value added and employment. With irrigation, the entrepreneurs are given the chance of greatly increasing their investments. But these investments are not forthcoming.

Only highly profitable investments are made; potentialities are 'skimmed off', rather than exploited in depth, and heavy investments with deferred profitability are sacrificed. Fruit growing, stock-breeding and forage crops are making little headway, which greatly restricts the field for development.

Private resources and short-term credit are for preference allocated to production which involves no risk, whose techniques are well understood, whose yields show little variation and whose prices are regulated or fixed by contract – such as rice and tomatoes. The lack of security of tenure only accentuates this trend.

The situation is further aggravated by the difficulty of disposing of produce. Since industry and incomes are insufficiently developed, the very restricted internal market offers no large-scale outlet for fruit or vegetables. In order to compete in international markets, they have to reach a critical volume of production and to have a strong marketing organization – which must be established in the first place for the internal market.

The outlets for possible irrigated crops may be closed because they enter into competition with dominant interests. Tobacco, cotton and sugar-beet are to a large extent checked, or even practically forbidden, in the interest of groups who produce or market these crops abroad. The low market price for meat impedes its production, and favours the established channels by which it is imported.

Even the irrigation-works have not always been carried out under the best conditions. Winter crops and early spring sowing are hardly possible on non-porous soils or soils which are subject to winter flooding; these should have been avoided. The distribution networks for each holding, left to the cultivators, have been badly constructed; irrigation by sprinkling, which gives much greater flexibility in use, is almost entirely absent.

The predominance of large and very large properties should also be noted. In most areas, over 80 per cent of the land consists of properties of more than 50 hectares and over 70 per cent of properties of more than 200 hectares; furthermore, over 70 per cent of the small proprietors have less than 10 hectares each and over 50 per cent have less than 5 hectares. Unless these small proprietors, who are underemployed on their own lands, can extend their cultivations by becoming tenant farmers or share-croppers they must go to swell the reserve of temporary labour for the large cultivations, together with the landless worker-peasants. Not all the full or seasonal unemployment, whether open or disguised, can be absorbed by agriculture, public works projects and industries for processing agricultural produce.

Nearly three-quarters of the land surface is occupied by owner and tenant farming; this is bound up with the predominance of big estates. Sharecropping is not very widespread.

The potentialities of the irrigated areas are of quite a different order to the methods of development used in existing, non-intensive dry agriculture. They constitute 'new lands' which cannot be exploited because the complementary investments, for preparing the ground, building roads and establishing commercial organizations, as well as the productive agricultural investments (livestock, farming implements and buildings) are altogether inadequate. Agriculture under irrigation is a pioneer form of agriculture, with a fundamental disequilibrium resulting from the fact that it is not geared to the needs of the local population, but to the most readily available and accessible foreign markets. The means of production are only exploited in so far as is profitable for the enterprise within the market economy. This pioneering agriculture has a very definite speculative tendency, favoured by the predominance of large cultivations wholly orientated towards the market. The small amounts of capital involved, and the precariousness of its involvement, makes it a wasting and depredatory form of agriculture, with scant interest in conserving the potentialities of land which is not fully exploited.

It is not sufficient merely to describe the negative situation in the irrigated areas; it must be explained, with the contradictions inherent in the operation of the various economic factors, and the solutions, and their limitations, must be understood.[7]

The immediate economic agents involved are the state and the entrepreneurs. Under the present hydro-agricultural arrangement, investments relating to irrigation, dams and the primary distribution network are carried out by the state, with public funds. The state levies a tax (which is not always paid) on the properties served, and the water is sold to the entrepreneurs to pay for the cost of maintaining the irrigation-works. These works are subsidized to a considerable extent by the community – whereas the land is rented or developed for a greatly increased land rent. Rents range from £7 or £14 per hectare for dry cultivation, to £40 or more for irrigated land.

In order to redeem this increased land-rent, agricultural entrepreneurs (whether owners or tenants) invest the additional capital required for irrigated cultivation, in such a way as to obtain high profits. The systems of production they adopt procure the maximum profit on the private capital and loans available to them.

There appears to be an important contradiction between irrigation and development – between the activity of the state and that of the entrepreneurs. Whereas the state invests £750 per hectare on irrigation (dams and the primary supply network), individual farms invest less than £150 in very unintensive development.

All economic calculations show that the entrepreneur, with a certain sum available for investment, can obtain a maximum profit by investing about £120 per hectare. The most profitable combination of products consists of rice, tomatoes and maize in very nearly the same proportions as in present development. With a high level of technology, the net return may exceed £40 per hectare, which represents 30 per cent of the capital invested by the entrepreneur. This capital is not tied up to any great extent: three-quarters of it is working capital, and the rest is in equipment.

Technicians and economists sometimes suggest that the blame lies with the Alentejan entrepreneurs, that their bad management is responsible for the economic and social difficulties of development. Calculations show that precisely the reverse is true. The entrepreneurs cannot be charged with 'management mistakes'. Taking the structures of cultivation and of the markets for produce and work into account, the system practised by them is easily the most profitable one. The difficulties of development have their origin in the economic and social structure within which they operate.

With heavier investment development becomes more intensive, but profitability diminishes. At £375 invested per hectare, the most profitable system of production would be one centred on dairy stock-breeding. Reckoning one dairy cow per hectare, together with her retinue of calves in the course of being reared, the additional capital would be almost wholly tied up in the animals. A pedigree dairy cow is worth over £150. Rice, tomatoes and grain-maize would occupy no more than half the irrigated surface, the other half being taken up by forage maize and sorghum. The soil would no longer be used only in the summer, but the whole year round: in winter it would bear forage crops, such as bersim, fodder cabbage, barley-vetch, vetch-oats and corn. The soil's utilization factor would be doubled. Two crops a year would be achieved, and full employment of the soil while wages and the use of manpower would be more than tripled.

This system is balanced technically: the forage courses clean the soil and improve its composition; the large-scale production of manure enriches the soil's humus. The heritage of land is not destroyed, but its fertility is increased.

The entrepreneurs, however, do not practise this system, for it is not in their interest to do so. For an investment of £375 per hectare, instead of £120, the net profit is less than doubled. The rate of return on the capital is almost halved. Entrepreneurs therefore find it preferable to rent more land for the non-intensive development of monocultures.

With intensive cultivation, the rate of profit on capital decreases. This point of view, however, is not in line with the interests of the community, for in this case it is the profitability of all capital taken together which must be considered, whether invested in development by the farmer, or in irrigation by the state. Now the profitability of all capital taken together increases with intensive cultivation.

There is thus a very clear contradiction between the general interest, which demands maximum profitability from the investments as a whole, and the interests of the entrepreneur. The profitability of the enterprise's capital is achieved at the expense of that of the capital invested by the state.

Calculations show that the profitability of all capital taken together goes on increasing up to a certain threshold, which corresponds to the system of intensive cultivation described above. This threshold is at a high level of investment, of the order of £375 per hectare.

If this system was practised in the irrigated zones in Portugal, an optimal distribution of investment between irrigation equipment and land reclamation would be obtained. How may this optimum level be approached, and the usefulness of the community's investment be increased?

If lines of production corresponding to the nation's needs had not been suppressed, the optimum level would already have been approximated, even without protection. With accessible outlets for beet and tobacco, and higher producer prices for meat, the optimum for the farmer would more nearly correspond to that of the public interest. It must be realized that such measures would constitute a complete volte-face in economic policy, and there is little sign of this happening.

In the absence of such a change, there is very little room to manoeuvre in. To bring investment in reclamation up to the same level as that in irrigation equipment, the state could decide upon a more balanced distribution of subsidies and loans. A part of these could be set aside for dairy stock-breeding, which is the only line capable of counteracting the inadequacies of the present methods of development. Controlled subsidies and loans would then have to be allocated for specific purposes.

Since the financial resources available to the state for hydro-agricultural works are limited, a reduction in the amount allocated to irrigation would work to the advantage of development. The irrigated surface, while more intensively cultivated, would also be smaller – by about 30 per cent. This would not be in the interests of proprietors and cultivators, who benefit from the differential land rent resulting from irrigation; the latter would dwindle as the area supplied diminished. It is not certain where such a policy would lead, since it clashes with these interests.

Thus the purely directive, centrally planned measures still conceivable – a prices and loans policy, or a better distribution of the state's investments soon run foul of the social and economic structure. Their scope is restricted by underdevelopment and domination. Under these conditions, it is practically impossible to create a form of agriculture conforming to the nation's needs, and making best use of the available resources.

Even the requirements of the local population, who are without jobs or income, are not properly met. The peasant families are deprived of the land which is monopolized by the big estates. Nor is it possible to establish semi-subsistence family agriculture, diversified and intensified to meet all needs.

A large section of the landless peasants, or of those who do not have enough land, have therefore to hire themselves out in order to make a living. There is no shortage of manpower. Cultivators are not obliged to take a labourer on full time in order to command his services, and they have no incentive to practise systems of production that will provide full productive employment during most of the year. Manpower is available on demand. Men can be hired by the day, the week or the hour, whichever will bring in the maximum profit per hectare, or per unit of capital invested, according to the seasonal work-requirement (which extends over a very limited period).

Most of the work is restricted to the two important peak periods of sowing and harvest. Sometimes there is a third, for cleaning the fields or for other agricultural tasks. During the rest of the year the work required for a single crop is very slight: guard work and light maintenance are all that is necessary. Single crops provide only a hundred, or sometimes fifty, days' work a year.

The monocultures of rice and tomatoes are incapable of providing full productive employment for the local labour-force; nor do they make full use of the land or water. They occupy the soil less than half the year (from April to September), whereas in a Mediterranean climate two crops a year are generally possible. Winter forage and vegetable crops could be grown on the same soil, and would require no watering as the winter is wet enough. They could be tended by the manpower already profitably employed on the summer crops.

Even diversification of the summer crops would enable the peak working periods to be spread out more. For rice, tomatoes and grain-maize, the sowing, cultivation and harvest of each come at about the same time; for forage-maize, sorghum, lucerne and sugar-beet, they are more spread out.

Some degree of crop diversification would also use the water more efficiently: the peak demand for water is restrictive, and it would be useful to have it spread out over a period.

Everything would be different if there was less concentration of land, if instead of estates and large enterprises there were traditional family cultivations; for in the latter, the aim is not to obtain a maximum net profit at the cost of considerable unemployment, wasted resources and squandered manpower. Once the fertilizer and the various supplies and implements have been paid for, the object is to achieve the maximum return from the work of the members of the family.

Family cultivation tends to create the maximum amount of wealth with the means at its disposal; and its aims approximate closely to the national interest. When one calculates the most advantageous system of production for family cultivation, it turns out to be quite different from the rice-tomato production pattern. Once again we find the balanced and intensive system of irrigated summer crops, winter forage and dairy stock-breeding. It uses the land, the water and the men to good effect, sustains the soil's fertility, and yields a high gross product and a large return from the work.

This is the system that tends to emerge among small farming proprietors. It is established, and becoming more widespread, in the irrigated zones of Badajoz in Spain, and in those rare areas of Portugal which have been parcelled out by the Junta of Internal Settlement.

Internal Settlement in Portugal resembles the experiments in Spain and Italy (Mezzogiorno), but is much more restricted and has practically been discontinued. In some irrigated zones, the state buys the lands of the big landed proprietors and subdivides them into family cultivations with two or three labourers. The farms are furnished with buildings, livestock and implements, and presented, fully equipped, to wholly or partially landless peasant families who pay in instalments.

Since this 'agrarian reform' is so expensive, it is necessarily limited. Land has to be bought at prices inflated by the potential effect of irrigation. The individual equipment, which has to be advanced in full, is often conceived by the technical authorities in a spirit of undue perfectionism.

The capital of the large concerns is left untouched by the reform. Equipment for cultivation has to be supplied all at once, since the would-be cultivators, agricultural workers, sharecroppers or small farmers, are without implements or livestock. They have no experience of running a modern, intensive cultivation. The success of the operation depends on effective, hence expensive, training. Only by working extremely hard can the new cultivating owners pay off the very heavy debts which weigh upon them.

Where 'internal settlement' has been carried out it has undoubtedly improved the social and economic situation, providing the population with more employment and higher incomes. Yet it cannot constitute a solution for the country as a whole, as it would cost more than the state can afford. Internal settlement found acceptance on a small scale just after the last war because of the political upheaval in Europe, but since then it has slowed down, and been discontinued. Finally, with the progress of technical evolution, the structure of family cultivation will not permit the fully profitable use of specialized equipment – which would itself constitute an obstacle to development later on.

In the absence of agrarian reform, family cultivation has therefore little chance of developing in Alentejo. It is not the only system, however, to encourage the fuller utilization of resources. On the big farms, and in the capitalist or socialist co-operatives in the developed countries, where there is little unemployment, labour has to be hired on a permanent basis. There may still be a few exceptional peak-periods of work, such as the thinning out of the beet or the grape harvest, for which seasonal workers are called in – though the latter are becoming harder and harder to find. Even the seasonal workers in Spain, who visit the beet and vine-growing areas, prefer permanent employment. The tendency is therefore to employ a permanent labour-force, and to deal with the peak working periods by means of mechanization and technological progress.

It is not often that a monoproduction, which is profitable when seasonal workers are paid only during the peak periods, remains the most profitable form of production when they are paid the whole year round.

Multi-product agriculture makes more profitable use of a permanent labour-force. Profits are high, and so are productive employment, gross output and added value. The interests of the entrepreneur and of the public no longer conflict to any great extent in the choice of products.

In southern Portugal far from achieving these conditions in order to do so, large-scale industrialization of the country would be necessary. This would absorb the unemployment, so that farming concerns would then be obliged to employ a permanent labour-force. However, industrialization is not occurring fast enough; so there is emigration.

Whichever way one turns, the progress of irrigated agriculture finds itself confronted with restraints which can only be removed by a far-reaching transformation of social and economic conditions.

Why not simply count on the appearance of new productions destined for the external market, as in the case of the tomato? The rising standard of living in the developed countries has led to an increase in the consumption of preserves, condiments and tomato-juice. The high potential and low wages in the irrigated zones of Portugal make it an important source of supply. The Anglo-Saxon food trusts appeared, the concentrate factories were opened, and the marketing arrangements established. There was a boom in tomatoes; tomorrow perhaps it will be the cauliflower or the gherkin. Why not simply wait until they arrive, then build development around them.

This, however, would be to take one of the causes of the disease for its remedy. A balanced agriculture cannot be created by adding one production to another according to the discontinuous needs of the dominant markets, any more than a balanced economy can be created by the addition of one mine to another mine. One form of mining can be added to another without fundamentally diversifying the economy.

And after all, there might not be another boom; on the contrary, there could very well be a slump in tomatoes. This depends on incomes and habits of consumption in the rich countries, and on the competition from the Mediterranean world. Economic dependence is accompanied by great vulnerability.

From the standpoint of a Portuguese producer in Alentejo, these markets are not only uncertain, but accidental. They are beyond the range of his ability to control, influence, or even predict. Dominated and distorted as it is, the agriculture of Portugal's irrigated zones is to a large extent beyond the control of the Portuguese agronomists and economists who wish to develop it rationally. It is quite unconnected with the country's real needs, and is 'overdetermined' by the operation of economic forces from outside.

Underdevelopment appears to be a cumulative process. In Algeria, as we have seen, it is an economic and social situation inherited from the colonial period. In the absence of colonialism it continues to flourish. In Portugal's case the irony is that production is held back for the benefit of big plantations and monopolies overseas. The mechanism of underdevelopment is independent of nationality, and will operate whatever the quality of the entrepreneurs. Most of the European farmers of Algeria and their Portuguese opposite numbers manage their cultivations well.

In the eighteenth century in England, and the nineteenth century in France or the United States, it was the 'captains of industry' (or agriculture) who developed a modern economy. In the dominated countries this game is no longer worth the candle, for the dice are loaded!

6. Results of the Process: Disorganization and Waste in the Irrigated Areas Inherited by Algeria

These processes have played a determining role in Algeria; it is not surprising therefore that the large-scale irrigation works involve waste and disorganization.

In the Cheliff valley, where the irrigation network extends over 50,000 hectares, the surface actually irrigated is less than 20,000 hectares (5,000 in the upper Cheliff region, 8,500 in the middle Cheliff and 5,700 in the lower Cheliff).

There is a considerable lack of proportion between the various irrigation works. The facilities for collection of water, the dams and pumping stations are all quite inadequate to supply the 50,000 hectares equipped for irrigation, so that the excess distribution networks remain unused and cannot pay for themselves. Yet the

Ghrib dam on the Cheliff (110 million cubic metres) and that of Wadi Fodda (a tributary of the Cheliff, 70 million cubic metres), and the pumping stations on the upper Cheliff, are capable of meeting the water requirements of more than 20,000 hectares. To the disequilibrium in the irrigation works is added a considerable wastage of water resources.

Run-off irrigation, which is the only form practised, is uneconomical in its use of water. With irrigation channels in the ground, it is difficult to appreciate what volume of water is being distributed to each parcel of land. The bad preparation of the land leads to an unequal distribution of water, and considerable losses. The channels also obstruct the working of agricultural machines.

Run-off irrigation is appropriate when accompanied by a high level of technology, as in the irrigated zones of California. The ground is made perfectly level and water is taken from the supply canals by siphoning, which enables losses to be well controlled. The water-towers are strictly programmed; a central 'brain' distributes the water to the various parts of the perimeter according to their surface-area and the requirements of each crop. In Algeria, however, due to the shortage of trained men, such a level of technology is difficult to achieve, and considerable amounts of water are lost.

Run-off irrigation also leads to delay in opening up land by holding back the development of intensive agriculture. The benefits of irrigation are postponed and diminished; revenue is inadequate for the amortization of the works.

On the other hand, irrigation by sprinkling enables the water to be brought much more rapidly under control, and entails little delay. Its flexibility in use favours complex schemes of rotation. Finally, and most important, it enables the consumption of water to be reduced, thus allowing the irrigated surface to be extended.

Calculated in economic terms, these advantages largely offset the difference in the costs of installation. Equipment for sprinkling is in fact 10 to 20 per cent more expensive than run-off irrigation. On the other hand, it has the advantage in terms of foreign currency, for Algerian industry is in a better position to manufacture the piping, pumps and most of the components required for sprinkling, than the bulldozers, and graders used in preparing the ground for run-off irrigation.

Sprinkling also makes it possible to water hilly regions. Exclusive concentration on run-off irrigation restricts the choice of zones to irrigate. The fertile slopes of the low hills surrounding some of the perimeters would, in many cases, have been more worthwhile to irrigate than the more humid plains, some of which require an expensive, perhaps prohibitive, complement of drainage and sweetening installations. A section of the lower Cheliff, now equipped for irrigation, is practically irremediable in this respect.

Taking the lack of water and technology into account, run-off irrigation is often the wrong solution. In certain cases, however, it can be justified: as when irrigable, homogeneous, well-drained and easily levelled land is plentiful; or when development is based on some perennial crop, such as citrus fruit, or on a simple form of rotation for which the methods of run-off irrigation are well understood. Lastly, sprinkling is not the best method when the water is too saline.

The uneconomic use of water must therefore be added to the inadequacy of the irrigation works as a factor which restricts the extent of development. Development, however, has evolved in an anarchic fashion. The lack of water has caused the amount of watering on the irrigated surfaces to be reduced as well, which leads to lower yields, and sometimes to the complete loss of all the money spent on cultivation. It also increases the salinity of the soil.

The water from the wadis is saline, so watering slightly in excess of requirements has to be allowed for. The salt deposits caused by intense evaporation are thus leached away by the excess water percolating through the soil. If watering is insufficient, these deposits accumulate year after year: the saline soil becomes infertile, and the capital in irrigation and land associated with it is destroyed.

In the citrus plantations even the trees are in danger and destruction can spread to this capital as well. The total loss could reach tens of thousands of dinars per hectare.

In spite of the lack of water, rice, which wastefully uses three times as much water as other crops, was established on over 1,000 hectares. Rice is justified in countries and climates where water is not a rare commodity – as in monsoon areas and some parts of the tropics where water is plentiful and the geomorphology of the valleys lends itself particularly well to rice-growing. In the dryer Mediterranean climate the deltas of certain rivers may also be suitable. In Algeria this is not the case, and rice-growing can only be justified if none of the land irrigated from a dam will support any other crop. But a dam like this is one of the least appropriate.

The sugar-refinery of El Khemis aggravates the shortage of water in the Cheliff area. The necessity of developing sugar-beet on the upper Cheliff means that new areas have to be equipped for irrigation.

In western Algeria the situation is equally chaotic. Irrigated cultivation is concentrated in the Oran perimeters of the Mina, the Habra and the Sig. It was a mistake to give priority to the irrigation of these littoral plains, which consist of deposits that are in many cases badly drained and sometimes threatened by the rising of a saline water-table. The sweetening of the soil required may prove more expensive than the irrigation itself.

The soil of the inland plains, on the other hand, seems generally of good quality, and would have been more suitable for irrigation. The choice of the littoral plains seems to have been due to the fact that, from the technical point of view, it was easier to supply them with water.[8] The flow of the wadis, and the sites for dams, appeared to be more favourable below the inland plains than above them.

The priority and choice of dams, from among the various possibilities, was often made on the basis of the price of a cubic metre of water. However, dams which can provide the cheapest cubic metre of water are not necessarily the most useful since it has later been discovered that their irrigable perimeters cost two or three times as much to equip as others would. In the last analysis, it would be more profitable to build slightly more expensive dams serving more suitable areas, for the cost of the primary and secondary supply and irrigation networks, and the preparation of the ground, are of equal importance, and must be taken into account. If a dam serves only unfavourable areas, allowance must be made for sweetening and drainage as well, which may double the expense of equipping land for irrigation.

Finally, all the expenses together do not constitute a criterion upon which to base a choice. The economic results of irrigation may vary extensively, according to the area (not to mention areas that are completely barren). From cost-benefit analysis, it can be seen that these results are five to ten times[9] more significant than the cost of water storage. When all is said and done, the price of the cubic metre stored is practically negligible in relation to the other economic quantities which have a bearing on the choice. Yet this inappropriate criterion was employed because the building of the dam precedes and eclipses everything else. The dam is a large and spectacular work – an occasion for great inaugural ceremonies. Like the tip of the iceberg, nothing else is seen, though it is the submerged part which is the most important.

In the Oran area, as on the Cheliff, there is a lack of proportion between the various irrigation works. The perimeters are over-equipped, and the development of urban needs was not foreseen: Oran and Sidi-bel-Abbès are short of water. Thousands of hectares planted with citrus (2,900 hectares in the Mina perimeter and 6,500 on the Habra) receive less than 75 per cent of the water that they need (less than 6,000 cubic metres per hectare, instead of 8,000 to 8,500). The plantations are in danger.

While on the Cheliff and in the Oran area the irrigation net-works are too wide, elsewhere one finds reserves of water not being used. Dams have been constructed without the perimeters they were to serve being equipped for irrigation, or even surveyed.

While there is a shortage of water in the west, at the opposite end of Algeria 110 million cubic metres, for the irrigation of 15,000 hectares, lie idle in the Cheffia dam (Wadi Bou-Namoussa, near Annaba, formerly Bône)! In 1962, when the dam was nearly finished, studies on development had not even been seriously begun.

Finally, in addition to the disproportion between the various irrigation works, and the shortage or wastage of water, the bad use to which this water is put must also be discussed. This is due, as in Portugal, to the fact that the crops under irrigation are far from being the most economic. Apart from rice, which has already been considered, the irrigated surface includes 2,000 hectares of cereals and 5,600 hectares of olives, confined to the Cheliff and Oran areas.

Cereals and olives make bad economic use of small quantities of water per hectare, and even more inefficient use of the irrigation networks – though the latter are just as expensive for these low-value crops, which were often already being grown before irrigation was installed. No additional investment has been required on the part of the enterprises concerned. This represents the least intensive form of development, and the one which makes the least profitable use of the communal irrigation works. Olives can be planted on the banks for protecting and restoring the soil; while cereal production can be intensified more economically in dry cultivation.

Even vines are to be found in the irrigated zones; these should have priority for conversion.

In 1962, market gardening and fruit growing (especially citrus) were the only systems intensive enough to make the irrigation-works pay. These, however, occupy barely more than half the irrigated surface, or about a quarter of the area equipped for irrigation.

Sugar-beet, occupying 2,500 hectares in the upper Cheliff, has only progressed appreciably since Independence, yet it had been envisaged in the Constantine Plan. It had previously been checked in response to the dominant interests of French producers.[10]

Cotton, which is almost entirely exported, occupies only 650 hectares, and forage crops 300 hectares.

Algeria imports sugar, textiles, meat and dairy produce – and even tomato concentrate, for which its irrigated zones provide conditions just as favourable as those in Alentejo. However, the commercial relations so long imposed on Algeria had prevented local production.

This 'vacuum' in development – apart from market gardening and citrus growing – must be filled. What the irrigated perimeters of Algeria need is an agriculture providing more jobs and income, which will use the irrigation more profitably; a form of exploitation is required that will lead to more activity beyond the confines of agriculture, especially in industry, thus constituting a true lever for development. These products would be orientated for preference towards the satisfaction of the nation's needs.

Conditions today have changed, and the speculative use of resources must no longer interfere with development. The land in the irrigated zones, which used to belong mainly to Europeans, now forms part of the socialist sector. It is now possible for production to correspond to the nation's interests – though the difficulties standing in the way of the practical exploitation of these possibilities are enormous.

Algeria can limit her foreign trade, and refuse to abandon her economy to disruptive and distorting effects from abroad arising from operation of the market. This does not mean that production for export should be excluded. If there are stable outlets for it, and if the income it creates per hectare is higher, it should be maintained and developed. On the other hand, if the amount of income created is equal, exports are always less worthwhile than production designed to replace imports. The volumes and prices of exports are seldom guaranteed, whereas internal needs filled by imports can be concretely ascertained. Since the internal market can be protected, it is easier to replace a foreign product here than to promote some product on the international market; foreign exchange is easier to save than to earn.

Finally, products are often exported in a crude form – their industrial processing takes place outside the country. Production destined for the home market, on the other hand, is processed on the spot, which multiplies its value.

To count only the creation of 'agricultural' income from sugar-beet production is to under-estimate it, for there is also the income created in sugar-mills and refineries. In addition to some tens of quintals of sugar, a hectare of beet produces two or three thousand forage units in the form of pulp, leaves and stalks – two to three times more calories than an average pasture in northern Algeria, or even than a hectare of corn in dry cultivation. In a balanced forage system, a hectare of beet will nearly support one dairy cow.

Bearing in mind also the productive employment created by the processing of produce derived from stock-breeding, especially the dairy industry, a hectare of sugar-beet is one of the most economically valuable crops there is. This fulcrum for intensifying agriculture is also a lever for agro-industrial development – though a difficult lever to control.

Factories, implements, specially bred cattle and technology all cost a great deal of foreign currency. In order to cover this expense, full use must be made of them as soon as possible. The sugar-mill of El Khémis is not working at full capacity, which reduces its effectiveness. Its installation was unfortunate, for the beet here is adversely affected by the dryness of the air and the hot winds from the south. Beet would be better confined to the Sahel perimeters, where it would have the benefit of a more temperate atmosphere and be practicable as a dry crop capable of withstanding the salinity of the soil. The Mondovi sugar-mill on the plain of Annaba (Bône) would thus be able to serve a complementary sector of dry cultivation, in addition to the irrigated Bou-Namoussa perimeter. It would be a mistake to install the factory at Guelma, so far from the centre of gravity of the supply area. After a few years, the extra transport required would cost as much as the factory itself!

Cotton-growing only attains its full significance in association with the textile industry. The oil extracted from the seeds should also be turned to account in the form of oil-cakes for cattle. Cotton is not a sufficiently intensive production when grown for export. The place assigned to it in production systems designed to provide more jobs and higher returns is therefore modest. The establishment of spinning and weaving extend the possibilities of enhancing the value of the crop. The mills could be allowed to pay for themselves before the chemical industry takes over with its synthetic fibres.

The tomato concentrate industry is already established on the plain of Annaba, where Tomacoop produce 3,000 tons of it. In the Bou-Namoussa perimeter, 1,200 hectares of tomatoes could be cultivated under irrigation; with over 1,000 hectares of dry cultivation, this would be enough to satisfy the demand. Before the production is extended for export, the risks of the market must be assessed, and the yields per hectare, as well as the productivity of the factories, must be greatly improved. It would also be desirable to move beyond the crude concentrate stage towards a more fully processed product.

Together with tobacco, a whole range of industrial crops can be envisaged, which could form a point of departure for true development.

Tobacco growing is still limited in extent – but, thanks to the protected[11] home market, much less so than it used to be, and considerably less than in Portugal. In order to broaden this foundation, other crops must be associated with it, such as summer and winter vegetables, potatoes, cabbages and roots – with which the internal market must be kept fully supplied, keeping prices down. All this is possible, for these activities can only lead to the fuller utilization of resources.

Yet only by the combination of intensive forage crops and stock-breeding can the objectives of development be fully achieved. With 15 to 20 per cent of beet, 20 per cent of cotton, 30 per cent of tomatoes, and a combination of irrigated forage maize and sorghum and winter forage, each hectare could still support more than one dairy cow.[12] The optimal use of land, water and men creates sufficient wealth to make the irrigation profitable. Taking into account the indirect effects of these productions on the processing industries, these systems make a considerable contribution to the national system in current use.

These profitable systems are also complicated; simplifying them in the interests of easier management leads to considerable losses. For the most efficient economic use of resources, activities must be developed multilaterally. On the other hand, losses also arise if the problem of managing complex producer units is not solved. Yet effective management of production and command of technology must involve specialization. This contradiction has to be resolved.

How can diversification and specialization be reconciled? In order to achieve this, the oversimple organization suitable for unintensive rotations must be superseded. All that is necessary to supervise a rotation of the cotton-wheat-fallow-wheat type, on a farm of a few hundred hectares, is a management committee, a good farm manager and an accountant.

An organization of this kind cannot handle a complex rotation consisting of four or five irrigated summer crops and winter forage crops, associated with a herd of several hundred dairy cows. Nevertheless, one has to rely on the experience acquired by the self-management workers, taking the men's capacity into account, and working methods should not be upset more than necessary. Experience shows that a working collective with its foreman can master a simple rotation on several hundred hectares.

The complex rotation could therefore be subdivided into four or five *ateliers* (literally workshops), each having only a few crops, which would thus be simple enough for a small gang of workmen to manage effectively. The old farm will become a co-ordination and service unit, where competent administration, book-keeping, supply-services and marketing will be more efficiently developed.

This arable farm would be associated with a livestock farm, also divided into several *ateliers* each comprising a number of cows suited to the capacity of a chief cowman and his gang of workers.

Though intensive production organized along these lines also requires greater technical competence than traditional methods, it makes more profitable use of it. The self-management workers should also be mobilized and allowed to participate in making decisions, as is shown by the experiment in progress near Annaba. Otherwise the method will not be well understood, and those concerned will lack sufficient motivation to achieve the objectives rapidly.

The development of the irrigated perimeters is difficult, and will involve exploiting the possibilities provided by the new social and economic conditions to the full. Yet it cannot be neglected. The proportion of irrigation capacity employed is so low, and water so inefficiently used, that it should have been possible to attain the same result with half the investment.

In order to correct this situation, the balance between

water-storage and distribution works also needs to be redressed, since they are everywhere slightly out of proportion. Dams and pumping stations should be built on the Cheliff and in the Oran area, while the Annaba plain needs to be equipped to use the water from the Cheffia dam. These works will make it possible for the surface actually under irrigation to approximate the area equipped. The works required to ensure that the existing installations are being fully used will lead on to works of extension properly so called. Policy is at present moving in this direction.

In all these operations past errors must be avoided. Algeria has only limited resources of water. Large-scale irrigation works constitute a heavy drain on public funds, and many of the installations are paid for in foreign currency. The capacities of the civil engineering firms and technical services are limited. None of these resources should continue to be squandered.

The projects must be carried out without giving way to technocratic haste. One cannot just pour concrete here and there, thinking that the rest must necessarily follow.

Decisions must be arrived at after rational preparation. In this sense, planning allows of a better choice of operations. The technical services entrusted with building the dams, extending the irrigation networks and ensuring that development takes place can eliminate the most glaring errors by getting together around a table. The planning authorities have already improved the procedure of choice appreciably through their arbitration, and by making the comparison and discussion of the projects take place systematically.

A large-scale hydro-agricultural complex is intricate, and difficult to manage. Various dams and pumping-stations are possible on the Cheliff, each capable of being carried out in several different ways, to supply one or more agricultural zones with water in varying proportions. Processing industries and ancillary installations must also be provided for, as well as the water-supplies to towns and industries. All these projects are interdependent: the choice of dams, areas to equip for irrigation, distribution and systems of development must all be made simultaneously.

It takes many years to equip a basin for irrigation. The balance between water resources available and water used has to be gone into at every stage. Planning in stages is therefore preferable to a definitive 'master-plan', with the dangerous rigidity it imposes on technical and economic thinking.

Such a progressive programme subject to revision is also quite distinct from the step-by-step pragmatism which led to the inconsistencies reviewed above, such as dams without irrigation networks, networks without dams, and installations without development. This programme ensures that the works will be in proportion to one another.

Finally, from among the various solutions technically possible, the most economic must be chosen. Posed in concrete terms, it can be seen that this problem involves thousands of unknowns and thousands of equations. It can be solved – but at what price? Can Algeria afford technology such as this? The question should be put differently: what one should ask is whether this technology pays. The saving in concrete will pay for it ten times over. Major irrigation needs this technology, or it will no longer be profitable and will lose all claims to priority.

Besides, good economic planning is cheaper than bad, since it relies on selective preliminary studies rather than exhaustive research.

It uses general schemes rather than costly pilot projects thus permitting economy in detailed research. In offices (and even cellars, since the offices are not big enough) heaps of papers accumulate over the years – definitive projects, all very detailed and complete, which have never seen the light of day. Geology, hydrology, climatology, plant and animal ecology, property ownerships, land use, sociology (occasionally), and economic analyses of the present and past situation, all these studies provide twenty times as much information as is needed for a rational choice, but not always the information that is necessary! To obtain this information it is sometimes quicker anyway to go to the site, for though reality may be richer than theory, it is often easier to decipher than the dossiers.

Once the choices have been made, it is of course necessary to draw up detailed plans. In the absence of rational planning, it is easy to see how the multiplicity of complete technical dossiers arises, for the works in which one or another group of interests had a stake have had a better chance of being adopted if the dossiers, upon which their claims rested, were more complete (or more illegible perhaps).

In Algeria, as in Portugal, large-scale irrigation provides a classic example of the distortions produced by economic domination. It was carried out much more for the benefit of the companies engaged in public works, speculative agriculture and the market of the metropolis, than in response to the country's needs. The enormous waste of resources was still further aggravated by the lack of planned co-ordination between the various operations.

Since Independence, Algeria has been in a position to redirect her economy, take national needs into account, and introduce planning.

Major irrigation, the industrial combines, the road networks and the urban infrastructure constitute 'heavy' sectors of the national economy. Their anarchic origin and bad management involve considerable waste. Consequently, while the planning authorities must be concerned with the general aims of the nation's economy and the particular objectives of socialist enterprises, they must also make every effort to manage these investments on rational lines. This will necessitate new techniques in planning, but, above all, in order to make the most of the new social conditions, it will involve basing choices on criteria that are really in accord with the national interest.

The planning authorities in Algeria have become aware of this aspect of planning, which is often underestimated.

7. *Providing the Missing 'First Agricultural Revolution' and Re-building the Abortive 'Second Agricultural Revolution'*

Food cereals, including hard corn, soft corn and to some extent barley, are consumed in Algeria in the form of semolinas (couscous, griddle-cakes) and flour (bread). They provide nearly 80 per cent of the calories consumed, the rest being mostly derived from fats and sugar. Meat, fruit, vegetables and dairy produce make up less than 10 per cent of the diet – which is not enough to supply all the vitamins, mineral salts and especially protein, that is needed.

As well as barely providing enough energy, the present diet is very unbalanced. Only the intensification and diversification of agriculture can make it possible to change over from a basically cereal diet to one that is more balanced and rich in protein. This will take time, and the cereal diet cannot rapidly be reduced. With the population growing at such a rate, overall needs will continue to increase.

Formerly, Algeria used to export grain, but during the last ten years she has begun to import it. Average production varies around 18–19 million quintals, with considerable deviation (in bad years it is less than 10 million, and in good over 25). In 1955–60[13] production and consumption were still balanced. With increasing population, the cereal deficit has already reached 3 million quintals.

At the average growth rate of 3 per cent a year, the population should increase from twelve million to eighteen million within fifteen years. The cereal deficit would then amount to nearly half the total requirement. Imports on such a scale (nearly 15 million quintals in 1983) would place a heavy burden on the Algerian economy.

There is now an appreciable danger of cereals becoming a strategic commodity employed by the over-producing countries to influence the politics of those with deficits.[14]

The problem of the cereal supply therefore looms very large, and production must be increased; the production of cereals cannot be *extended* however, and in the better-watered areas and the irrigated perimeters it may even have to give way to more intensive production.

Cereals will also give way to erosion and the progress of pastoral stock-breeding in the marginal areas. The struggle against erosion and the protection of cereal-growing may check the diminution of the areas devoted to it, but cannot enable them to be extended.

Increased production of cereals can therefore only be achieved by improving yields.

Non-intensive cereal-growing is the system of cultivation most prevalent in Algeria. It covers 6 million hectares, as against only 600,000 for vineyards and orchards, and a few tens of thousands for annual irrigated crops.

Biennial rotation (alternating cereals and fallow) is the form most widely practised. Triennial rotation (one-third fallow, two-thirds cereals) is employed on part of the best-watered and most fertile northern plains, and is also gaining ground in the over-populated areas.

Triennial rotation was most prevalent in the moist and temperate lands of Europe. At lower temperatures, the organic content of the soil becomes less impoverished and with a more even distribution of rainfall is less affected by erosion. The yields of grain are on average higher; the decrease is less marked, and the land can be cultivated two years running without impairing its fertility.

A considerable increase in production has been achieved in these countries by replacing the fallow period by forage or food legumes. Forage crops involve a closer association between agriculture and stock-breeding. Manure is plentiful, and the nitrogen from the legumes has led to increased yields.

In the last three centuries this trend towards intensification has become widespread throughout the whole of western Europe. It has been possible to create a considerable surplus of wealth, thus contributing to the accumulation of capital necessary for industrialization.

In Algeria this 'first agricultural revolution' – as it is usually called – has remained very much in embryo. Dairy stock-breeding, or the production of food legumes (beans, lentils, chick-peas, peas, kidney beans) have been developed on the farms of some settlers and peasants; but while 3 million hectares are still laid fallow, in 1966 legumes occupied less than 60,000 hectares, cultivated forage 61,000 and industrial crops (cotton, tobacco, beet) less than 20,000.

Instead of intensification with increased fertility, the land in Algeria has been over-exploited for grain. This is the result both of the requirements of the speculative commercial agriculture established on the best land, and of the increasingly pressing needs of the subsistence agriculture driven back on to the poorer land.

During the last century, without stock-breeding, manure or fertilizer, the quest for the highest immediate yields, followed by attempts to arrest the decline in fertility, took the form of an increasing over-exploitation of the soil.

At the beginning of the nineteenth century, the Algerian peasants used to sow their grain on unploughed land, after the first autumn rains. The seed was then lightly ploughed in; it was practically impossible to use the traditional swing-plough before the rains came. The sowing spared the soil, which, despite its fragility, was thus able to maintain its fertility. Unwelcome plants were checked by using the fallow for grazing and by weeding it every year.

At first the European *colons*, relying on the peasants' long experience, adopted these methods of a balanced subsistence agriculture. However, this equilibrium was soon to be upset by the development of commercial grain production.

In the records of Algerian colonization for 1852 mention is made of the fact that, with one or two ploughings, grain may be cultivated several years in succession without the use of fertilizer. The large-scale destructive exploitation of the soil had begun. Algeria's land could not stand up to such treatment, and yields declined catastrophically; it is recorded that, by about 1870, in Sidi Bel Abbès they had fallen from 15 to 5 quintals per hectare.

In order to escape ruin, the grain producers had to find a new equilibrium. After various trials, they were obliged to fall back on the biennial cereal-fallow rotation familiar since ancient times (it was already being practised in the Sahel and on the high plateaux during the Roman period).

The soil was impoverished; to obtain higher yields it had to be cultivated at a greater depth. Deep ploughing brought fresh layers of sub-soil to the surface, which became part of the arable land. It became necessary to preserve the life of the soil by using manure, which could be provided by the ever more powerful teams of draught animals. Improved varieties of grain were also developed, as well as a better method of preparing the soil (by harrowing).

It was under these conditions of partially restored production that machines first made their appearance. After the First World War 'dry farming' was imported from North America; this involves ploughing fallow land (two or three stubble ploughings and one tilling) to create a loose and powdery layer of earth designed to prevent the soil from drying out, and to allow the autumn rains during the fallow period to be retained and carried over to the following year's cereal crop. To some extent this storage is illusory, but in any case the weeding needs to be done more thoroughly.

However, this impetus to yields is obtained at the expense of still further impoverishing the soil. With more ploughing and better aeration, another franction of the soil's humus is consumed, thus freeing a certain quantity of nitrogen. Since the ploughed fallow is no longer protected by its carpet of vegetation, erosion by wind and water becomes more marked.

Yet mechanization is expensive; to make it pay, more had to be extracted from the soil. Dry farming, with its two or three stubble-ploughings was no longer enough.

'Full fallow' was invented, which involves 'various multiple operations spread over a period of fourteen to sixteen months'. This represents the ultimate refinement in destructive exploitation of the soil. Fully ploughed fallow land can no longer be used as pasture; and the numbers of cattle are also reduced by the replacement of draught animals by mechanization. The soil receives less and less manure, so that its reserve of humus is still further depleted.

The agricultural authorities note that 'cereal yields follow the diminution in the amount of humus'. After recovering at the beginning of the century, fertility is once more on the wane. 'The development of mechanized cultivation shows a decline in yields, which have fallen from 15 – 20 quintals per hectare before the war (1939) to 12 – 14 in recent years.'[16]

Yet there are great advantages to mechanization. The ploughing can be done rapidly, whenever required; while the destruction of weeds, the fine preparation of the soil for sowing, and the deep ploughing which increases the amount of water held represent exhaustion and degradation of the soil? It should be treated with large amounts of manure and fertilizer in order to avoid these dangers.

With the passing of the era of animal traction, only dairy or meat stock-breeding can provide manure in sufficient quantity. Here too, the quest for big, quick profits does not operate in favour of animal productions.[17]

Since the 'first agricultural revolution' never took place, there was a lack of manure; and the orientation of the 'second revolution' that of tractors, machines and fertilizers, was altogether wrong.

Phosphate fertilizers were used, though only to a small extent; potash even less. For the expensive nitrates reliance was placed on the dwindling resources in the soil. Even in 1959 there was a programme for developing the production of cereals in which the word 'fertilizer' was never once mentioned. Both in fact and in theory, 'mechanized cultivation' had too long been given priority.

The very mechanical equipment displayed a lack of balance. Super-mechanization developed in the modern sector, and great harvester-threshers were imported for the harvest, to the detriment of local employment.[18] The refinements in the cultivation of the soil also made for over-equipment, while traditional agriculture on the other hand was short of the most basic tools and implements.

Algeria today must therefore simultaneously redirect her mechanization, develop the use of fertilizer and hybrid seed on a massive scale, and change over from non-intensive cereal growing to intensive production systems associated with stock-breeding.

The use of hybrid seed and fertilizer is the first objective. The outlay for the cultivator and the national economy would be recovered within the year.

Within the next ten or fifteen years, Algeria can rapidly reduce her present imports, then meet her own needs. In the better-watered regions of the north, the combination of seed and fertilizer will make it possible to obtain seven quintals of grain more per hectare, and four more in the areas where the rainfall is less than 400 mm.[19] This operation is all the more important in that Algeria is already producing her own phosphates and will soon be producing nitrate fertilizer too, in her new industrial complexes.

With the use of fertilizer, the raison d'être for the over-exploitation of the soil by increasing mechanization disappears. Mechanization needs to be reconsidered, giving due attention to the necessity of conserving the soil and achieving full employment.

Most important, the massive use of phosphates, nitrates, and occasionally potash, will enable the fallow land to be brought under cultivation, which cannot be done at present without exhausting the soil. The growing of weeded plants could be widely practised – in association with forage crops, stock-breeding and the use of fertilizer. Even triennial rotation will be feasible in the better-watered areas (Sahel, and Plains of Tell Atlas).

Intensive rotations will provide three or four times as much employment and income as the present non-intensive methods of cereal cultivation.

Depending on the region, one or two hectares of cultivated winter forage (vetch-oats, bersim) are required to feed one dairy cow. 300,000 dairy cows could be established on 1·5 million hectares of the most fertile land in northern Algeria. Cattle for meat and improved breeds of sheep could be located more to the south, farther from the centres of consumption.

First of all Algeria could absorb her imports of meat and dairy produce;[20] next, she could meet the needs of her growing population, and finally improve their diet (which is deficient in animal protein), raising it to the level of the developed countries.

Intensification of the 6 million hectares of non-intensive cereal cultivation is the only way to increase the employment and incomes of the millions of workers on the land, and meet the growing needs of the twelve (which will soon be eighteen) million Algerians.

Heavy investment is necessary. Prime livestock will have to be imported, or else bred on the spot – which will take time. The 300,000 dairy cows alone represent an investment of about one million dinars. The agricultural capital must be doubled or trebled altogether.

This cannot happen all at once. Algeria has lagged too far behind, and too many negative features remain to be corrected. It will be an outstanding achievement if she manages to attain these objectives within fifteen or twenty years.

8. From 'Impossible' Full Employment to Labour-investments: Small-scale Water Works, Rural Reconstruction, Agrarian Reform

The first agricultural revolution never took place, industrialization is inadequate, and the second agricultural revolution has misfired. The European economy's 'spontaneous sequence' of advances is no longer possible for Algeria. For too many years investment has been directed towards other objectives than the creation of jobs and the satisfaction of the population's needs.

Yet only through industrialization, the development of the irrigated perimeters and the intensification of all Algerian agriculture, can the underemployment and unemployment be rapidly absorbed. The normal processes of investment demand equipment, foreign currency, men with technical training, and considerable financial means. However, these resources are too limited to create a sufficient number of immediately productive jobs.

Agrarian reform should also, in principle, diminish underemployment in the private sector. However, Algeria does not have large estates; there is no large unexploited reservoir of land available. It will not therefore provide many new jobs.

Consequently, in view of the scarcity of arable land in Algeria, the large, unused work-force will persist if these methods are adhered to.

It would be logical to employ this predominantly rural work-force at least expense (on the spot therefore) to increase the productive potential of the soil. This will mean tackling its chief limiting factors which, in Algeria, are the lack of water and the degradation of the soil by erosion. Water must be made available without recourse to expensive equipment, which can only be achieved by means of small-scale irrigation over small areas, installed by the peasants themselves using local resources. Erosion must be combated by building banks, creating plantations, and planting forage crops in alternate strips. The fertility of degraded soils should be restored as far as possible by limiting the use of mechanization. These operations constitute 'rural renovation'.

Small-scale irrigation and rural renovation can only be achieved on a collective basis. They conflict with the private ownership of small parcels of land. For these two reasons, these labour-investment operations will require a massive mobilization of the peasants; for this is the only way of guaranteeing that they will be widely carried out, and properly maintained and used. It is therefore important for the peasants to realize that the operation's aims are in line with their own interests.

All this cannot be guaranteed if only material incentives are offered, or if only the unemployed are hired at the work-sites.[21] Mobilization like that of the successful ploughing campaign is required, though more sustained and deep-rooted. Agrarian reform can provide the right conditions for this.

In addition to the projects of small-scale irrigation and rural renovation, full employment could be ensured for several years by the reforestation of Algeria – putting immense stretches under timber.

The productivity of the soil on each hectare affected by small-scale irrigation and rural renovation may be doubled or tripled. Labour-investment therefore makes it possible to wait until industry and modern intensive agriculture can provide enough jobs. It also increases production and the possibilities of investment, hastening industrialization in the long run. It is no mere stopgap remedy for unemployment, but a potent resource for development.

NOTES TO CHAPTER 14.

1 *Op. cit.*, p. 220.
2 In a situation of underemployment, the measure of the increase in the community's income (a criterion of social welfare) is equal to the increase in income from employment and in net exports. *Cf.* J. Lesourne, *Le calcul économique*, p. 33.
3 There is a certain analogy to the situation of Cuban sugar with respect to the United States' market.
4 And also those of petrol (500,000 tons in 1969 and 1970).
5 *Problèmes de l'Algérie indépendante*, in the magazine *Tiers-Monde*, Presses Universitaires de France, Paris, 1963.
6 René Dumont, *op. cit.* See the cheapness of seasonal fruit-juices and Kvass in Moscow, and the massive scale of their distribution.
7 To this end, I shall rely on the extensive economic studies carried out by the Junta of Internal Settlement (Lisbon), and by myself.
8 Perhaps also because of the milder climate.
9 At present value.
10 When René Dumont was sent to Algeria in 1940, he was given only one instruction by the Ministry of Agriculture: to prevent the development of sugar-beet! It would therefore be unfair to blame the Algerian farmers for shortcomings due to restrictions imposed by Paris. The first sugar-refinery in Algeria dates, in fact, from the last war when the links with the mother-country were relaxed.
11 To many economists this protection seems questionable – especially in France, where excessive protectionism held up agricultural modernization and even industrialization during the first half of the present century. One should realize that in Algeria and the other underdeveloped countries it is not a matter of preserving the backward-looking structure of a market economy, but of protecting the growth or adaptation of economic activities that are in the country's interest. It is less a question of protecting profits than of safeguarding the most productive use of the nation's resources. Free trade has always been preached by the advanced countries, for it serves their ends. In the backward countries, some degree of protection has always proved useful in creating the right initial conditions for the growth of a market economy. Even today, our economy would collapse if the European market was not protected. Corn, sugar, pork, poultry and butter production, as well as many of our industries would be wiped out. All that would remain in France would be choice wines, Cognac, Roquefort, subsistence agriculture – and millions of unemployed! What should we say if such a process of underdevelopment were imposed upon us by some political and economic

sphere more powerful than our own? Let us be clear, though, that protection must be progressively lifted in France, in the interests of adapting and increasing the efficiency of every branch of our agriculture and industry.

12 With two crops, one in summer and one in winter, the soil's co-efficient of utilization is over 180 per cent.

13 Since 1905, the quantity of cereals, vegetables, dried fruit, milk and meat per head of the population, produced by non-European agriculture in Algeria, has constantly declined (R. Dumont).

14 In their book *Famine 1975*, the Paddock brothers give a very clear exposition of this policy. The world surpluses located in North America, Argentina and Australia may be made available in proportion to the political docility of those who ask for it. The example of India is significant.

15 Under 5 quintals per hectare, cereal growing ceases to be profitable commercially. With yields of between 5 and 3 quintals, it can continue at a subsistence level. Pastoral stock-breeding, on the other hand, is quite profitable with one sheep per hectare, However, although it provides a marketable product and a monetary profit, it feeds and gives employment to fewer men than the subsistence cereal cultivation it tends to replace. The peasants abandon farming to swell the ranks of the underemployed and unemployed. This is a tendency not to be encouraged in the present economic situation. Assistance to farmers and the distribution of seed could be advocated in the dry years, in these areas. The pressure from sheep-farming could also be reduced by establishing fodder reserves (of non-spiny cactus), regulating the price of mutton, and organizing sales campaigns to diminish the accumulation of livestock.

16 Mentioned by G. Mollard in *Evolution de la production du blé en Algérie*, Editions Larousse, Paris, 1950.

17 Even the rearing of sheep on the stubble-fields was discontinued in the interests of the 'full fallow'. However, Algeria is not Latin America, and large reserves of land from estates did not exist. There was a limit to the possible extension of commercial grain cultivation. Mechanized cultivation led to a fall in production, or at any rate prevented it from being increased. In order to maintain their incomes, cultivators had to increase their outlay and begin to intensify. Stock-breeding and industrial crops were developed, though only to a very small extent. In some areas the fallow land was sown. Lentil growing spread in the Sersou. However, in this climate, the cultivation of the fallow land without fertilizer or manure led to further impoverishment of the soil, and lentil and grain production soon declined.

18 In private concerns, harvester–threshers are more profitable than reaper–binders for more than 6–7 quintals per hectare, though the national economy demands a yield of 15 quintals per hectare. Moreover, for the harvester–thresher rapid storage of the grain is necessary, so that more equipment for storage and transport is required. In theory it should allow harvesting losses to be reduced, but in practice the opposite is more often the case, on account of the thresher's ventilators and grills not being properly adjusted. Finally, it will soon be possible to manufacture binders (apart from certain components) in Algeria, whereas the possibility of manufacturing harvester–threshers is still remote.

19 A dressing of sixty units of phosphoric acid and nitrate (divided into two spreadings, in the autumn and the spring) in fertile areas, and of forty units in average areas, are profitable (cf. the work of the FAO project, *Algérie 8*).

20 In 1965, Algeria imported 8,000 adult cattle for slaughter, 3,000 tons of meat, and the equivalent of 70 million litres of milk.

21 These methods are not to be excluded completely; they may provide a supplementary impetus, rather than being the driving force of the movement.

CHAPTER FIFTEEN

Decentralized Management and Planning for the Socialist Self-Management Sector

1. The Initiative Passes to the Management Committees

The National Office of Agrarian Reform played a useful role just after Independence by stabilizing the situation and restoring various services which had become disorganized. Afterwards, repeating the experience of other socialist countries, it demonstrated once more that agriculture does not lend itself to administrative management.

A centralized, hierarchical administration becomes hopelessly entangled among the many day-to-day decisions relating to the several thousand farms scattered throughout the country. The situation gets out of hand and in order to bring it under control again, there is a tendency for ineffective administrative measures to proliferate, paralysing the producers.

The cultivation plans devised by the central authorities are ill-adapted to the concrete conditions on each farm, and supplies and loans are distributed without taking the imperatives of production at the base into account. Breakdowns occur, blocking production. The returns from the socialist sector, worked out in the aggregate for each administrative district, do not allow the farm committees to know their own financial results.

The Office for Agrarian Reform was therefore dissolved, and in 1966 initiative was handed back to the farms, who devised their own cultivation plans, which were presented to the district administration for approval. They prepare their own programme of requirements which they submit at the beginning of the season. The loans made available for these programmes are more in line with what is needed. Each management committee has a cheque-book for the purchase of goods and services, and the returns for each committee are individually accounted.

A quarter of the farms which until 1967 had not managed to balance their books, have shown profits since then. During the summer of 1968, shares were allotted to the producers.

Self-management has thus proved capable of prolonging the existing systems of production. After an initial drop, production has stabilized and started to recover. It sometimes happens, moreover, that the fall is exaggerated by an increase in the quantities consumed by the producers themselves, and a corresponding reduction in the amounts of produce commercialized.

With its present organization, the self-management sector must be capable of equalling, then exceeding, its previous results. The normal techniques, such as fertilizer, hybrid seed, treatment, implements, and so on can be assimilated; more difficulty would be encountered with technical and economic organization. General information, loans, supplies, and the sale of produce still need to be improved.

Good technical and financial management of existing activities will not be enough. Even under socialism and self-management, the modern sector perpetuates the dependence, disequilibrium and vulnerability of colonial agriculture, and its failure to meet the social and economic needs and objectives of present-day Algeria.

2. Intensification through Changed Organization, Direct Control and Looser Management

Industrial crops, the association of agriculture with stock-breeding, and the processing of products locally will lead to the emergence of a complex agro-industrial organization. This is adumbrated in the more fertile areas, such as the Cheliff perimeter and the plain of Annaba with their industries and service units, Tomaco-op (tomato concentrate), Tobaco-op, the manufacture of fruit-juice, and machinery and repair depôts. A regional economic service will be needed for the direction and demarcation of functions and organization within these combines.

The creation of specialized *ateliers* within each diversified and intensive farm must not result in cumbersome administration. The number of workers, turnover, area of land, and quantities of livestock and equipment must not exceed a certain level, so that the gang in charge of a single *atelier* can take direct control of it. Above this threshold, the gang and its foreman could no longer be on top of their job.

It would then be necessary to replace direct control by the gang with a cumbersome and inefficient set of detailed records. Analytic accountancy attempts to record not only every economic fluctuation in the farm, but also in each crop, each parcel of land, and even each farming operation. On the basis of these figures, it claims to be capable of very accurate 'costing', in spite of the fact that fluctuations in yields from year to year may make manufacturing prices vary by 100 per cent. Though it records only the past, it claims to be a tool for economic prediction. A rear-view mirror, even one with several facets, can only enable a person to look behind, not in front.

It is a beautiful dream to have all the figures describing a farm's economic activity, down to the smallest detail, available on one's desk without ever having to set foot on the land – but in fact it often remains just a dream. For dozens of farms the recording of this mass of figures is never completed, but continues to mount up, choking the department and even the electronic accounting machines. In the end there may not even be an ordinary farm account available.[1]

In the last analysis, this comes from mixing up the various management tasks of prediction, organization and control, all of which the analytic monster proposes to deal with simultaneously.

For the moment, however, the self-management sector has escaped this trap, which has not always been avoided in the agriculture of other socialist countries.[1] At the most, one can only point to a few isolated instances, from which the Algerians, having little tendency to dogmatism, soon drew the lesson.[2]

In self-management, a simple and usable farm account is needed, so that the farm's overall results can be appreciated; a simplified account is also required for each independent *atelier*.

3. Planning Production while Respecting the Initiative of the Committees

For the reorientation and transformation of production something quite other than detailed analyses is required.

In many management committees the numbers of the permanent workers have increased. If the committee is allowed to make its own decisions, it will try to make profitable use of this extra manpower. On the plain of Annaba, the suppression of the fallow period and the change to continuous cultivation indicate a trend towards intensification.

Nevertheless there is still considerably less manpower in the self-management than in the private sector. The majority of the fertile land is in the hands of a minority of workers. Under-employment, unemployment and the use of temporary labour still persist. In selecting the most paying product, a management committee interested in profits will not necessarily fix on the most intensive systems of production. So long as the distortion in the economy remains uncorrected, the interests of the individual enterprises and the aims of the national economy will continue to be very much out of step with one another.

Through loans, prices and investment the state can guide production towards industrial crops, vegetables, fruit, forage and stock-breeding. With such a great disequilibrium, these measures will not be effective; they are limited, and in some cases involve risks. Prices paid to the farms cannot be manipulated at will; retail prices must be taken into account. The 'artificial' reduction of the price of bread below that of grain in the USSR resulted in its being used for feeding livestock. If processing factories are built to provide an outlet for industrial crops, there is no guarantee that they will be supplied.

On the other hand, a plan of production cannot be dictated to every management committee. Though it may appear to conform to the general interest, if the plan is conceived by a remote, centralized planning authority it is sure to be ill-adapted to the farm's actual capabilities. Their losses, and the difficulty of adhering to the plan will make the producers wary of it, and their discouragement and misrepresentations will impede production.

Detailed production plans adapted to the capabilities of every farm could, in theory, be worked out, but this would involve two or three months' work on the part of a highly-qualified specialist – and such men are in very short supply. It will be a long time before the planning and agricultural authorities have a tenth of the necessary staff.

Even if such intensive plans of production were 'tailor-made', they would still seem ponderous and out of line with the enterprise's and the producers' interests. Being badly understood, they would not be adhered to.

If production plans are to be properly carried out, they must be drawn up by the producers, with regard to external factors, to make them fall into line with the country's economic objectives.

For self-management an economic service is required to explain the new economic orientation, advise the committees on organization and help them work out a plan of cultivation, a programme of supply and an estimated budget at the beginning of the season, as well as the farming accounts at the end of it; its functions would be advice and education rather than administrative supervision.

In each area, this economic service would constitute a link between the planning authorities and the producers. After being adopted by the administration, the plan of cultivation becomes a sort of contract between the committee and the community, by which the former agrees to adhere to the plan, and the latter to supply the means for it to do so.

While the plan of production is conceived with a view to creating the maximum wealth for the country, the farming enterprises should try to make as much profit as possible in carrying it out. Otherwise objectives fixed as regards quantity might be achieved at too high a cost. This is why a supply programme and budget of expenditure, however elementary, must be drawn up at the start of the season.

Profit-sharing would also encourage this, though this incentive is not without its drawbacks. The total profit depends more on the quality of the farm in the committee's charge, than on the quality of its management. Even if a rent corresponding to the fertility of the soil is deducted, the possible profits will still vary according to the technology and equipment possessed by the farms.

Ideally, the profits shared out would be related to the difference between expected and actual profits. Making due allowance for the effects of the weather during the year, this difference would be the best index of the quality of the committee's work. Unfortunately, neither accurate prediction, nor the measurement of results are easy. The committee and the administration may differ in their estimates. Only by discussion or 'negotiation' can estimates be established which, if not absolutely fair, must at least be acceptable to both sides.

This method would have the advantage of making a mutually educative dialogue take place between the committees and the cadres.

Management in the socialist sector of agriculture cannot be reduced to handling the multiple day-to-day decisions required in carrying out an imperative, centrally-worked-out plan. This would be detrimental both to the enterprise's efficiency and to the country's economic objectives. Decentralized management and the planned guidance of agriculture through negotiation and education may be a better way of resolving the conflicts between the interests of the small community in charge of an enterprise and the national interest.

NOTES TO CHAPTER 15

1 Dumont has observed this in the Cuban people's farms.
2 Analytic accountancy could be retained as a special check on certain selected farms (samples).

CHAPTER SIXTEEN

From the Outdated Model to the Original Path

The study of Algeria's 'underdevelopment' clearly shows that it cannot be equated either with non-development or with mere economic backwardness.

If there are primitive communities or purely archaic societies in the world, living at subsistence level, without material wealth, very few of them have remained untouched by colonial invasion, plundering and entanglement with the modern economy. The majority have not escaped repression; some even spring from the disintegration of civilizations that were once more stable and sometimes prosperous. Non-development, strictly speaking, is only a minor factor in underdevelopment.

The underdeveloped countries are in reality those which have been subjected to economic domination. Penetration by a dominant economy is effected by means of trade; it is facilitated and tends to be perpetuated through the political control of a metropolitan country.

Part of the nation's resources are thus diverted for the benefit of more powerful foreign interests. This results in a 'modern sector', of commerce, agriculture, mining and even industry organized and directed to accord with the dominant economy's needs, existing side by side with a 'traditional sector', which is repressed or exploited.

The wealth diverted to the profit of the metropolitan country is generally derived from mining or agriculture. Apart from extractive industries, or agricultural industries concerned with preliminary processing, industrialization merely consists of activities which complement the dominant economy.

Without adequate industrialization, and with a large part of the population reduced to subsistence in the 'traditional' sector, the internal market cannot be other than very restricted; because of the lack of tariff protection, it is soon saturated, thus preventing the creation of internal trade networks as well as the development of agricultural and industrial production to satisfy the needs of the local population.

Even bare subsistence upon 'traditional' agriculture may sometimes be threatened. This happens when an export agriculture corners a large share of the richest land for the development of its plantations, or for the creation of unused latifundia. There is no longer enough land available to provide the rural population with jobs or incomes. Poverty may then become extreme.

Because of the existence of a sector geared to external markets, the social needs felt by the population constantly increase in quantity, quality and diversity, while the possibilities for satisfying them remain stagnant, or decline. Even the workers of the modern sector (those at least who have permanent jobs) appear relatively privileged. Fleeing from poverty, and attracted by the urban façade, the peasants come to the towns in search of work, which the inadequate industrialization cannot provide. Slums and unemployment are the result.

The situation thus created is aggravated by the population explosion,[1] and by the infertility or degradation of the land. Poverty is then transformed into the threat of famine.[2] If they are not the underlying cause of underdevelopment, these phenomena frequently accompany it, and are attended by further difficulties, which must be treated very seriously.

The importance of the modern sector, the form and nature of its activities, and the degree of the traditional sector's repression depend on the character and needs of the dominant economy; these determine which of the local sources of wealth will be chiefly exploited. Economic distortion is a general feature of underdevelopment, though in each country the distortions are created historically within the particular limits imposed.

Thus the social and economic situation, the structures and

forms of production inherited by each country, constitute a point of departure that is both specific and inevitable. Any economic and political strategy taking account of these realities must therefore be original. The extent to which a country is geared to international trade, the degree of irrationality of its economic structure, the extent of unemployment, and the relative scarcity of land, technicians, capital, etc., are essential factors which vary from country to country.

These requirements are not formulated purely in response to a desire for rationality. Any strategy which neglects them will eventually, after repeated corrections, be compelled to take them into account by the pressure of the facts. This is shown by the experience of the European people's democracies, which imported the Soviet 'model' into very different sets of circumstances.

The 'model' concept is therefore out of date, and must be replaced by the concept of an 'original path'.

Algeria's example clearly illustrates the weight and diversity of constraints inherited from the past, and the need for an appropriate strategy.

This is not to say there are no lessons to be drawn from the experiences of others; it does not mean that principle and method can be abandoned in social and economic analysis, or in the definition of aims. The general object of a strategy for development must be to get the economy on its feet, while providing full employment for the population, and satisfying their social needs, which must involve industrialization, and the reorientation and intensification of agriculture. The basis of this strategy is that the process of 'underdevelopment' should not be reproduced or perpetuated. Although the approaches to development are many the direction is the same: a head-on-struggle with the dominant economies, with every form of economic or political imperialism.

NOTES TO CHAPTER 16

1   Massive use of vaccines, serums and antibiotics has reduced mortality in the
    Three Continents from 3 or 4 per cent a year at the beginning of the century,
    to between 1 and 2 per cent. However the birth-rate has remained at between
    3 and 4 per cent – hence the 'explosive' population growth rate of 2 to 3 per
    cent a year.
2   *Cf.* R. Dumont and B. Rosier: *The Hungry Future*, André Deutsch, London,
    1969.

Attempted Summing Up

RENE DUMONT

1. The Pillars of Modernization: Birth-control, Action against the Privileged Minorities and the Dignity of Labour

There is everywhere a limitation on agriculture's capacity for expansion and this tendency is likely to increase. The UNESCO congress of September 1958 has shown us the perils of exhausting, destroying, and polluting the limited resources of our biosphere. This means that prudence must be exercised with regard to population growth, and that the spread of North American power must be checked. Many South Asian countries have hardly any new land to reclaim. Irrigation is a tremendous lever for expansion, but requires vast amounts of capital, and must be followed up by very intensive cultivation – which has requirements of its own. Non-agricultural productions (such as petroleum yeasts, algae, aquiculture, and syntheses) are extremely demanding. The population explosion of recent years has made development everywhere more difficult. According to Han Suyin, the increased poverty to which it gives rise will foster revolution. There is a danger of widespread mental retardation due to lack of protein; an overpopulation of apathetics. The 'wretched of the earth', from the Andes to the Brazilian *sertao*, are no more inclined to revolt than was the lumpen-proletariat of nineteenth-century Europe.

The capacity for production thus created must be used first of all to meet the needs of the new segments of the population. Land reclamation, the building of roads, dwellings, schools, dispensaries and hospitals – all this expenditure on behalf of the extra mouths leaves little with which to raise the living-standard of the existing population. Let us not forget, finally, that birth-control is also an essential form of respect for women – who in backward countries are, all too often, despised. The women of China have been aroused to a genuine revolutionary enthusiasm[1] by their newfound dignity.

After the rising flood of population, the second obstacle to rapid development is the existence of the privileged minorities denounced by Yves Lacoste.[2] We have seen how, everywhere, with the real political and economic power in their hands, they take an unduly large share of the national revenue, and play along with the dominant economies. They generally devote an inadequate proportion of the tax receipts to investment or development. Capitalism in the poor countries shows little sign, in general, of repeating the Japanese 'miracle', or even that of the Ivory Coast. It seems to me that it only has some chance with the more primitive workers of Asia, in Thailand or Korea for example, or in Hong-Kong and Formosa, where a certain level has already been attained.

Massive imports of luxury goods for the use of the rich deplete the foreign currency reserves and reduce the capacity for buying equipment. The same applies to the export of profits, savings and capital, which has assumed dramatic proportions in South America, and is spreading in other places. This bad example encourages corruption in administration, which may lead to material losses far greater than the sums actually stolen. Dishonest officials give preference to those expenditures which best lend themselves to speculation, and these are not necessarily the ones most favourable to development. In Eastern Nicaragua, for example, some of the public works officials, instead of providing facilities on the rivers that are already navigable, are giving preference to a very expensive and largely premature road network.

An honest government, dedicated to the general interest and therefore to that of the workers, can safeguard economic independence (Tanzania) and seek the solutions that will do most to foster social and economic progress. It would thus be impelled to free itself from domination and reduce social injustices – without striving for the Utopian ideal of complete equality. Yet it would also seek to uphold respect for, and the dignity of, all those who work; and their right to work as in the case of Cuba. For the untouchable or the illiterate black peasant, this dignity and right, essential at the very outset of development, are much more important than the phoney freedom of elections which they understand little.

Yet an honest government, especially if it claims to be socialist, should also begin to cultivate a respect for freedom of expression. This need not necessarily imply a proliferation of more or less demagogic parties nor the adoption by some regimes of caricatures of European parliaments before the level of development to justify them has been attained. This freedom could be reconciled with a single party system, provided the party strives constantly to maintain the widest possible flow of information and communication, and the frankest possible dialogue between the leaders and the base. The recent trial in Tunis (September 1968) is an example of what must be avoided: here, unacceptable opinions were heavily penalized as conspiracies iust as they are in fascist or communist countries.

2. The Accepted Foundations of Development: Investment, Planning and Technical Knowledge

These three factors are generally considered first when one proposes to accelerate growth. In placing the above conditions before them, I have had no intention of minimizing their importance. More capital is required for the accumulation of equipment than could ever be provided by foreign aid, even increased to the extent I shall demand. Greater internal efforts are needed, in which taxation will play an important role: private saving has proved much less important in the backward countries than it was in nineteenth-century Europe.

The limited resources available for investment provide an incentive to make the best possible use of them in development, which means that the latter must come within the general framework of a plan. The plan will first specify in general terms what collective and individual needs are to be given priority; it will then be possible to study and then suggest the most economic methods of satisfying them. The idea of planning, long opposed by the Americans, is now accepted to some extent everywhere; it is even to be found in the Ivory Coast and in South Korea. As is demonstrated by the series of examples we have just been studying, planning does not at all imply centralized direction of the whole economy, or even the collectivization of the principal means of production.

Though industrial progress is necessary to development, the export of mineral oils and ore – extractive industry – may, as Paul Bairoch rightly emphasizes, 'constitute a mortgage on future development: the export of profits, the depletion of underground resources, the use of foreign capital equipment, the failure to extend operations into processing.'

The most productive modern equipment can only be brought into play with the aid of a constantly growing army of ever more highly qualified engineers, technicians and skilled workers, pending the arrival of programmers and management advisers. Economic independence cannot be assured when factories and workshops remain chiefly in foreign hands, as in the Ivory Coast. This conclusion calls into question the whole system of education, which in backward countries has until now too slavishly followed the European system which used to give and continues to give undue emphasis to Law and the Humanities, at the expense of scientific, technical and professional training.

A general culture of great value could be founded on a more intimate acquaintance with the village and the soil, with the city and its trades, based on an essentially technical education – which should not be despised as it has a direct bearing on the increase of production. Economic planning logically involves planning in employment and education. By combining manual work with both theoretical and practical studies, at every level of education, it would be possible to form an *élite* who do not despise manual labour. This contempt, which we saw chiefly in connection with India, though it is also true of Africa, is a fundamental obstacle to the development of the backward countries.

The shortage of technicians is considerably aggravated by the brain-drain from the backward countries to Europe or North America, which affects Asia to a large extent. This most harmful form of the plunder of the Three Continents is encouraged by the intolerance of corrupt governments who reject useful revolutionary elements, likely to contribute to the ending of their privileges. While India is terribly short of statisticians, Professor Mahalanobis estimates that 35 per cent of those in the United States are Indian. But India cannot afford many of them, and they too, lacking a national or political conscience, go in pursuit of higher wages.

3. The Local Search for Appropriate Roads to Socialism

The government of a tropical country that had recently achieved political independence, if it claimed to have some particular socialist orientation, might attempt to clarify some general principles of action, which it would itself have to define. It might seek first of all to control the commanding heights of the economy; this would make it possible to eliminate luxury and semi-luxury imports, or reduce them by means of taxation. It could then encourage only those investments recognized as priorities in the plan of modernization. Credit control should be introduced very early, at this stage, with the aim of increasing (judiciously oriented) productive investment. The first object of taxation should not simply be to achieve a certain amount of budgetary revenue, but to introduce taxes and subsidies in a way likely to contribute to the rapid expansion of production and employment, as well as to diminish inequalities in income.

It is a delicate matter to decide to whom this control should be entrusted, for many corrupt administrations, especially in Latin America, offer little grounds for hope. The decisive impulse must, however, come from the state, if the object is to satisfy the needs of the community while protecting the interests of the weak. Any determined move in this direction would therefore presuppose that power was already in the hands of the people's representatives. This also applies to the preferential organization of the economy towards the home market, or to the creation of large blocs of backward countries who may be too small to achieve genuine development on their own. It would then be possible for them to free themselves from domination, by reducing the role played by exports to the wealthy countries. As Chairman Mao rightly says: 'politics is in command'. It is therefore of primary importance for the producers to achieve the reality of power. It is also necessary that they should not be betrayed by their representatives, as happened, and all too obviously still does happen, in the parliamentary oligarchies of South America, or under Stalin's heirs.

The series of problems concerned with the management of the economy, and the relative importance of the public and private sectors then arises; also, within a socialist perspective, the attempt to expand the former progressively. In this area one should be very cautious. I noticed the prudence exercised in Zambia and Tanzania, in contrast to the precipitate haste of Mali and Guinea. Doctrinaire rules are very dangerous in this area, for decisions on the best date and degree of any collectivization raises a whole series of questions, especially those relating to feasibility and timing. The administration must be competent and honest if collectivization is to be carried out on a large scale; especially if planned terror along neo-Stalinist lines is to be avoided – even if it goes by the name of 'the dictatorship of the proletariat'.

In many sectors even the advisability of collectivization may now be open to dispute. In Sweden's dynamic economy excessive differences in incomes are avoided by means of taxation and other policies (the salary range is from one to five, as opposed to one to fifteen in France). This opens up a whole range of possibilities for humane socialisms – which should respect the initiative, responsibility and dignity of the individual much more, not less, than capitalism. Herein lies the great interest of self-management, in spite of the initial difficulties of putting it into practice which must be overcome.

Thus a whole series of very varied socio-economic experiments could develop, to which we will not deny the name of 'socialism' – provided they respect man and his personality, the labourer and his dignity, reduce injustices and allow some degree of individual flowering within a framework of dedication to the local community and to the national interest. On the other hand, whenever a privileged minority seizes power, political leadership, and the lion's share of the national revenue – while rejecting the right of others to hold opinions different from their own (whether they be pro-Russian as in Egypt, or pro-American as in Tunisia) – then it ceases to be a true socialism, whatever the Soviet or fascist leaders may pretend.

4. Plunder or Regulated Markets?

Socialism, like the Kingdom of Heaven, appears to be more difficult for the rich to enter; at least so the example of the United States, or even western Europe, would tend to suggest. In April 1964, at Sian, the Chinese authority greeted me with the Maoist catechism: 'In France, as elsewhere, 90 per cent of the population belong to the working class, who have an interest in creating the revolution.' I replied that when over half the workers possessed private cars they tended to become bourgeois. For once he was nonplussed, even visibly disturbed.

Yet the events of May–June 1968 – the spring of Prague and Paris – show that the socialist ideal, which has nowhere in the world found satisfactory concrete expression, still exerts a considerable attraction on a large section of youth. They are in revolt against the abuses of North American imperialism, and a growing proportion, especially since the occupation of Czechoslovakia, are also ranged against post-Stalinian neo-imperialism. Other young people, considered more moderate and often Christians, protest against the fundamental injustice perpetrated on the backward peoples of the Three Continents, and are keenly aware of the rising tide of hunger.

For the benefit of those who pin their hopes on charity, I have tried to display the very narrow limits of such a policy in order to guide them also towards political action. Anyone who claims to be a socialist[3] should exert pressure on their government to oppose the pillage of the Third World and to increase its multilateral contribution to development (less open to suspicion of politico-economic pressure than a bilateral contribution). The Soviet government has never agreed to provide a guaranteed amount of aid, even limited to 1 per cent of its national revenue.

Before one can talk of aid, the various forms of exploitation must be attacked, beginning with the deterioration in the terms of trade. It would thus be more important to organize the market in mineral and agricultural raw materials on a world-wide basis, leading progressively to the world planning of production. Price stabilization would be ineffective unless efforts were made to adjust production and consumption, preferably by expanding the latter, which could if necessary be subsidized. If the rich countries agreed to buy larger amounts of processed agricultural produce and industrial goods under preferential conditions we should have to reorientate our economic activity; this would involve upsetting some of our cherished habits, our immoderate love of the *status quo* and of tradition. The Mansholt plan for the renovation of European agriculture, keenly debated at Brussels, cautiously suggests that less should be paid for fats, and that milk-protein should be more highly assessed – which is what I was demanding as early as 1946. It urges concentration into large modernized farms, which are the only ones capable of keeping production costs down to a minimum. Our own agriculture is highly protected, though we buy cheaply from the backward countries. 'Woe unto the poor,' sigh the rich. The Mansholt plan aims to reduce Europe's overproduction by extending fallow land, whereas what it ought to do is to tackle world under-consumption by putting an end to malnutrition.

In 1969, surplus milk will cost the French taxpayer over four million new francs. This will make it possible to continue stockpiling more than 300,000 tons of butter in European refrigerators – which is turning rancid, and will one day have to be thrown away. It would be less expensive, the specialists assure me, to manufacture whole powdered milk and transport it in sealed casks to countries suffering from malnutrition. This would also safeguard the stock-breeding of Brittany and other overpopulated areas, as well as the future intelligence of millions of children in the tropics. Of course this would be only a temporary solution pending the satisfactory development of stock-breeding in the tropics. True aid to the backward countries demands intelligence, flexibility and the ability to adapt to new situations, rather than great sacrifices. In fact it could make an important contribution to the economic expansion of our agriculture and industry, satisfying our communal needs and providing a vital minimum for all, without claiming the prerogatives of North America.

'Will not this increased aid,' some revolutionaries ask me, 'help to reinforce and perpetuate the reign of those privileged minorities whose unfortunate effect upon development you have yourself underlined?' This is a very delicate problem, because, after denouncing the many defects and malpractices of the Indian leaders and officials, I could not have prevailed upon myself to suggest that the deliveries of American corn should be halted in the middle of a famine. Yet a great deal of it would be misappropriated by speculators and dishonest officials. Increased poverty does not automatically produce a more revolutionary tone.

However useful it might appear to subject the increased aid to greater controls,[4] if these were exerted solely by the contributing country, it would also increase the political character of the co-operation. This is why I suggested that the distribution should be controlled by international bodies, even though these may themselves suffer from the encroachments of bureaucracy, and often represent an up-dated form of neo-colonialism. It is impossible to solve all the problems concerned with development, or with the excessive inequalities between nations or individuals, within the space of a few lines. Yet we must begin to tackle them more seriously, after deeper study of past experiences. We must then try to go forward – feeling our way – taking into account at every stage the results of the experiments that are piling up every day.

5. *The Three Continents: A Common Front Against Imperialism*

Let me conclude with this admission: fundamentally, we, the various socialist families of Europe, are all at sea. Those who cannot bring themselves to justify Soviet Stalinism or neo-colonialism with the aid of a broad interpretation of Marxism – Leninism, can refer to the great tradition of Utopian thinkers from Saint-Simon to Fourier and Proudhon or, in order to water down the totalitarian element, they may invoke some anarchist ingredient taken from Bakunin or Kropotkin.

None of this seems to me very up-to-date, or really adapted to the completely novel, specific and very varied conditions of under-development. The latter have almost nothing in common with the situation in Europe at the start of the Industrial Revolution in the nineteenth century. The backward races are brutally confronted by very different economic problems of development, within the context of a new international situation dominated by two great powers, each defending its own radically distinct ideology and interests, ill-adapted to the backward countries. The history of the Third World, and its colonization, has helped to give those who are not yet westernized an outlook, a style of life, concepts and ideals that are very different from our own. The delay in their development, involving the domination of their economies, makes it advisable to adopt a different strategy – that of a common front against imperialisms, beginning with the development of economic relations with one another.[5]

The peoples of the Three Continents cannot look to some sacred text for the answer to all their problems. The progressives in the developed countries should help them to carry on the fight on several fronts. They should bear in mind that in the long run no progress will be possible without birth-control – clearly a progressive concept, as is confirmed by the reaction of the Roman Curia. It would be a good thing for them to diversify their anti-imperialism – for there are several forms of imperialism, two of them dominant and consequently slightly different. Besides, the threatened famines of the years ahead cannot be staved off without recourse to the masses of surplus cereals available from North America; this does not at all imply, however, that every condition laid down by Washington should be accepted. Since America must in the end negotiate in Vietnam, it is no longer necessary to believe that she can do whatever she wants.

The peoples of the Three Continents are approaching their majority; quite rightly they are attempting to throw off their corrupt tutelage, whether of external origin or arising from their own privileged minorities, who often side with the foreign domination. We must help them to emancipate themselves more rapidly by increasing our material and cultural contribution; sometimes also by discussing their problems and attempting to clarify them. There must, however, be no hint of that paternalism which, in August 1968 at Prague, was pushed to its caricatural conclusion, when the Russians explained in detail to the Czechs exactly what they had to do in order to be recognized as 'normal'. This act of overweening presumption conjured up for me the image of Prague psychiatrists being judged by semi-lunatic Muscovites – for those who live in a closed world, deprived of information, attempting to defend the privileges of a caste of bureaucrats, cannot have all their wits about them.

Some talk of nothing but aid, while dissembling their all too obvious plundering of the Third World. Others talk only of exploitation, while denying the possibility of effective co-operation, so that teachers and technicians become discouraged. Like colonization – against which it has nevertheless had to struggle – co-operation has both positive and negative aspects. A blanket condemnation of imperialism is therefore oversimple, and much too easy. Ways must be found of improving the situation within the present framework until the latter can be changed.

Some people go so far as to suggest that the Three Continents should cut all their ties with the developed world. Though this would certainly be inconvenient for the latter, it would be even more so for the backward countries if they had to manufacture all their own equipment. The various schools of progressives in the developed countries tear one another to shreds, and accuse each other of being 'false Marxists'. Nevertheless, in default of a common ideology they must find some common programme of action if they wish to be effective. This could be developed on the basis of reducing exploitation and increasing aid to the Third World – an indispensable form of international solidarity. Maximizing production, diminishing social injustices on a global (rather than a purely national) scale, and improving communication between men and their general participation, with a view to greater liberty – these aims could be accepted as common principles.

The Third World socialisms have only just made their timid appearance. They will evolve, encounter many difficulties, and sometimes fail before they can be reborn from their ashes. Yet in this way they may finally succeed in constructing original forms of socialism better adapted to their actual situation than our own off-the-peg models, made to fit bodies with other measurements. Humanity's hope of one day achieving a more humane form of socialism will to a large extent rest on these socialisms of the Third World. Should they fail completely, it is hard to see who else in our time could reasonably take up the torch.

The moral preoccupation of men such as Nyerere and Kaunda is a pledge of success. Socialism, as I conceive it, cannot be reduced to an economic schema based chiefly on the struggle between the classes, which is said to be still happening in China. Its aim is to achieve a communal society, and this will necessitate an improvement in moral standards. Moreover, this necessary intervention of morality adds another dimension to the strictly scientific character of socialism. Castro, at the end of 1968, spoke of Marxists and Christians working in conjunction. This seems very interesting to me, who am neither a strict Marxist, nor a believer – for these two essential forces will have no future unless they can adapt.

6. Managing Without 'The Truth': Reforms and Revolutions

We cannot discover a political 'truth' which does not exist; yet we can try to progress, step by step, towards a better world, without claiming that we can ever reach perfection. Agriculturalists often act before subjecting their proposals to absolute scientific tests. They do not ignore either common sense or intuitive syntheses. Yet the recognition that there is no absolute truth changes the character of the struggle, for it means that we must respect those who think differently from ourselves[6] and allow them to develop in their own way.

This, however, only applies to those who do not attempt to hinder the development of their contemporaries: exploiters such as United Fruit or the corrupt bureaucracy of Moscow with its censorship must be regarded as enemies. Yet they should be persuaded rather than liquidated, convinced rather than intimidated. The basic struggle is initially directed against the two great imperialist oppressors: the United States for the Third World and its black population, and the Soviet Union for eastern Europe and Russia itself. Tolerance of the intolerant would be weakness, but the form of the struggle is not immaterial; the end never justified the means, especially not in Prague.

A student at the 'Agro' told me that my course, which to some extent reflects this book, was woolly and ambiguous: he was right – because the reality I try to grasp is too complex to be schematized overmuch, without distorting it out of all recognition. One student at a lecture at ENSET[7] thought the developed countries would never agree to give real help to the poor countries because they benefit by exploiting them. Revolution in the rich countries was the only answer, he believed.

At first, when I call to mind the appalling spectacle of the children of north-east Brazil, of eastern Uttar Pradesh, of India north of Benares, or Biafra, I am inclined to agree with him. On further reflection, I feel that the chances of such an enterprise succeeding during the little time that remains to me on earth are very slight. There would therefore be some justification for a determined effort of reform, influencing public opinion in various ways to reduce the exploitation of the Third World, with more effective collaboration in the latter's true development as its aim.[8] Only to the extent, however, that it does not involve abandoning any revolutionary action justified by a serious analysis of the

M

situation. Yet we can rely only on those revolutions whose starting point is respect for man and not on those which talk of dictatorship, and condemn the Czechoslovak attempt at a more humane form of socialism[9] without even trying to understand it.

All the same, since 1929, when I started my career at Tonkin, decolonization has been achieved, thanks to the socialist world and the hard struggles of the Vietnamese, Algerians, Kenyans, Cubans, etc. It was not unimportant that these people should have had the support of a fraction, however tiny, of public opinion in France. Now even the United States find themselves compelled to negotiate. The struggle that must be carried on for the Third World's benefit is the hardest and most vital there is. Hitler and two world wars, followed by the world-wide imperialism of America and an endless Stalinism – these provide us with enough excitement for this century. Yet for the Third World of today, or even for Europe, the threat of fascism is even greater than before; it must therefore be the primary target of our struggle, for which we shall have to adjust our tactics at every stage if we are to defend ourselves better than we did in 1933.

In conclusion, the problems of socialisms and development prove to be extraordinarily complex. In an essay of this kind I could not treat them in their entirety, but have had to confine myself to an outline. But they will dominate our lives and those of our great-grandchildren; are we going to leave them a world in which it will be possible for them to live?[10]

NOTES TO THE CONCLUSION

1 'An increase in the area under active cultivation is an essential prerequisite for the growth of agricultural productivity' which, as Bairoch shows us, dominates the whole of development. This presupposes birth-control in Africa.

2 *Géographie du sous-développement*, Presses Universitaires de France, Paris, 1966.

3 To claim still to be a socialist in France, when the SFIO will not shake off American influence, nor the communist party free itself from Moscow's grip, and when so many of the left are so extremely unrealistic, is to give proof of staunch optimism.

4 In order to achieve an annual growth-rate of 6 per cent, the Third World would have to invest 125 thousand million dollars, out of a total gross product of 310 thousand million dollars in 1968!

5 But only 6 per cent of Africa's trade is inter-African; 21 per cent of the underdeveloped countries' external trade is among themselves.

6 'Freedom is always the freedom of those who think differently' – in the unambiguous words of Rosa Luxembourg, a true socialist, who was killed by a German officer in 1919.

7 *The Ecole normale supérieure d'enseignement technique* at Cachan, a suburb of Paris.

8 'If we succeed in overturning the old hierarchic spirit of the University which works from the top downwards, and in creating powers which work from the bottom upwards, we shall have thrown a brand into authoritarian society which sooner or later will ignite all the forms of power. To take reformism to its limits in the University is, in the middle or long term, to be revolutionary with respect to the whole society.' Paul Ricoeur, introduction to *Conception de l'Université*, Editions Universitaires, 1969.

9 For which Jan Palach made the supreme sacrifice: Let us salute him! Perhaps history will one day tell us that the invasion of Czechoslovakia saved us from the super-Yalta which seemed to be brewing between Moscow and Washington.

10 'The Third World has made rather a bad start, and the likelihood of its getting more rapidly under way in the near future is very slight,' concludes Paul Bairoch, who stresses the progress made by China. Apart from organization, system and management, success or failure will be determined more than anything else by population growth.

Selected Bibliography

AMIN, Samir, *Le Dévelopement du Capitalisme en Côe D'ivoire*, Paris Publications Paris.

AMIN, Samir, *L'Economie du Maghreb*, Paris Publications, Paris, 1966.

BAIROCH, Paul, *Diagnostic de L'Evolution Economique de Tiers-Monde 1900–1968*, Gauthier Villar, Paris, 1969.

BARAN, Paul Alexander, *The Political Economy of Growth*, Monthly Review Press, London, 1953, New York, 1968.

BETTELHEIM, Charles, *Planification et Croissances Accelerée*, Maspéro, Paris, 1965.

BETTELHEIM, Charles, *La Transition Vers L'Economie Socialiste*, Maspéro, Paris, 1968.

BOREL, Paul, *Les Trois Revolutions du Dévelopement*, Les Editions Ouvrières, Paris, 1968.

CHESNEAUX, Jean, *Le Vietnam*, Maspéro, Paris, 1968, *The Vietnamese Nation*, Current Books, Australia, 1966.

DENIS, Henri, *Histoire de la Pensée Economique*, Presses Universitaires de France, Paris, 1960.

DESPOIS, Jean, *L'Afrique du Nord*, Presses Universitaires de France, Paris, 1949.

ETTIENNE, Gilbert, *Studies in Indian Agriculture: The Art of the Possible*, University of California, 1968, Cambridge University Press, Cambridge, 1968.

FETJÖ, François, *Historie des Democraties Populaires Après Staline*, Editions du Seuil, Paris, 1969.

GERVAIS, Servolin and Weill, *Une France Sans Paysans*, Editions du Seuil, Paris, 1967.

GOREZ, André, *Le Socialisme Difficile*, Editions du Seuil, Paris, 1967.

GUEVARA, Ernesto Che, *Reminiscences of Cuban Revolutionary War*, Allen & Unwin, London, 1968, Monthly Review Press, New York, 1968.

GUTELMAN, Michel, *L'Agriculture Socialisée à Cuba*, Maspéro, Paris, 1968.

JALEE, Pierre, *The Pillage of the Third World*, Monthly Review Press, New York, 1968, London, 1970.

JULIEN, Claude, *Canada: Europe's Last Chance*, St Martin's Press, New York, 1968.

KRIEGEL, Annie, *Les Communistes Français*, Editions du Seuil, Paris, 1968.

LACOSTE, Yves, *Geographie du Sous-Dévelopement*, Presses Universitaires de France, Paris, 1965.

LE CHAU, *Le Vietnam Socialiste*, Maspéro, Paris, 1966.

LEWIS, Oscar, *La Vida, a Puerta Rican Family in Culture of Poverty*, Random House, New York, 1966, Secker & Warburg, London, 1967.

LONDON, Arthur, *On Trial*, Macdonald, London, 1970, Panther, London, 1968.

LOYER, J, *Black Power,* Edi, 1968.

MARTINET, Gilles, *La Conquête des Pouvoirs*, Editions du Seuil, Paris, 1968.

MEISTER, Albert, *L'Afrique Peut-Elle Partir?*, Editions du Seuil, Paris, 1966.

MEISTER, Albert, *Socialisme et Autogestion, L'Experience Yougoslave*, Editions du Seuil, Paris, 1964.

MENDE, Tibor, *China and Her Shadow*, Thames & Hudson, London, 1961.

MENDE, Tibor, *Un Monde Possible*, Editions du Seuil, Paris, 1963.

PADDOCK, W and P, *Famine 1957*, Little, Brown, Boston, 1967, Weidenfeld & Nicolson, London, 1968.

PHILIP, André, *Les Socialistes*, Editions du Seuil, Paris, 1967.

RYAD, Hassan, *L'Egypte Nassérienne*, Editions de Minuit, Paris, 1964.

SAKHAROV, Andrei Demitrievich, *Progress, Coexistence and Intellectual Freedom*, Norton, New York, 1968, André Deutsch, London, 1968, Penguin, London, 1969.

SOLZHENITSIN, Aleksander Isaerrich, *The First Circle*, Collins, London, 1968, Harper & Row, New York, 1968.

STAWAR, André, *Libres Essais Marxistes*, Editions du Seuil, Paris, 1963.

SUYIN, Han, *China in the Year 2001*, Basic Books, New York, 1967, F. Watts, London, 1967.

SUYIN, Han, *Birdless Summer*, Putnam, New York, 1968, Jonathan Cape, London, 1968.

TOURRINE, Alain, *Le Mouvement de Mai, ou le Communisme Utopique*, Editions du Seuil, Paris, 1968.

TROTSKY, Leon, *History of the Russian Revolution*, Gollancz, London, 1965, Sphere, London, 1970, University of Michigan Press, Ann Arbor, Michigan, 1957.

Index